Y0-DKZ-467

# ACROSS THE ATLANTIC

AFRICAN IMMIGRANTS IN THE UNITED STATES DIASPORA

---

*EMMANUEL YEWAH & 'DIMEJI TOGUNDE*

# ACROSS THE ATLANTIC

AFRICAN IMMIGRANTS IN THE UNITED STATES DIASPORA

*EMMANUEL YEWAH & 'DIMEJI TOGUNDE*

Common Ground

First published in Champaign, Illinois in 2010
by Common Ground Publishing LLC
at On Diversity
a series imprint of The University Press

Selections and editorial matter copyright © Emmanuel Yewah & 'Dimeji Togunde 2010;
Individual chapters copyright © individual contributors 2010

All rights reserved. Apart from fair dealing for the purposes of study, research, criticism or review as permitted under the applicable copyright legislation, no part of this book may be reproduced by any process without written permission from the publisher.

Library of Congress Cataloging-in-Publication Data

Across the Atlantic : African immigrants in the United States diaspora / editors, Emmanuel Yewah and 'Dimeji Togunde.

    p. cm.

Includes bibliographical references and index.
ISBN 978-1-86335-788-3 (pbk : alk. paper) -- ISBN 978-1-86335-789-0 (pdf : alk. paper)
1. Africans--United States--Social life and customs. 2. Africans--United States--Social conditions. 3. Africans--Ethnic identity--United States. 4. African diaspora.
5. Immigrants--United States--Social life and customs. 6. Immigrants--United States--Social conditions. 7. United States--Emigration and immigration. 8. Africa--Emigration and immigration. I. Yewah, Emmanuel. II. Togunde, 'Dimeji. III. Title.

E184.A24A28 2010
973'.0496073--dc22

# Table of Contents

**Chapter 1: Towards a Fresh Perspective in Understanding African Migration to the United States Diaspora** .................... 1
*Emmanuel Yewah & 'Dimeji Togunde*

**Chapter 2: Media Representation of America and Youth Migration Intentions** .................................................. 7
*'Dimeji Togunde, Ayobami Ojebode, Amanda Vocke*

**Chapter 3: Imagined America in African Texts and the Desire to Migrate** .................................................. 39
*Emmanuel Yewah*

**Chapter 4: The Recent African Immigrant (RAI) as the Radical Other** ...................................................... 61
*Emmanuel D. Babatunde*

**Chapter 5: Reproducing African Communities in the US** .......... 75
Settlement Patterns and Social Organizations
*Bridget Teboh*

**Chapter 6: African Émigrés in the UNITED STATES** ............ 95
Negotiating Ethnic Identities, Majority-Minority Statuses, and Negative Media Co-Representation
*Anthony A. Olorunnisola*

**Chapter 7: Emigration and the Social Value of Remittances in Nigeria** ................................................... 127
*Ayokunle Olumuyiwa Omobowale*[1],
Mofeyisara Oluwatoyin Omobowale[2] and
Olawale Olufolahan Ajani[3]*

**Chapter 8: Religious Institutions** ........................... 137
Mode of Adaptation for African Immigrants in the U.S.A.
*Emmanuel K. Twesigye*

**Chapter 9: The African Diaspora's Impact on Homeland National Identity** ................................................... 149
*Okechukwu Iheduru*

# Acknowledgement

This book grew out of our recognition of the synergy between teaching and scholarship as a hallmark of higher educational institutions as well as our scholarly interests, experience in the classroom and those of the contributors. It seeks to fill important gaps in current literature on African immigration to the United States and to provide multidisciplinary theoretical and empirical insights to students in several of our courses, including "Africa: Myth and Reality", "Issues in US Immigration", and "Social Change and Development in Africa", who have continued to be fascinated by immigration issues.

This volume will not have been possible without contributions from our colleagues who worked diligently to ensure the completion of their chapters. Several other colleagues have encouraged us throughout the process: Professors Leonard Berkey, Diana Ariza, and Scott Melzer, all of Albion College. There are other colleagues whose critical comments have enriched some of the chapters in this volume. These include, Professors Dianne Guenin-Lelle of Albion College, Ekema Agbaw of Bloomburg University, Kenneth Harrow of Michigan State University, Cilas Kemedjio of The University of Rochester, and Dr. Sylvester Osage of Pennsylvania State University. We also want to thank Professor Olakunle Ogunbameru and Mr. Agunbiade Ojo of Obafemi Awolowo University, Nigeria for their assistance in data collection for one of the chapters. We offer our special thanks and gratitude to Linda Clawson, Secretary of Modern Languages & Cultures Department, Albion College for painstakingly combing through the manuscript and for ensuring that it conforms to the publishers formatting requirements. We would also like to thank the anonymous reviewers and, especially Kathryn Otte, Publishing Director, Common Ground Publishing at the University of Illinois Research Park for her effectiveness, promptness, and attention to details. We extend our gratitude to other members of Common Ground Production and Marketing Team.

We particularly thank Albion College for generous financial support provided us through Yewah's Howard L. McGregor Endowed Professorship in the Humanities and Togunde's John S. Ludington Professorship in the Social Sciences.

Lastly but not the least, this could not have been accomplished without the unconditional support and love of our families. To our spouses, Marie-Louise and Oluwaseun and children: Temitope, Roy, Abisola, Raisa, Kristelle and Olapeju, we lack the words to express our appreciation for bearing with us as we spent countless hours away from home to bring this project to fruition.

Emmanuel Yewah<br>'Dimeji Togunde

Contributors

**Dr. 'Dimeji Togunde** is Professor of Sociology and Chair of the Department of Anthropology/Sociology at Albion College, Michigan, USA, where he holds the John S. Ludington Endowed Professorship in the Social Sciences. He also is Chair/Director of Ethnic Studies Program. His academic work intersects the areas of African development, family demography, immigration and Africans in the United States diaspora. His extensive publications in these areas have appeared as book chapters and in several scholarly journals including *the Journal of Asian & African Studies, Journal of Developing Societies, Journal of Children & Poverty, West Africa Review, International Journal of Sociology of the Family, International Review of Modern Sociology, Africa Development, and the International Journal of Interdisciplinary Social Sciences*. Professor Togunde has made numerous presentations at regional, national and international conferences. In 2009, he delivered the Distinguished Africanist Lecture at the University of Delaware, USA. In addition to serving as routine reviewer for several academic journals, he sits on the editorial board of the International Journal of African Studies. He is also the Editor-in-Chief of the International Journal of Social & Management Sciences. Professor Togunde earned a Ph.D. degree in Development Sociology from Cornell University, Ithaca, New York, USA.

**Ms. Amanda Vocke** is a 2010 graduate of Albion College, Michigan USA, where she majored in French and Spanish with a Concentration in Public Policy. While at Albion, she was a Fellow of the Undergraduate Research, Scholarship, and Creative Activity (FURSCA) and a member of the Gerald Ford Institute for Public Policy. She also served as a research assistant and student mentor for Dr. Togunde's seminar class on Immigration.

**Dr. Emmanuel Yewah** holds a Ph.D. in Comparative Literature from The University of Michigan, Ann Arbor. He is the Howard L McGregor Endowed Professor of Humanities in the Modern Languages and Cultures Department, Albion College, Michigan where he teaches French and Francophone Studies. He has served on the Board of the West African Research Association as well as on the Executive Council of the African Literature Association. His research interests range from (anti) dictatorial narratives, African detective fiction, filmic adaptations of African literary texts, and postcolonial theories, to African visual cultures (Film and Photography) and African writers' contributions to discourses on migration and Human Rights. He has pioneered a field of studies in Law and African Literatures in which he explores the questions of evidence, memory, disciplinary autonomy, and legal storytelling, as well as cross-examines the many "misunderstood relations" that exist between African literatures and the indigenous and received traditions in the law. He has published extensively in these areas and in a variety of avenues including *Research in African Literatures, The French Review, L'Harmattan, African Identities Journal, Africa World*

*Press, Theatre Research International, Africa Today, The International and Comparative Law Review*, etc.

**Dr. Ayobami Ojebode** holds a PhD in Development Communication from the Department of Communication and Language Arts, University of Ibadan, Ibadan, Nigeria. Currently a Senior Lecturer, he teaches communication research, development communication and communication ethics. He is the coordinator of postgraduate programs in his Department. Dr. Ojebode's research interests include development communication, indigenous communication, and media studies in general. He is on the editorial board of the Journal of Communication and Language Arts. He has received visiting fellowships at the African Studies Center at the University of Leiden, Netherlands; University of Oxford's Centre for Research on Inequality, Human Security and Ethnicity (CRISE); and at the College of Communications, the Pennsylvania State University (USA). A prolific scholar, he has published several articles in national and international journals and has co-edited two scholarly books.

**Dr. Emmanuel D. Babatunde** is a professor of Anthropology and chair of the Department of Sociology & Anthropology at Lincoln University, Pennsylvania, USA. Prior to his appointment as chair, he has served as Director of Honors Program for Talented Students from 1993- 2006. Dr. Babatunde has a Doctor of Philosophy from Oxford University in Anthropology in the area of Development and Culture. He earned another Doctor of Philosophy from London University in Comparative Education and an M.Litt. in Social Anthropology exploring how marginalities and minorities seek the verbalization of views unique to them. Dr. Babatunde has published extensively and served as a consultant to numerous renowned international institutions such as the UN, the UNICEF. He has done such distinguished post-doctoral fellowships as the year long Sasakawa Foundation funded Japanese Studies Seminar, the yearlong American Association of Colleges and Universities and is a Fulbright Senior Program Specialist, with expertise in globalization and the marginalization of Sub-Sub-Saharan Africa. He has been successful at writing grants that seek to utilize strengths inherent in African cultures to find solution to some of African social problems. While on Sabbatical during the 2005-2006 Academic year, he served as the Archie Mafeje Fellow at the Africa Institute of South Africa.

**Dr. Bridget A. Teboh** is an Assistant Professor of History at the University of Massachusetts-Dartmouth. She holds a Ph.D. in African History from the University of California Los Angeles (UCLA). Her B.A. (Hons.) is from the University of Yaoundé, Cameroon and a DUEF (Diplôme d'Université d'Etudes Françaises) from Université Jean-Moulin, Lyon III, France. She specializes in African History; African-American Women's History, Women's and Gender studies, and Oral history. Her research interests are colonialism, post-coloniality, historical biography and life writing, women's *ikah* [power], historical ethnography, and women's history. Dr. Teboh has served as a Ford Foundation and International Studies and Overseas Program (ISOP) Scholar-in-Residence and Research Affiliate of the University of Yaoundé. She has contributed several scholarly articles and book chapters including the most recent, "Locating Women in Early 20th Century Moghamo History," in *Emergent Themes and Methods in African Studies: Essays in Honor of Adiele E. Afigbo* eds. Toyin Falola and Adam Paddock (Africa World Press: Trenton, New Jersey, 2009). Dr. Teboh's current projects include *"Unruly Mothers, Combative Wives: Rituals, Women and Change in the Cameroon Grassfields c. 1889-1960,"* a study of British and German colonialism in West Cameroon in the late19th and early 20th centuries; and *Herstory: The Life and Times of "Madame Maternity,"* a political figure and veteran health worker.

**Dr. Anthony A. Olorunnisola** is Associate Professor and Head of Department of Film/Video & Media Studies at the Pennsylvania State University, University Park, U.S.A. He earned a Ph.D. in Mass Communication from Howard University, Washington; D.C. Dr. Olorunnisola has research interests in the transformations of African media systems and in transitions of persons of African descent and has contributed several essays to local and international journals and book volumes. He is editor of *Media in South Africa after Apartheid: a Cross-Media Assessment* (Edwin Mellen Press, 2006) and editor of *Media and Communications Industries in Nigeria: Impacts of Neoliberal Reforms between 1999 and 2007* (Edwin Mellen Press, 2009). He is Guest Editor of a special issue of the *Journal of Communication and Language Arts* (2009) and Guest Editor of a special issue of the *International Journal of Social & Management Sciences* (June 2010); both issues are focused on Media and Political Culture in Africa. He is also lead co-editor (with Keyan Tomaselli) of *Political Economy of Media Transformation in South Africa* (Hampton Press, forthcoming 2010). Dr. Olorunnisola reviews for several and serves on editorial boards of three academic journals.

**Dr. Ayokunle Olumuyiwa Omobowale** holds a Ph.D. in Sociology from the University of Ibadan. His thesis was on *Political Clientelism and Rural Development in Selected Communities in Ibadan, Nigeria*. His research interests lie in African issues related to the Sociological fields of Development, Rural, Political, Medical and Urban studies. He is the recipient of the University of Ibadan Postgraduate School Award for scholarly publication in 2007. At present, he is a lecturer in Sociology at the University of Ibadan, Nigeria. Dr. Omobowale also served on the Editorial Board of the *International Encyclopaedia of Revolution and Protest* published in March 2009 by Wiley-Blackwell Publishing. He has published articles in renowned African Studies journals such as *African Spectrum, African Identities, Journal of Asian and African Studies and Journal of Modern African Studies* as well as made book chapter contributions.

**Ms. Mofeyisara Oluwatoyin Omobowale** holds a Master of Arts (M.A.) degree in Applied Anthropology. She is currently a doctoral student in Anthropology at the University of Ibadan. Her research interests are in Applied Anthropology and Gender Studies. She has published articles in edited volumes and books.

**Mr. Olawale Olufolahan Ajani** holds a Bachelor of Arts (Hons.) in Archaeology and a M.Sc. in Sociology from the University of Ibadan. His scholarly focus is in Medical Sociology, Sociology of Development and Demography.

**Dr. Emmanuel Twesigye** is a professor in the Department of Religion at Ohio Wesleyan University, USA. He currently holds the Aden S. and Mollie Wollam Benedict Professor of Christian Studies and Sharp-Davis-Trimble Professor of religion. He had previously served as Chair of the Department of Religion and Director of Black World Studies at the same institution. Prior to joining the Ohio Wesleyan University in 1989, Professor Twesigye was Professor and Chair of the Department of Religion and Philosophy at Fisk University in Nashville, Tennessee. He has also served as President of the Ohio Academy of Religion as well as Fellow of the National Endowment for Humanities at Princeton University. Professor Twesigye has published a number of major scholarly books and articles. These include: *Religion & Ethics for a New Age* (New York: UPA, 2001); *African Religion, Philosophy, Christianity in Logos-Christ: Common Ground Revisited* (New York: Peter Lang, 1996); *The Global Human Problem: Ignorance, Hate, Injustice and Violence* (1988). Dr. Twesigye completed his Ph.D. in Philosophy and Religion at Vanderbilt University.

**Dr. Okechukwu C. Iheduru**, PhD University of Connecticut is currently Professor of Political Science in the School of Politics and Global Studies at Arizona State University, Tempe where he also served as Director, African and African American Studies Program. Professor Iheduru had previously been Assistant and Associate Professor of International Relations at the James Madison College, Michigan State University, East Lansing, Michigan where he also served as Chair of the International Relations Field. His publications include *The Political Economy of International Shipping in Developing Countries* (University of Delaware Press, 1996), over 50 scholarly papers in local and international journals and book chapters, and more than sixty academic and professional paper presentations. Dr. Iheduru has held visiting professorships and fellowships at Rhodes University, Grahamstown; the University of Johannesburg, Johannesburg; and at the Africa Institute of Southern Africa and the Human Sciences Research Council, both in Pretoria. He is a recipient of the Lilly Endowment Teacher-Scholar award (1995), the Fulbright-Hays Faculty Research Fellowship (2000-2001), and the Zebulon Pearce Distinguished Teacher Award from Arizona State University in 2009. Since 2008, he has been writing a weekly column on Thursdays for *Business Day* newspaper on economics and politics in Lagos (Nigeria).

# Chapter 1
## Towards a Fresh Perspective in Understanding African Migration to the United States Diaspora

*Emmanuel Yewah & 'Dimeji Togunde*

African migration to the United States Diaspora has followed different patterns ranging from forced exit as in slavery to voluntary emigration. The discourse on migration among African scholars has now shifted to a strong focus on the recent Africans immigrants to the United States. Available evidence indicates that the proportion of this new flow of immigrants outnumbers those who came in the "waning years" of slavery. Although the reasons for the recent African migration have been well documented by scholars in various disciplines, the increased wave of African immigration is generating intense debates both in the media and books because of its impact on socio-economic, political, demographic, and cultural landscapes in the United States.

The growth of African diasporic communities in the United States is especially intriguing given the interaction between the countries of origin and the society of encounter, that is, the United States. This ongoing interaction has been taking different shapes and forms ranging from contributions to political activities and/or participation in home politics, cultural diffusion and exchange, educational development, and various creative media products such as literature, art, music, and remittances flow to the role of religion as a mechanism for coping with adjustment challenges and for spiritual growth.

While the push and pull factors that trigger African immigration have been well documented, the role of the United States immigration policies have been recognized as well. With respect to reasons for African migration, major factors such as wars, famine, ecological disasters, weak economic bases, political instability, globalization, and returnees' role in spurring further migration have received empirical support in the literature (Arthur, 2000, 2009; Takyi & Konadu-Agyemang, 2006; Togunde & Osagie, 2009). While the United States immigration policies and visa requirements have been widely recognized by many as strict, the fact remains that they have served as catalyst in promoting African immigration. Prominent among these are the 1965 Immigrant Act, the 1980 Refugee Act, the 1986 IRCA (Immigration Reform Control Act), and the 1990 Diversity Lottery Visa Program. Additionally, the creation of Africana and Diaspora studies in several United States universities has attracted a significant number of African intellectuals. This was made possible in part by the 1965 Immigration Act which gave preference to skilled immigrants and the relatives of those already in the United States to rejoin their family members. Moreover, the United States government and other agencies such as the Rockefeller Foundation and the Ford Foundation began to offer grants and scholarships to Africans to enroll in graduate schools in diverse disciplines. Furthermore, the 1980 Refugee Act, signed into law by President Carter aimed at broadening the scope of forced migrants that would be allowed to enter the United States. Prior to this, only refugees from communist countries were given permission to enter the United States. This resulted in many refugees from war-torn, drought-stricken African countries – Ethiopia, Liberia, Sierra Leone, etc. to enter the United States for sanctuary. While these refugees are scattered all over the United States, the pole of attraction remains major urban centers such as Minneapolis/St Paul, Minnesota, Washington D.C and its environs, Boston, Massachusetts, and New York city.

The 1986 pro-immigration bill promulgated in response to the public outcry against increased illegal immigrants and signed into law by President Reagan, granted amnesty to a substantial number of immigrants from various continents including Africa. The bill allowed immigrants who had entered the country illegally and those who had overstayed their visas to regularize their status to permanent residency. The Diversity Visa Lottery Program which was created by the 1990 Immigration Act seeks to inject new skilled manpower into the American labor force and to diversify the pool of immigrants from countries that had, hitherto, been underrepresented. It allows a total of fifty five thousand immigrants annually from various countries around the globe to enter the United States as permanent residents. Available evidence suggests that within the 1990-2000 decade, about twenty thousand Africans came annually from various African countries through this program (Konadu-Agyemnag et al, 2006). Although it has been argued quite passionately that this program contributes to brain drain from Africa especially, the literature has also recognized that the remittance flow resulting from emigration of highly skilled Africans serve as a compensating mechanism for socio-political and economic development in countries of origin. For instance, Nigerians abroad remitted $10 billion into the country, the highest in sub-Saharan Africa and "the sixth highest destination of remittances from citizens of developing nations in the diaspora", according to a 2009 World Bank report. In the 2008 World Bank Report, other recipients of remittances in the top ten were Sudan $1.2 billion, Senegal and Uganda with $0.9 billion each, South Africa $0.7 billion, Lesotho $0.4 billion, Mauritius $0.3 billion, Togo $0.2 billion, and Mali $0.2 billion.

Despite the burgeoning interest in African migration and its effects, however, there remain gaps in knowledge in this field. For instance, in existing books on African migration to the US diaspora (Konadu-Agyemang et al, 2006; Arthur, 2000, 2009; Apraku, 1993; Falola & Afolabi, 2007a, 2007b; Falola et al 2008; Falola, 2009) there is insufficient attention given to pre-migration departure plans and how they impact migration decisions and adjustment at the country of destination. Some of these books, with the exception of Konadu-Agyemang et al (2006) and Arthur (2009), make perfunctory references to pre-migration plans and characteristics without discussing how immigrants' experiences connect with their homeland. In their insightful collection of essays, Konadu-Agyemang (2006), paid considerable attention to how: pre-migration cultural endowment, "pre-existing patterns of social organization", pre-migration educational attainment, and pre-informal trading experience, have all engendered a semblance of linkage with African immigrants' homeland. Despite this significant scholarly endeavor, pre-migration characteristics such as media and literary representation of the United States, socialization experiences including exposure to oral traditions, religious identity and pluralism which become important tools for immigrants to cope and to navigate through the complexities of their new society have received little or no attention in the literature. This book is an attempt to fill in these gaps. On the one hand, media and literary portrayal of the United States, create certain impressions of America with respect to the economy, the socio-cultural environment, the political culture, educational system - all of which influence potential migrants' mental preparation, sense of awe and desire to visit/live in the United States. On the other, media's representation of Africa and of Americans of African descent in the United States may influence the way African émigrés imbibe African American worldview and their culture.

Moreover, the acculturation and assimilation challenges confronted by African immigrants as do other groups have yet to be analyzed within the context of the socialization experiences that expect Africans to be strong, resilient and successful amid difficulties. Given the multiethnic nature of most African countries, experiences regarding ethnic dynamics may play a major role in shaping ethnic relationships and cultural integration at the country of destination. Since migration does not just occur in a vacuum and since it is a complex process that involves planning, information gathering about destination, risk-taking, overcoming intervening obstacles, the title of this book "Across the Atlantic" is deliberate as it seeks to capture a vast expanse of geographical space and at the same time to offer a fresh perspective on the current debate on African migration to the United States Diaspora.

While the chapters are scholarly, directed at an academic audience, the multidisciplinary approaches employed would appeal to a general readership, especially those who may be interested in learning about Africans in the rapidly growing multiethnic society. Given the impact of print and visual media in generating images that shape public perceptions of any society, journalists and writers would find this book useful, particularly, as it sheds light on the pertinent role that they play in triggering the decisions to migrate. Furthermore, this book will be useful for teachers and students interested in how literature creates the desire and fantasies to want to migrate to the United States. Additionally, the field of ethnic and cultural studies would be enriched by discussions of ethnic identities, role of African cultures and traditions in remittance flows, religious adaptations, and how African immigrants cope with stress in the United States. Anthropologists, family sociologists, and economists would be enlightened by the discussion of how African cultures and traditions play major roles in remittance flows. Scholars and students in Political Science would find the discussion of how Diasporas impact the reconstruction of homelands' political identities highly informative. Finally, in light of the complex nature of the field of immigration, the book would be an invaluable resource as it utilizes an interdisciplinary perspective to examine African migration.

**Structure of the book:**

This volume expands on the growing interest in scholarship on pre-departure and post-immigration experiences of African immigrants in the United States Diaspora. Multidisciplinary in its approach, the collection brings together a select group of accomplished African scholars. It begins by exploring African migration intentions from two perspectives. First, it brings to the fore the complex role that media plays in creating both positive and negative images of the United States and how those images in turn spur or deter the desire to migrate to the United States. Second, it analyzes how African writers' responses to their real or imagined experiences with America help to generate the interest of their readers to contemplate emigrating. These two perspectives set our current book apart from other works published so far. Given the recent phenomenon of media globalization and the free-trans-border flow of media products, the chapter by Togunde, Ojebode, and Vocke explores the role of visual, lyrics, and print media in creating the intention of Nigerian youths to migrate to the United States. Using multiple methodological approaches such as surveys, content analyses, and focus group discussions, Togunde et al examine if young people are engaged in any selectivity process in their treatment of information about the United States. The paper seeks to detect if there is any evidence of selective perception, selective exposure, and selective retention. Yewah's chapter draws from a wide array of texts (dealing with some aspects of America) including essays, memoirs, documentaries, philosophical treatises, and literature to discuss African writers' ability to create "imagined communities." Yewah explores how readers are in turn enticed and immersed through different narrative techniques to think about migrating to the United States.

As mentioned earlier, the literature on immigration is replete with information regarding challenges that immigrants face upon arrival at their destination and how differences in cultural values and life style account for disparity in achievement. The chapter by Babatunde brings in a new perspective by examining aspects of African cultural repertoire that have enabled African immigrants to thrive in the face of uncertainties in the US. Moreover, in an attempt to provide detailed information regarding some of the practices of community building and (re)creation of identity utilized by African émigrés, the chapter by Teboh explains settlement patterns and social organizations of Africans in the United States. Drawing on multiple sources such as primary and secondary data and archival materials, the author examines very clearly how three major spheres: African foods, cultural festivals and conventions, and use of African language serve as adaptation tools and as link with pre-migration cultural practices among Cameroonian immigrants in the United States. Furthermore, the idea of how pre-departure majority-minority contestations among African ethnic and racial groups in their countries of origin are carried over to shape their acculturation experience in the society of encounter is discussed in the chapter by Olorunnisola. The novelty of this chapter hinges on how cumulative negative media representation of Africa and Africans shapes identity and race relations between Africans and majority population on the one hand and how it creates cultural rifts between Africans and African-Americans on the other.

In a new approach, the chapter by Omobowale et al highlights sociocultural importance of remittances as a derivative of social organizations of African family. Its goal is to accentuate the role that African culture plays in the expectation and the responsibility bestowed upon an emigrant. Drawing on surveys and interviews, this chapter elaborates on the importance of family bond as well as African values of interdependence, of sharing, and of being "your brother's keeper", to explicate why African émigrés feel obligated to send money or other goods back to their countries of origin.

While the role of religious traditions and practices in the adaptation process of African immigrants has been explored in previous books, the chapter by Twesigye is unique for two reasons. First, the author draws on his personal life story and experiences to buttress the importance of pre-migration religious orientation and values in shaping response to acculturation shocks in the United States. Second, Twesigye recognizes the creation of new religious institutions and how different African immigrant groups and their leaders utilize these institutions partly as a response to "a higher spiritual calling", desire to worship according African socio-cultural norms, and as a source of self-employment, particularly as it is difficult for most African immigrants to transfer skills gained in their home countries to the American labor force. Furthermore, the chapter highlights African immigrants' creation of churches or mosques in an attempt to preserve the integrity of their religious, moral and cultural heritage and for them "to feel at home."

In recognition of the fact that the socio-political and cultural impact of African immigrants in the diasporas are not limited to the society of encounter, the chapter by Iheduru fills an important gap regarding immigrants' political impact on their homeland. It extends the exploration of the effect that the Diasporas have had on home country culture and society by focusing, in particular, on the construction and reconstruction of homeland national political identity. Drawing primarily on the Ghanaian and Nigerian experiences in the United States as a case study, the chapter elaborates on the repercussions of the connection between the homeland's changing impressions of its Diasporas and of themselves. The effect of African Diaspora cyber-citizenship and cyber political activities on the conception of African national identity is discussed.

## References

Apraku, Kofi K. (1991). *African Emigrés in the United States: a Missing Link in Africa's Social and Economic Development*. New York: Praeger.

Arthur, John A. (2000). *Invisible Sojourners: African Immigrant Diaspora in the United States*. Westport CT: Praeger.

_____. (2009). *African Women Immigrants in the United States: Crossing Transnational Borders*. ____ : Palgrave Macmillan.

Falola, Toyin, Niyi Afolabi (eds.). (2007). *The Human Cost of African Migration*. New York: Routledge.

_____(eds.). (2008a). *Trans-Atlantic Migration: the Paradoxes of Exile* New York: Routledge.

_____ (eds.). (2008b). *African Minorities in the New World*. New York: Routledge.

Konadu-Agyemang, Kwado, Baffour K. Takyi, John A. Arthur (eds.). (2006). *The New African Diaspora in North America: Trends, Community Building, and Adaptation*. Boulder CO: Lexington Books.

Togunde, D., Osagie, S. (2009). *Icons of Progress: Returnees' Effects on Decisions by Nigerians to Migrate to the U.S*. International *Review of Modern Sociology, Vol. 35. No 1 (Spring)*

# Chapter 2
## Media Representation of America and Youth Migration Intentions

*'Dimeji Togunde, Ayobami Ojebode, Amanda Vocke*

### Introduction

Migration of people from what is now known as Nigeria is an ancient practice dating back to the pre-colonial periods. A combination of economic, political, religious and natural factors had been responsible for such migration (Onwubiko, 1986). Such factors included trade, war and conquest, the trans-Saharan and trans-Atlantic slave trade, religious movements such as the jihads and missions, as well as famine and outbreak of diseases, and climatic changes (Barrios, Bartinelli & Strobl, 2006).

British conquest and colonization brought Nigerians greater opportunities for volitional trans-Atlantic migration. In the post independence era, migration to the West rose as Nigeria, and many other African countries, experienced economic hardships occasioned by the adoption of structural adjustment measures, and as persecutions of pro-democracy activists during military rule worsened (Okome, 2002; Takougang, 2003; Ekpu, 2005). Migration has thus been on a steady rise in Nigeria. This is much more so among young and educated people. As Adesina (2007:5) observes, one in every five Nigerian undergraduate students wants to leave the country after graduation in search of better economic opportunities abroad. Specifically, in a more recent study (Togunde and Rinkinen, 2009), a highly significant proportion of youths intend to migrate to America in order to live in a safe environment, and with better infrastructures. Another recent study that takes into account the role of African returnees in stimulating further emigration to the US observes that returnees shape the representation of the US African diaspora through their economic success, life styles, mannerisms, and frustrations, all of which influence peoples' desire to visit or live in the United States (see Togunde and Osagie, 2009).

The characteristics of African-born immigrants in the US support the observation that most Africans migrating to the US are highly educated and many are young. The Journal of Blacks in Higher Education (JBHE), analyzing the 1997 United States census figures, showed that African immigrants are the most highly educated group in the United States (JBHE, 1999-2000). Results of the 2000 United States census show exactly the same trend. As presented by Schmidley (2001), of all the groups of immigrants in the United States, African immigrants have the greatest proportion of holders of a college degree. Whereas 49.3% of African immigrants have a college degree or higher, only 44.9% of Asian immigrants, 32.9% of European immigrants and 11.2% of Latin American immigrants in the United States have a college degree. Only 25.9% of South American and 19.3% of Caribbean immigrants have a college degree (Schmidley, 2001). The proportion of African immigrants in the United States with a college degree is greater than the proportion of US citizens with a college degree which is 24.4% (US Census Bureau, 2003). Nonetheless, the studies noted, African immigrants earn lower income than non-African immigrants with similar educational qualifications (JBHE, 1999-2000; Schmidley, 2001).

With reference to age, the 2000 Census figures also showed that in the United States, the proportion of African immigrants aged 25-54 was 69.0% which is higher than 41.7% for the native-born population (Schimidley, 2001). Most African immigrants are immediate college graduates and fall within the critical work force in the United States.

Nigerians constitute a large number of African immigrants in the US. Grieco (2004), citing statistics from the US Department of Homeland Security Office of Immigration, showed that in 2002, Nigeria had the highest number of immigrants obtaining legal permanent resident permit in the US (8,129) followed by Ethiopia (7,574).

Though Nigerians seeking migration are such a large number and are highly educated people in their most productive years, studies in migration from Nigeria have not been robust. Migration has been explained away as a resort by those escaping the push factors of poverty, unemployment and infrastructural inadequacy in Nigeria (Adesina, 2007, Nwajiuba, et al., 2007; Togunde and Osagie, 2009; Togunde and Rinkinen, 2009). Studies have also focused on migration to the West in a way that suggests a monolithic definition of the West. Not only these, the place of cultural institutions, including the media, in galvanizing or limiting migration has not been explored in the Nigerian context. This chapter intends to fill this gap by focusing on young Nigerians' migration intention and the possible role the media play in creating this intention. In this case, we focus on intention to migrate to the United States of America.

The question of why people migrate has attracted a plethora of theoretical disquisitions especially in the last four decades. The earliest of these theories is the pull-push theory which explains migration as a product of two forces sometimes complementary, other times working in isolation. Push forces are those factors that lead people to decide to leave their places of residence—heavy taxation, oppressive laws, infrastructural collapse, unemployment—while pull factors are those that attract people to a particular destination (Lee, 1966). Another is the network theory which suggests that precious migrants' friends and family members, residing at the destination, provide valuable information, links and impetus that tend to ginger migration intentions (Fleisher, 2007; Pajeras, 2007; Gelderbom, 2006; Wentzel, Vilijoen and Kok, 2006). The cumulative causation theory suggests that with each successful migration in a community, more individuals in that community tend to want to migrate. Value expectancy framework suggests that intention to migrate is provoked when people realize that the values driving their goals can be easily attained somewhere outside their origin (De Jong, Johnson and Richter, 1996; De Jong, Richter and Isarabhakdi, 1994).

As useful as these theories are, we found that they do not explain the possible influence of such societal agencies as the media. In an era of media globalization and free trans-border flow of media products, it is incomplete to account for international migration intentions without factoring in the media.

**Image of America in Non-American Media**

In most parts of the world, America is generally perceived politically in media as the biggest superpower, although there are variations in the ways countries present these perceptions. From the perspective of European countries such as Germany and Great Britain, the United States military is depicted as the superpower of the world, often considered too powerful and controlling of other countries around the world. The Germans' impression has been predicated on their experience with the United States during World War II and the Vietnam War (Enzensberger 2002). Thus, the United States is perceived negatively as a "democratic watchdog," aiming to force its political ideologies and ideals on less fortunate countries. Despite these negative impressions by the Germans, they highlight the positive aspect of the United States' political power. During World War II, the United States was able to save Germany from Hitler's reign of terror (Enzensberger 2002). Furthermore, the dominant sentiment among former American colonies is that their rights were violated by hostile takeover and imposition of the United States' ideals, without any regard to the opinions, history, culture, or political situations in their countries (Hamilton Paterson 2002).

In the Middle East and Asia, political perception of America as a dominant superpower still persists (Waseem 2004). In most African countries however, the United States adopts a laissez-faire approach to political and economic crises afflicting the continent. Since political and strategic interests primarily dictate the United States' foreign policies, the country has restricted its physical presence and influence in military and political affairs in African countries. As a result, most Africans view the United States as being ignorant of other cultures (Hargreaves 1998).

Media portrayal of the United States in Pakistan depends on prevailing socio-economic and political circumstances in Pakistan and neighboring countries. During periods of relative peace and political tranquility, the Pakistani opinions of the United States tend to be positive and it is considered as a non-threatening ally. But during military coups and political unrest, the Pakistanis tend to appreciate the support and sympathy of the United States, but are suspicious of its subtle dictation of democratic ideals (Waseem 2004).

In some African countries such as Rwanda and Darfur, the United States has played a major role in quenching political and economic crises. Such assistance and presence of the US has produced positive perception that the country provides aid to other countries that need its support (Hargreaves 1998).

Until recently, media around the world has often portrayed the United States' economy in a positive light. The US is perceived as the richest country in the world—a land flowing with "milk and honey." The notion of a prosperous nation seems to be contributing to the increasing immigration to the United States in the last 40 years (Wallerstein 1992; McKenzie, Gibson, & Stillman 2007; Khadiagala 2001). For example, in Lebanon, the people of Beirut have always seen the United States as a place of economic boom that will allow some of their emigrants to come and live the life of a royalty (al-Shaykh 2002).

Culturally, media portrayal of America has produced mixed feelings in several countries through comic books, newspapers, televisions, and movies. On the one hand, the British media tends to highlight America's cultural diversity (Buruma 2002). Furthermore, American movies seen in Africa have been viewed as capable of heightening the desires to visit and live in America especially when Hollywood produces special effects and paints romantic, luxurious, high-tech cars and buildings. To most Africans in urban areas, American living conditions is portrayed as a paradise on earth where there is no poverty (Ambler 2002). A study of Nigerian newspapers' portrayal of America and Europe however shows that though most news stories about the US originated from US-based news agencies, the stories were mostly (66%) negative focusing on crimes and crisis (Ojebode, 2009). Moreover, Indians seem to admire how American comic books portray American heroes to children, and how this influences children's knowledge and appreciation of these heroes as people they can look up to (Chaudhuri 2002). On the other hand, Indians seem to portray America as ignorant of other cultures (Chaudhuri 2002). In fact, in some African countries such as Kenya and Tanzania, the stereotype in the media is that the United States is a country full of cowboys (Hargreaves 1998). In Europe, through television shows, American programs are often dubbed into the maternal languages of various countries, thereby providing opportunity for their citizens to learn about American culture. In Italy, for instance, the Italians will dub classic American television shows like Dynasty where luxurious styles of American culture are shown. The Italians will use the ideals of the show to create perceptions that Americans dress in extravagant clothes. These clothes make them look as if all Americans are rich and live in large houses with plenty of space (Gruber 2002).

In Australia and New Zealand, the media shows troubling images of America where violence and abuse take place. The impression created in these countries is that the United States is one of the most dangerous countries in the world with a high crime rate. Access to guns is considered to be responsible for the violence and dangerous living conditions in the United States (Ellis 1998). In addition, media in some West Africans countries such as Cameroon and Ghana portray the United States as a racist society where minorities especially blacks of African descent are discriminated against. As a result, there is some anxiety and fear among potential migrants from Africa that they will also be treated unfairly if they come to live in the United States (Amin 2005). The fear is even more pronounced in South Africa where there is perception that racism in the United States surpasses that of South Africa's apartheid (Jackson & Faupin 2007). The media in Europe also paints racism as a negative part of United States' culture, where minorities are treated as second class citizens (Marinot 2000).

Though direct studies of what the audience see and its effects on their intention to migrate to the US are rare, several studies suggest that consumption of media products that paint a nation positively can stimulate, in the consumer, intention to migrate to that nation. For instance, Mai's (2004) study of migration intention of young Albanians strongly suggests that Italian television strongly motivated young Albanians' intention to migrate from Albania in search of modern life. In fact, he described the television as a catalyst that responded to and stimulated the young people's desire to break away from the traditional communist home. Mai's (2004) study is quite helpful. However his work cannot be generalized to the Nigerian and American contexts. The prevailing political situation in communist Albania was a strong push factor to the young people. This makes it difficult to draw a line between the influence of the media as a pull factor and that of the prevailing circumstances at home.

## Theories of Media Effects

The exact influence of the media on individuals and societies has been the concern of scholars, politicians and public commentators starting from World War II when Nazi's successful use of propaganda led to the conclusion that the media had powerful effects on their audience. This assumption, which was known as the hypodermic needle or powerful effect theory, has been roundly criticized for portraying societies as homogenous and the audience as totally helpless and incapable of screening or criticizing messages. The assumption was also criticized for lacking scientific or empirical foundations (Severin and Tankard, 2001; Folarin, 2002; Baran and Davis, 2003).

Media theorizing witnessed a paradigm shift with the works of Paul Lazarsfeld and his colleagues who proved that the media indeed had limited effects. Employing thorough scientific and empirical approaches, Lazarsfeld and others were able to prove that a network of interpersonal relations, group commitment and other intervening variables mitigate any unbridled power of the media (Lazarsfeld, Berelson and Gaudet, 1944). According to them, rather than rushing at people like a wild gale and overpowering them, media messages pass through opinion leaders who screen information and pass on items that would help others share their views., They called this the two-step flow theory—the idea that messages pass from the media through opinion leaders to opinion followers (Baran and Davis, 2003).

From the works of Lazarsfeld and his colleagues, other theoretical positions such as the individual differences theory and the social categories theory directly or indirectly sprang (DeFleur, 1970). The former stated that individuals are so different that media influence will vary from person to person, while the latter argued that membership of certain social groups—political party, religious groups, age, income level—predisposes people to being influenced in the same way by media messages (DeFleur, 1970).

Still on the factors that might mitigate the effects of the media, Leon Festinger articulated the theory of cognitive consistency, which held that "people consciously or unconsciously work to preserve their existing views" Baran & Davis, 2003:145). When people receive such information as is contrary to their beliefs and views, they experience cognitive dissonance, a kind of psychological discomfort. To minimize dissonance, people embark on a number of processes called the selective processes. First is selective exposure that argues that people tend to expose themselves to messages that are consistent with existing beliefs and attitudes (Baran and Davis, 2003; Griffin, 2003). Next is selective retention that states that people tend to remember best and longest those messages that are most meaningful to them. Third is selective perception, which states that people alter the meaning of messages so that they become consistent with pre-existing beliefs and attitudes. Our search for any studies that examine young Nigerians' selectivity with regards to information about developed nations did not yield any fruit.

In this study, we explore the extent to which the media influence the migration decisions of young people in Nigeria. We examine the image of the US presented in the Nigerian media and whether this influences the migration intentions of young people. We want to examine if young people engaged in any selectivity process in their treatment of information about the US.

# Method

Depth and quality for a study of this nature call for a multifaceted approach to the inquiry. Therefore, we adopted both quantitative and qualitative approaches. We studied the views of young people through a survey, media messages through content analysis and asked for further qualitative explication through focus group discussions. In this section, we present the methodological choices we made in the course of this research and first, we begin with the procedure of the survey.

## Procedure for the Survey

The analysis in this section derives from a 2006 survey of 678 students in two South-Western Nigerian universities located in Ile-Ife (Osun State) and Ibadan (Oyo State). The interviews were conducted between May and July, 2006 by the principal investigator and a team of trained research assistants. Funding for this project was provided by the Faculty Development Grants and the John S. Ludington Professorship at Albion College. Participants were surveyed regarding their socio-economic and demographic variables as well as on their plans towards future migration. The surveys also elicited information about students' prior travelling experience to the United States. This question is followed by an inquiry that aims to detect whether or not students plan to visit or migrate to America within the next five years as well as reasons for wanting to do so. For respondents who wish to migrate to America, they were asked to give the most important reason for intending to migrate from Nigeria.

To enable us to achieve the goals of this paper, respondents were asked about various perceptions about the American economy in Nigerian media as well as where those perceptions come from. We then queried students about their views regarding images and pictures of America in the Nigerian media in addition to perception of America created in the American media accessible to them.

To enhance the depth of our analysis, two additional questions included whether or not they actively and currently participate in the annual United States Lottery Visa program; and whether or not respondents perceive the United States as a land of socio-economic opportunities. The diversity visa was part of the 1990 Immigration Law to enable about 55,000 residents of many developing countries to come annually to the United States as permanent residents. Our argument is that an active participation indicates serious intent to move to the United States. For the latter question, our rationale for including it derives from an assumption that perception of the socio-economic landscape in United States may shape peoples' expectations and migration intentions.

As a unique study that focuses on migration intentions of undergraduate students, the choice of the two universities was dictated in part by the presence of academic colleagues who later helped in linking us with reliable research assistants/field workers, and by the socio-economic diversity of the two universities. As two premier public universities, we are confident that information garnered from students who come from wide-ranging backgrounds would shed light on an area of inquiry that has not yet received adequate attention in the African migration literature. Yet, we recognize that had we got more funding, we would have expanded the sample size to include students from other universities in the region.

To ensure uniformity in data collection techniques and to increase sampling accuracy, a two-stage sampling approach was employed. First, in each university, residential block of hostels for males and females were identified. At the second stage, within each block, the number of rooms was also identified, and a systematic selection of rooms in randomly selected blocks was undertaken. Structured questionnaires and follow-up interviews were conducted with eligible students in selected rooms. For both universities, a total of 1500 questionnaires were administered, however, only 678 students participated fully in the study, which is equivalent to 45% response rate. The fact that students in both universities were preparing for end of semester examinations was responsible for the modest response rate. Despite the difficulty of sampling a larger pool, the robustness of the data is reflected in the variability of the students' characteristics such as age, sex and educational level (or total years of education). Surprisingly, majority of the students are single and are full-time students who do not work at all.

We proceed with the empirical analysis by showing in Table 1 the percentage distribution of the respondents' demographic and socio-economic characteristics. Next, in Table 3, we present a descriptive analysis of various dimensions of media portrayal of America; respondents' past and future migration plans; and reasons for planning to migrate to America or stay in Nigeria. Both Tables 4 and 5 show a series of bivariate analysis to connect the relationship between various perceptions of America with the likelihood of visiting or moving to the United States. For these two tables, we invoke Pearson-Chi-Square to assess significant relationships.

Table 1 shows demographic and socio-economic profile of the respondents. The average age of the sampled population is 22.4 years; their ages range from 16 to 31 years. There is a higher proportion of males than females (55.2% vs. 44.8%). Students' total years of schooling range from 13 to 18 years, with an average of 15.7 years. The sampled population consisted of first year students through fifth year students. Those students are predominantly single (93.1%), and they are also overwhelmingly full-time students who do not work at all (94.4%).

Table 1: Respondents' demographic and socio-economic characteristics

| Variables | Frequency | Percent |
|---|---|---|
| Age in years** | | |
| 16 | 8 | 1.2 |
| 17 | 24 | 3.5 |
| 18 | 63 | 9.3 |
| 19 | 43 | 6.3 |
| 20 | 77 | 11.4 |
| 21 | 55 | 8.1 |
| 22 | 80 | 11.8 |
| 23 | 80 | 11.8 |
| 24 | 66 | 9.7 |
| 25 | 59 | 8.7 |
| 26 | 48 | 7.1 |
| 27 | 27 | 4.0 |
| 28 | 19 | 2.8 |
| 29 | 10 | 1.5 |
| 30 | 18 | 2.7 |
| 31 | 1 | 0.1 |
| **Average age of respondents= 22.4 | | |
| Grouped Age of Respondents | | |
| 16-19 | 138 | 20.4 |
| 20-23 | 292 | 43.1 |
| 24+ | 248 | 36.6 |
| Sex | | |
| Males | 374 | 55.2 |
| Females | 304 | 44.8 |
| Educational level in years** | | |
| 13 | 83 | 12.2 |
| 14 | 116 | 17.1 |
| 15 | 113 | 16.7 |
| 16 | 136 | 20.1 |
| 17 | 84 | 12.4 |
| 18 | 146 | 21.5 |
| **Average years of education= 15.7 | | |
| University level of Education | | |
| First year student | 135 | 19.9 |
| Second year student | 158 | 23.3 |
| Third year student | 130 | 19.2 |
| Fourth year student | 159 | 23.5 |
| Fifth year student | 96 | 14.2 |

| Marital Status | | |
|---|---|---|
| Single | 631 | 93.1 |
| Married | 47 | 6.9 |
| Occupation | | |
| Full-Time Student (not working at all) | 640 | 94.4 |
| Full-time Student (but combines trading) | 38 | 5.6 |

## Procedure for Focus Group Discussions

The focus group discussions (FGD) were meant to provide deeper insight into the influence of media images of the United States on young people's migration intention. In the FGD we wanted to know what young people thought about America and the factors responsible for this opinion. This entailed asking open-ended questions on their sources of information about America, their perception of American, and their migration intention to America.

We selected a government university, a private university and a government polytechnic. In each school, we conducted four focus group discussions drawing participants from across departments and disciplines. A total of 96 students took part in the twelve discussions. From the discussions, we were able to identify, among others, media outlets and products mostly patronized by students. The most often mentioned of these were the ones we selected for content analysis. We considered newspapers, magazines, music and movies. Interestingly, television and radio were not as often mentioned as the media mentioned above.

## Procedure for the Content Analysis

We selected two newspapers: the Nation and the Nigerian Tribune; and a hard-news magazine, Tell. We discovered that young people patronized a myriad of soft-sell magazines out of which we selected two: Ovation and Encomiums Weekly. The most often mentioned American movie by our respondents was Prison Break. Others were True Lies and Madea's Family Reunion. It is customary for Nigerian musicians to visit United States and sing about life and experience in the United States in their albums. We purposively selected available tracks released by these musicians.

In all, we analyzed 151 editions of the Nation; 147 editions of the Nigerian Tribune, and 23 editions of Tell. We also analyzed 8 editions of Ovation and 12 of Encomiums Weekly. We studied the three films named above and the songs released by five Nigerian artists about their life in the United States. For the newspapers, our selection cut across the year 2007; we chose six randomly selected months of the year and analyzed all available editions released in those months; for the hard-news magazine, we chose every other edition.

In all our analysis of the media product, we were guided by the question: what image of the United States is offered by the media? For the newspapers and magazines, we constructed 12 content categories:
1. An opulent nation meant for the rich
2. An equal opportunities nation for foreigners; a nation flowing with milk and honey
3. A nation where democracy thrives
4. Promoter of peace and democracy in other nations; philanthropic nation
5. A land of scientific and technological innovation
6. A nation that rewards its people
7. A nation of heroes and heroines
8. A nation ridden with crime and insecurity
9. A land troubled by natural disasters
10. A nation troubled by social problems
11. A land of turbulent politics
12. A nation whose foreign mission went wrong

In addition, we categorized all stories into two directional groups: positive stories about the US, and negative stories. As the categories suggest, all stories that fell into the first seven categories were positive; those that fell into the last five were positive. Two independent coders worked on these two sets of content categories as a way of ensuring inter-coder reliability. Using Holsti's inter-coder reliability formula (Wimmer and Dominick, 2000), we obtained a reliability index of 0.7.

## Findings

We consider it more useful to present the result of the content analysis first. It appears more logical to first consider what is in the media before considering whether or not these influence young people's migration intentions. In the content analysis section, therefore, we answer the question "what is the image of America in the media accessible to young people. We follow this with the survey findings that connect this image with migration intention. The FGD comes last which provide further insights into the survey claims. We round off the section by identifying the common themes across the bodies of data we have presented.

### The image of America in Nigerian and American Media

We present the result of our content analysis under three subsections: the image of the US presented in the Nigerian print media; the image of the US presented in Nigerian popular music and the image of the US found in the American films Nigerians watched.

## The Image of the United States Presented in Nigerian Print Media

Our analysis of media content showed that the US enjoyed remarkable space in the Nigerian media. Comparing the number of stories about the US with stories about all other nations put together, we discovered that more than one-fourth (26.7%) of all foreign stories were about the US. We concentrated on stories about the US and coded 1,585 such stories from the selected newspapers and magazines. Table 2 presents the results of the analysis.

Table 2: The Image of the US in Nigerian Papers

| S/N | | The Nation | | Tribune | | Tell | | Soft Sells | | Total | |
|---|---|---|---|---|---|---|---|---|---|---|---|
| | | F | % | F | % | F | % | F | % | F | % |
| 1. | Opulent nation | 0 | 0 | 43 | 5.9 | 16 | 8.7 | 34 | 52.3 | 93 | 5.8 |
| 1. | Equal Opportunities | 22 | 3.6 | 42 | 5.7 | 14 | 7.6 | 10 | 15.4 | 88 | 5.5 |
| 1. | Where democracy thrives | 61 | 10.1 | 0 | 0.0 | 0 | 0.0 | 1 | 1.5 | 62 | 3.9 |
| 1. | Promoter of democracy; philanthropic | 110 | 18.2 | 86 | 11.7 | 8 | 4.3 | 5 | 7.7 | 209 | 13.1 |
| 1. | Scientific and tech innovation | 0 | 0.0 | 83 | 11.3 | 46 | 25.0 | 2 | 3.1 | 131 | 8.2 |
| 1. | Rewards people | 21 | 3.5 | 0 | 0.0 | 0 | 0.0 | 13 | 20.0 | 34 | 2.1 |
| 1. | Heroes/heroine | 0 | 0.0 | 0 | 0.0 | 20 | 10.9 | 0 | 0.0 | 20 | 1.3 |
| 1. | Crime | 109 | 18.0 | 32 | 4.4 | 28 | 15.2 | 0 | 0.0 | 169 | 10.6 |
| 1. | Natural disasters | 0 | 0.0 | 15 | 2.0 | 8 | 4.3 | 0 | 0.0 | 23 | 1.4 |
| 1. | Social problems | 55 | 9.1 | 92 | 12.6 | 26 | 14.1 | 0 | 0.0 | 173 | 10.8 |
| 1. | Turbulent Politics | 12 | 2.0 | 81 | 11.1 | 8 | 4.3 | 0 | 0.0 | 101 | 6.3 |
| 1. | Wrong foreign mission | 214 | 35.4 | 258 | 35.2 | 10 | 5.4 | 0 | 0.0 | 482 | 30.2 |
| | Total | 604 | 100.0 | 732 | 100.0 | 184 | 100.0 | 65 | 100.0 | 1585 | 100.0 |

The predominant image of the US presented in the papers is a negative one. The greatest proportion of the stories (30.2%) presented the country as one whose foreign mission has gone sour. Expectedly, most stories in this category deal with the war on terror, several of them focusing on the heavy casualty the US was incurring especially in Iraq. An example of these is Nigeria Tribune's "3000th US Soldier Killed in Iraq" which states that "the day after Saddam Hussein's execution, the death toll for Americans killed in the

Iraq (sic) war reached 3,000 as President Bush struggles to salvage a military campaign that has scant support" (Nigeria Tribune, January 2, 2007:43).[1]

Others in this category focused on President Bush's handling of the war. "President Bush is, indeed, very dangerous, harmful and downright arrogant" (Oladeinde, 2007:7) and "President Bush should have the courage to admit his own mistakes" (Cohen, 2007:20)[2]. Yet others focused on the human rights abuse that was brought about by the Iraqi war and the way it was prosecuted. Olatunji (2007:40) writes:

> Under the cover of fighting terror, the Bush administration has emasculated the robust foundations of the liberties Americans fought to institute and have come to take for granted. The right to receive and impart information is under steady assault, and so is the right to privacy...it denies to foreigners suspected of terrorism all the protections of the Geneva Convention and other international accord.

Other stories of rights abuse presented gory events such as the shooting of several civilians and a 15-year old passer-by by US soldiers in Afghanistan who also "forced AP and AFP photographers at the scene to delete their photos they had taken" (The Nation, March 5, 2007:58).

Still on American foreign policy, stories condemn America's foot-dragging about the Darfur crisis. In "Spineless on Sudan", Ktistof (2007:20) compared Bush with the French President Mr. Sarcozy praising the latter for taking courageous steps such as pushing to send a European Union force to Darfur while Mr. Bush's aides are "still discussing whether he should give a primetime speech on Darfur to ratchet up the pressure"

Next in proportion to, but much fewer than, stories describing American foreign mission as having gone sour were stories describing the country as promoter of democracy in other nations, a peace-loving and philanthropic nation. These stories constituted only 13.1% of the total number. Among them were The Nation's "US Pushes for Kosovo Independence" and Tribune's "US Government Denies Endorsing Buhari".

Other prominent images of the US in the papers were that of a nation troubled by social problems (10.8%) and a nation plagued by crime and insecurity (10.6%). On the former, the Tribune (January 1, 2007) had "'I blame Posh and Co' says mother of girl killed by anorexia" which discussed the death of a girl, Sophie, who "spent a fortune on magazines full of pictures of celebrities" and starved to death trying to be like the celebrities "who make being thin attractive and glamorous"; Williams (2007:21) lamented the failure of efforts to improve race relations and promote integration by integrating whites and blacks in the same schools in the US, Abah (2007:12) wrote "Las Vegas: the City of Sin", describing the city as "the meanest town on earth, a representation of all that is extreme"

On crime and insecurity, stories published included Adeyemi's (2007:14) "Man attempts to roast wife"; Bob's (2007:9) "A gift of marijuana" which is the story of a 13-year old whose "father, mother and grandmother smoked it [marijuana]" and to whom marijuana was presented as birthday gift by parents. On this same theme, The Nation gave prominence to Poulton's (2007:21) "Guns are the great American specificity". Poulton commenting on Cho Seung-Hui's shooting on April 16 2007 of 32 fellow University students and then of himself in Virginia, wrote:

> Cho bought his guns openly and legally at gun shops. Yes, America has gun shops!...Nothing about this is strange in Virginia where any adult may purchase one pistol every month...The guns statistics make America unique; 25% of private citizens have a firearm. More than 200 million firearms are in private hands. 40% of men own at least one gun. 10% of women own a firearm. Only 14% of people in large urban areas own a firearm—that would be huge in Europe, but seems small in USA...there are more than 30,000 gun deaths every year...three times more than in comparable countries...a dozen children are killed by firearms every day...more than 20 times as many as in the other 25 advanced industrial nations

The Nation repeated this report a week after it was first published. Though we coded it only once, we noted that the repetition was the paper's attempt to call attention to this feature of the American society.

Put together, negative stories about the US in Nigerian print media accounted for 59.6%. However, it is important to note that the image of the US varied from one genre of the print media product to another as the fig 1 depicts:

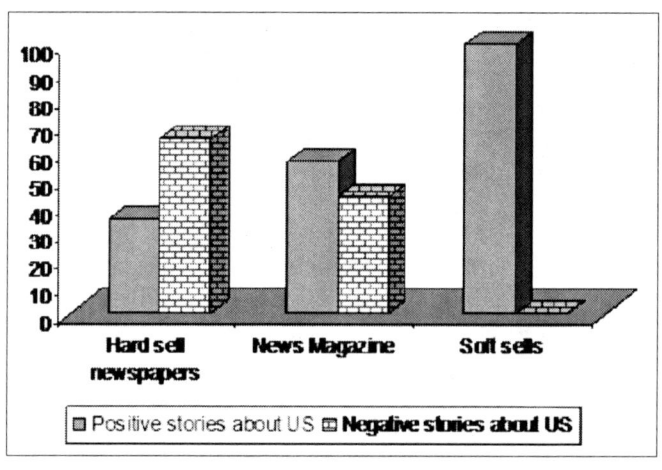

Figure 1: Proportions of positive & negative stories about the US by different genres of Nigerian newspapers

The predominant image presented in the newspapers was negative; the one in soft sells was a positive one. In fact, the soft-sell magazines had not a single negative story about the US. More than half of the soft-sell stories (52.3%) present the US as an opulent nation meant for the rich. These stories report the visits of the rich in Nigeria to the US for holiday, business and medical care. Encomiums Weekly had such stories as "Saint Obi's wife delivers baby boy in US" (December 11, 2007, Pg 4); "Kanu Nwankwo budgets N100m for father's burial; flies in special casket from America" (December 11, 2007, Pg 7); "Top industrialist, Tunji Sunmonu on holiday" (October 9, 2007; Pg A22, and "Biola Adegoke off to US" (December 4, 2007, Pg 3).

A smaller proportion of soft-sell stories (15.4%) presented America as a nation of equal opportunities for both citizens and immigrants; a land flowing with milk and honey. Ovation reported an "Interview with Jumoke in New York". Jumoke, a Nigerian, had become so influential in New York that "many African Americans have named their boys Jumoke" (Ovation undated, Pg 35)

The image presented in the magazine (Tell) was more positive than negative. We noted that Tell magazine did not maintain a foreign page but had a section titled Panorama where, in most cases, light issues were presented. Most of the positive stories presented by Tell recorded scientific and technological breakthroughs as well as oddities in the US. The magazine published stories such as Fabiyi's (2007:13) "Surgery not for adults", and Abah's (2007:16) "A final bye to meningitis". But not all of the stories celebrated America's technological and scientific breakthroughs. A few, such as Aleem's report of the birth of Jiejie, a baby with three arms, and the confusion among surgeons in Texas Children Hospital over which of the arms to amputate, and Abah's "Stem research and a moral burden" rather show scientific dilemma.

To sum up this subsection, we would say for the most part, on the pages of Nigerian papers, the US is not a nation flowing with milk and honey. While it is presented as a place for the rich to visit by soft-sell papers, a place of oddities and scientific innovation by the magazine, it is presented as a nation whose policy on terrorism is wrong, a nation troubled by crime and social problems in the hard-news dailies.

## The Image of the US in Nigerian Popular Music

During our focus group discussions, participants identified Nigerian musicians that have sung about visits to the US. Frequently mentioned were Bright Chimezie, late Gbenga Adeboye,[3] Abass Akande Obesere, Ayinde Wasiu and Adewale Ayuba. We sought and analyzed the lyrics of these artists.

Two images of America emanated from our analysis of the lyrics. The most predominant of these is the image of a land flowing with milk and honey; a place where Nigerians are 'making it' well enough to afford lavish social parties and sponsor musicians. In the album, Exposure, Gbenga Adeboye briefly presented the lavish welcome and courteous hospitality he received from Americans:

> (Translated) They came to pick me with a long sleek car; in length it was second only to trains. It was known as Stretch limousine. With it they took me round. The whites whom we adore were the ones adoring me. They opened the car door for me, made tea for me, even made my bed for me.

Others, such as Wasiu Ayinde and Alabi Pasuma discussed such reception as well. The former usually gives a long list of Nigerians in different parts of the US who warmly received him, lavishly entertained him and sponsored or supported his musical shows.

In Bubble Dance, Adewale Ayuba dressed in a shirt with the colors and patterns of the American flag, stressed the abundance of food in the US compared with Lagos, Nigeria when he said:

(Translated) There is a kind of food we ate in America

If we get such to eat in Lagos; we all will be big

Food such as Kentucky chicken, and McDonalds

And a kind of biscuits called 'gira' in America

Take a look at Ade, my lead drummer

Take a look at Afaro who beats the small drum

Was this how (fat) they were when they left Lagos?

...America is great/sweet

Nigerians, facelift our country

In other words, unlike Americans, Nigerians are scrawny and skinny because of malnutrition. Basic survival needs, especially food, constitute the central allure in Ayuba's songs about America.

Abass Akande Obesere, in OBTK, also underscored the abundance of food in the US. In the US he and his team ate:

(Translated) Burgher in the morning

Gira in the afternoon

Kentucky in the evening

And when it gets dark, we 'urinated there'[4] with whites...

We ate chicken so much that

Fowls began to flee from us

Within weeks, our buttocks bloated up;

Our cheeks bloated up, and our stomachs bloated up too

As the fourth line shows, Obesere went further to discuss the moral laxity in America. He narrated his and his team's sexual recklessness with white American ladies in explicit expressions:

I saw a white lady in New York City, then I began singing, saying if I am unable to 'urinate there' with this white lady I will commit suicide. Within a jiffy, I 'urinated there' with her.

In the above excerpts, we noted that the musician did not assume the position of a moralist trying to condemn a practice but rather he was celebrating his triumph.

The second image of the US presented in the lyrics is that of hardship people, especially immigrants in America faced. Lyrics that present this image are very few. Gbenga Adeboye, in London Yabis, discussed the problem of marital instability in Europe and America. He expressed shock about the fact that children can ask their parents to be arrested and jailed. In vivid details, he painted the picture of immigrants laboring in Europe and America:

See how they work: Cleaning job 6pm to 8am

Cleaning assistant: 9.00-11.00

Or kitchen porter: 9-11

Security: 11-5

No rest, no break; back to 6pm-8am

He went on to describe the filthy and despicable jobs that Nigerians in Europe and America pick up: washing corpses, working in hospices and washing public toilets:

> toilets blocked with human excreta...and with pads drenched with menstrual blood. You must use the hands with which you eat to pack faeces and pull out sanitary pads before you can flush the toilets...as if you're a prisoner.

He talked about the high cost of living in Europe and America. Everything the immigrant earned was swallowed up by bills:

> Bills for electricity, bills for water; bills for gas, bills for even the air they breathe in, bills for light. If he passes excreta he pays; if he urinates he pays; if he spits he pays. Bills after bills...that's why they cannot come back home

The life of the immigrant as presented by Gbenga Adeboye is indeed an unattractive one.

Unpleasant experiences of immigrants presented in the lyrics included distrust and misunderstanding by citizens. According to Bright Chimezie, when he was eating the Nigerian delicacies he took to the US, some citizens thinking "he's committing suicide o; the black man "wey dey" here is committing suicide oo" called on the police. And Adewale Ayuba was insulted for spitting while chewing Nigerian dental sticks.

In sum, by far the more dominant image of the US presented by Nigerian musicians whose songs we studied was that of a nation of opportunities flowing with milk and honey. Very few present the other side of life in the US.

## The Image of the US Presented in American Films Young Nigerians Watch

In each of the focus group discussions we had, discussants mentioned Prison Break as one of the American films they were watching. Most discussants had not finished watching the film for it is a long one. Prison Break is an American serial television series now available in DVD formats in Nigeria. Produced in three seasons with each having about 22 episodes, the film is characterized by suspense and intrigues. The story revolves around a man who was sentenced to death for a crime he did not commit, and his brother's desperate plan to help him escape the sentence. The man, Lincoln Burrows, was found guilty of murdering the Vice-President's brother Terence Steadman. Lincoln's brother, Michael Scofield, determined to get him out made connections with prison staff and inmates. At the end of Season One, Michael, Lincoln with six other inmates escaped Fox River State Penitentiary. In Season Two, the escapees moved to locations across America. Lincoln was, towards the end of the Season, exonerated of all charges against him while his brother, Michael was sent back to prison to face homicide charges.

In the film, life in the US is presented as characterized by intrigues, crime and violence. Agency personnel commit murder to cover tracks; a girl was mistaken to be Sara and was shot dead at a phone booth and Lincoln Burrows could just have been executed for a crime he did not commit.

True Lies, an Arnold Schwarzenegger film, was the next frequently mentioned. A 1994 film, True Lies revolves around Harry and Helen Tasker. Secret agent Harry was to track down stolen warheads smuggled into the US by a radical Islamic group. Harry was assisted by fellow agent Albert Gibson with whom he was trailed by Aziz, the leader of the Islamic group. The trail led to a restroom and later a hotel where fighting ensued. Aziz escaped but the group succeeded in arresting both Harry and his wife, who had all along thought her husband was a computer salesman. Harry and Helen managed to escape before the terrorists would blow up the hideout and Harry with Albert succeeded in blowing up the terrorists' convoy. Harry then went to rescue his daughter who had been kidnapped by the terrorists. Taken on the surface, the film presents the US as a nation with advanced technology. The film also shows the nation as apprehensive of terrorist attack. There is also a large dose of violence in the film.

The third most famous American film among our discussants was Tyler Perry's Madea's Family Reunion. It is the story of a black community held tightly together by a matriarch, Madea. Madea, energetic, selfless yet firm and at times brutal, is ordered by a court to foster Nikki who had been under foster and had experienced abuse. Madea's niece, Lisa, is engaged to a rich banker, Carlos, but was consistently abused by him. Madea's disdain for injustice found expression in her suggestion to Lisa to 'swat Carlos like Serena and Venus swat the tennis'. Contrary to Madea's reaction, Victoria, Lisa's mum wanted Lisa to continue to endure the abuse obviously because of the financial gains accruing to her from Lisa's engagement to Carlos. Lisa's sister, Vanessa, kicked against it and during the family reunion; a fight ensued between Vanessa and Victoria, her mum.

Before the service began on their wedding day, Carlos gave Lisa another beating but Lisa, remembering Madea's advice, poured hot grits on him. Lisa appeared in church alone, unkempt and in casual wears and declared that she was not getting married. "For the past five years, I have been beaten everyday". Frankie, a caring, if at times brash bus driver, walked up to Vanessa, to whom he had been engaged, and asked that they move straight to the altar and get married. Vanessa, after the initial shock, acquiesced, and they were married. The rejoicing and celebration that followed showed that the wedding received the approval of the community.

Running through the film is the theme of the indomitable American spirit. The vast compound on which the family reunion was held was owned by a former slave family and forebears of the black community in question. They, with sheer hard work, bought the property from their masters and rose from slaves to landowners. Nikki rose from a never-do-well runaway and a truant to a top-of-the class student on her way to becoming a lawyer.

Madea, with little or no formal education, held the community together and would gladly fight and be sentenced in order to protect members of her black community. Greed and selfishness, gambling and indecent dressing are parts of the features of the community but the inspiring words of elderly Myrtle assisted by May suggested that these vices were alien to the community.

The image of the US presented in the most often mentioned films is dual. In some we see the picture of a nation characterized by violence, crime and intrigues; in others we see the picture of a determined people daring all odds. There is affluence as well as poverty.

## Findings from the survey

Table 3: Respondents' perception of America, possible sources of and influence of information

| Variable | Frequency | Percent |
|---|---|---|
| Perceptions about American Economy in Nigerian Media | | |
| Stable and lots of jobs | 283 | 41.7 |
| Best in the world (the most prosperous nation) | 391 | 57.7 |
| Corrupt/selfish/exploitative society | 4 | 0.6 |
| Is America a land of socio-economic opportunities? | | |
| Yes | 483 | 71.2 |
| No | 195 | 28.8 |
| If yes, where do you get the perception that America is a land of socio-economic opportunities? | | |
| Shared experiences with returning or visiting migrants | 135 | 27.9 |
| TV/Media | 188 | 38.9 |
| Both people and media | 68 | 14.1 |
| Own perception (through reading books) | 92 | 19.1 |
| Why is America not a land of socio-economic opportunities? | | |
| Prevalent of Crime/ Poverty | 93 | 47.7 |
| Perception of Racism | 25 | 12.8 |
| No such place/ other countries are prosperous | 77 | 39.5 |
| Media Images and Pictures of America in Nigeria | | |
| Beautiful/ Lovely/Paradise | 226 | 33.3 |
| Civilized/Developed economically and politically | 282 | 41.6 |
| Rampant with crime and pornography | 170 | 25.1 |
| Media Portrayal of America in American Media | | |
| Developed/High-Tech country | 238 | 35.1 |
| Orderly/Just/Trust in Government | 93 | 13.7 |
| Beautiful/Paradise | 106 | 15.6 |
| Violent/Corrupt/ Pornography/moral decadence | 241 | 35.5 |

| | | |
|---|---|---|
| Has Respondent traveled to America? | | |
| Yes | 49 | 7.2 |
| No | 629 | 92.8 |
| If no, does respondent wish to visit within the next 5 years? | | |
| Yes | 594 | 94.4 |
| No | 35 | 5.6 |
| Does respondent desire to move to America within the next 5 years? | | |
| Yes | 374 | 55.2 |
| No | 304 | 44.8 |
| If yes, what is single most important reason for desire to move? | | |
| More work/Better economic conditions | 177 | 47.3 |
| Safer/Better infrastructures | 197 | 52.7 |
| Why does the respondent not wish to move (or migrate) to America? | | |
| Patriotism/ Love of homeland | 171 | 56.3 |
| Social/ cultural ties to family and friends | 93 | 30.6 |
| Negative feelings/ perceptions of racism | 40 | 13.1 |
| Do respondents regularly participate in the annual U.S. Visa lottery program? | | |
| Yes | 271 | 40.0 |
| No | 407 | 60.0 |

Table 3 presents respondents' perceptions of media portrayal of America in Nigeria. It is discernible that slightly more than half of the students believe that America is the most prosperous nation in the world, while 4 out of 10 perceive America in terms of its economic stability and availability of job opportunities. When respondents were queried about whether America is a land of socio-economic opportunities, a large proportion (7 out of 10) answered yes.

Further investigation regarding the sources of their perceptions indicate that information from the media has shaped their knowledge (27.7%); followed by approximately 20% whose views come from shared experiences with other Nigerians (e.g. returnees). Yet, 1 out of 10 derives their impressions from both people and media, and 1 out of 7 collects their perceptions from books. Of the respondents who did not believe that America is a land of socio-economic opportunities, prevalence of crime and poverty (13.7%) is their biggest reason. Furthermore, 4 out of 10 respondents think that America is civilized and highly developed economically and politically. Interestingly, 1 out of every 3 surveyed students hold the impression that America is portrayed by the media as beautiful and lovely place ("a paradise on earth"). Despite positive images of America, a significantly large proportion (25.1%) see America portrayed as a nation plagued with crime and pornography.

Moreover, as shown in table 2, there are clear differences between how respondents view media portrayal of America in the Nigerian media compared to perceptions of America in the American media. While there is a slight decrease in the proportion of students who think that American media portrays America as a developed and technologically advanced country (35.1%), there is a significant increase in the proportion that hold the impression that the United States is a violent, corrupt, and morally decadent society (35.5%). Furthermore, there is a significant drop in the proportion of students who think that American media conveys America as a beautiful and lovely place (15.6%) compared to the proportion who responded to media images of America in the Nigerian media (33.3%).

Still on Table 3, findings show that an overwhelmingly large proportion (92.8%) of the respondents had never visited the United States. Of those, a significant number want to visit within the next 5 years (87.6%). In addition, our investigation regarding whether or not students would want to move and live in the United States shows, however, that only 55.2% desire to migrate to the United States. Further inquiries behind their motivations to migrate to America reveal that desires for better economic opportunities (26.1%) and safer living conditions (29.1%) are the two important reasons. Among those who do not desire to move to America, interestingly 1 out of 4 mention patriotism and love of homeland as the major reason. Other reasons mentioned for lack of motivation to migrate include social and cultural ties to family and friends and perception of racism in America.

In Table 4, we begin our analysis with data showing the relationship between perceptions of American economy and desire to visit or not visit America. Evidently, respondents' favorable perception of American economy is directly related to desire to visit. In other words, portrayal of America's economy as stable and the most prosperous nation in the world influence desires to visit the United States. Interestingly, although small in numbers, respondents who think that the media perceives America as a corrupt, selfish and exploitative society also desire to visit the United States. Furthermore in an attempt to determine the consistency of students' responses, an inquiry regarding whether or not students perceive the United States as a land of socio-economic opportunities reveals no significant difference between those who aspire to visit and those who do not. Yet, sources of respondents' perceptions as a land of socio-economic opportunities indicate that almost 9 out of 10 desire to visit the United States. But among those who do not believe that America is a land of socio-economic opportunities, negative perceptions of America as a society filled with crime and poverty as well as racism appear to have significantly reduced the desire to visit America.

Furthermore, findings show that overwhelming proportions of students who think that America is a beautiful and lovely place; and is civilized and developed economically and politically are more likely to plan to visit the United States. Again, it is surprising that 4 out of 5 among those who hold an impression of America as a country full of crime and pornographic images also plan to visit America.

Data examining students' opinions on America's image in the American media and its influence on the propensity to visit America produces similar findings as in the previous paragraphs. In large numbers, students are significantly more likely to visit America in light of America's portrayal as a high-technologically developed society; an orderly and just society; and as a beautiful paradise "on earth." Although depiction of America in American media as a violent and corrupt society decreases the likelihood of wanting to visit America, the fact is that 4 out of 5 of students who hold this impression still want to visit the United States.

Table 4: Respondents' perceptions of America and desire to visit or not visit America

| Variable | Desire to visit America | Do not desire to visit America |
|---|---|---|
| Perception about American Economy in Nigerian Media** | | |
| Stable and lots of jobs | 83.7 | 16.3 |
| Best in the world (the most prosperous nation) | 90.3 | 9.7 |
| Corrupt/selfish/exploitative society | 100.0 | 0.0 |
| Is America a land of socio-economic opportunities? | | |
| Yes | 88.8 | 11.2 |
| No | 84.6 | 15.4 |
| If yes, where do you get the perception that America is a land of socio-economic opportunities? | | |
| Shared experiences with returning or visiting migrants | 91.1 | 8.9 |
| TV/Media | 89.9 | 10.1 |
| Both people and media | 89.7 | 10.3 |
| Own perception (through reading books) | 84.8 | 15.2 |
| Why is America not land of socio-economic opportunities?* | | |
| Prevalent of Crime/Poverty | 82.8 | 17.2 |
| Perception of Racism | 76.0 | 24.0 |
| No such place/other countries are prosperous | 85.7 | 14.3 |
| Media Images and Pictures of America in Nigeria | | |
| Beautiful/lovely/Paradise | 87.6 | 12.4 |
| Civilized/Developed economically and politically | 90.1 | 9.9 |
| Rampant with crime and pornography | 83.5 | 16.5 |
| Media Portrayal of America in American media** | | |
| Developed/High Tech | 92.0 | 8.0 |
| Orderly/Just/Trust in Government | 86.0 | 14.0 |
| Beautiful/Paradise | 87.7 | 12.3 |
| Violent/Corrupt/Pornography/moral decadence | 83.8 | 16.2 |

**$\chi^2$ (chi-square) tests are significant as p<0.01 level; * $\chi^2 tests$ are significant as p<0.05 level

Table 5: Respondents' perceptions of America and desire to migrate or not migrate to America

| Variable | Desire to migrate to America | Do not desire to migrate to America |
|---|---|---|
| Perception about America Economy in Nigerian Media | | |
| Stable and lots of jobs | 55.1 | 44.9 |
| Best in the world (the most prosperous nation) | 55.2 | 44.8 |
| Corrupt/selfish/exploitative society | 50.0 | 50.0 |
| Is America a land of socio-economic opportunities? ** | | |
| Yes | 65.2 | 34.8 |
| No | 30.3 | 69.7 |
| If yes, where do you get the perception that America is a land of socio-economic opportunities? | | |
| Shared experiences with returning or visiting migrants | 67.4 | 67.4 |
| TV/Media | 62.2 | 37.8 |
| Both people and media | 54.4 | 45.6 |
| Own perception (through reading books) | 59.8 | 40.2 |
| Why is America not land of socio-economic opportunities? | | |
| Prevalent of Crime/Poverty | 31.2 | 68.8 |
| Perception of Racism | 32.0 | 68.0 |
| No such place/other countries are prosperous | 31.2 | 68.8 |
| Media Images and Pictures of America in Nigeria | | |
| Beautiful/lovely/Paradise | 54.9 | 45.1 |
| Civilized/Developed | 56.0 | 44.0 |
| Rampant with crime and pornography | 54.1 | 45.9 |
| Media Portrayal of America in American media | | |
| Developed/High Tech | 58.4 | 41.6 |
| Orderly/Just/Trust in Government | 53.8 | 46.2 |
| Beautiful/Paradise | 54.7 | 54.7 |
| Violent/Corrupt/Pornography/moral decadence | 52.7 | 47.3 |

**$\chi^2$ [chi-square] tests are significant as $p<0.01$ level; * $\chi^2$-tests are significant as $p<0.05$ level.

In Table 5, it is clear that media portrayal of the American economy determines the likelihood of migrating to the United States. However, the negative perception of America as a corrupt, selfish and exploitative society discourages a significant proportion (50%) of the respondents from wanting to migrate to the United States. Interestingly, a much larger percentage (about two-thirds) of those who hold the impression of America as a land of socio-economic opportunities is significantly more likely to migrate than their counterparts. Furthermore, it is important to note that respondents who obtained first-hand information from visiting or returning Nigerian emigrants regarding America's fortune as a prosperous society are significantly more inclined to move (67.4%), while those who derive their information from the media come in a distant second (62.2%). Not surprisingly, only one-third of those who hold the perception of America as racist and full of crime and poverty desire to migrate. Moreover, in an attempt to compare how the influence of media portrayal of America in Nigeria differs from effects of America's image in American media, we detect no significant differences in desire to migrate. Nonetheless, in both instances, positive images of America are associated with increased desire to move to the United States.

### Results of Focus Group Discussions

We started from our discussants' general aspirations, how easy or difficult it was for them to realize their aspirations in Nigeria, and whether they thought it was easier elsewhere to realize their aspirations than it was in Nigeria. Without exception, our discussants wanted to be rich, or at least comfortable, and able to plan for their future. A discussant from one of the University of Ibadan groups captured the aspirations of young Nigerians in these words:

> All of us want basic comfort: a decent job, basic infrastructure and facilities, stability so that one can plan for the future and security. Anything beyond that is greediness.

All discussants agreed that it was difficult to realize these aspirations in Nigeria and that it was easier elsewhere.

> It's not easy—especially for people from poor background. Feeding, ordinary feeding is difficult, not to talk of fun. You want to have fun in Nigeria but you can't go out in the night because of insecurity......our government doesn't care for anybody...the money your parents give you isn't enough.

Without exception, the first country mentioned by our discussants where it was easier to realize one's aspirations was the United States. And almost without exception, everyone wanted to go to the US. "If I get a US visa today, I will abandon my studies and zap[5]", said a final-year university student. More than half of our discussants had applied for the US visa lottery before and would apply again; most of those who had not applied before would apply for the lottery.

Our discussants painted the image of the US in incredibly romantic strokes. According to a discussant, in the US,

> You have your own money...even the government is paying because you are dependent. The opportunity to have money and lay hold of the things you want is greater there...

Another said:

> Jobs are available for youths so students don't need to worry. There is 100% employment in America. The economy is better than Nigeria's. Security is

better: whenever anything happens to their people, the government takes it serious. The infrastructure is better. Take the example of telecommunications: whenever you dial once in America, it goes through. If it is here, they will say network failure.

Commenting on the welfare services in the US, and comparing those with the situation in Nigeria, a discussant said:

> In the United States of America, I heard of it, when a child attains the age of 18, the government takes over (his) responsibilities. So children there do not resort to evil practices such as 419[6] as we do in Nigeria. But in Nigeria, there's no provision for any employment even when you graduate. That is why we experience corruption.

Another added:

> Newly born children are taken care of (by the US government) right from when they are born. This makes it possible for parents not to bother much about their children. Even the poor in America get food to eat and some money from government.

Summing up the image of America as it exists in the minds of young Nigerians, a discussant who had applied for the American visa thrice, said with definite confidence:

> America is the best, and the most beautiful place, and a place to be. My immediate sister just got to the US and she called me and said Nigeria is truly bad and dirty. America loves their citizens. They do not go to school during summer when the sun is hot...even they pay less to go to school and they have more facilities. America is not like a land flowing with milk and honey...It really is a land flowing with milk and honey.

Simply put, nearly all of our discussants felt that America was everything good that Nigeria was not.

Very few and much less confident were those who thought that in America people experience hardships and difficulties. These minority voices spoke about individualism in America:

> In America, everyone is on his/her own; in Nigeria, we lean on one another all the time. Your neighbor in America doesn't even care about you. Does he even know you exist?

They also spoke about the harsh weather conditions and what they called "excessive freedom given to children" in the US.

> It is not in everything they (Americans) are better (than Nigerians). We have a better weather. And the issue of child abuse; what we can do here as training the child, they can't do it in the US. They call it child abuse.

Another said:

> There are places in America that are worse than Nigeria such as the ghetto in Chicago.

We want to stress that these were the voices of the very few among our discussants.

We sought to know from where our discussants got their romantic picture of the US. The most common source of information about US was friends and relatives living in the US. Common responses were: "I have enough information. My people are there [in America]" "my bishop told me about America" "my sister just got to the US and she called me" "my friends live there...when they come home, they give us information".

Again, one of the minority voices cautioned:

> People who live in America, when they come home they do not tell us the whole story. You never know what they did in America. They tell you only the bright side. They don't tell you what they do. Many of them don't even have the opportunity to come back home.

Next to human and interpersonal sources of information about the US were the media. Newspapers, magazines, television and fiction were sources of information about the US.

> You watch American films and you see that things are working in that country...there is electricity twenty-four-seven[7]. Things are just working.

But most discussants affirmed that the media show both the pleasant and the unpleasant aspects of American life.

> The films also tell us a lot about the evil in America. You watch films and you see that they kill people in America anyhow...the insecurity in black neighborhoods... it's not everything (shown in the films) that is good.

Yet, to most of our discussants, the US is the place to be. We thus wanted to know if the image received in the media influenced our discussants migration intentions. Most of our discussants believe the vision of America they receive in the media positively influences their intention to go to the US. Discussants put it this way:

> It is what you see that you believe: even if the country [America] is good and you don't hear about it, you won't even know it exists. You will not aspire to go there. Seeing is believing...America pops up everywhere (in Nigeria)...My very desire to go to America was influenced by a coca-cola advert. Your knowledge about America is a subconscious thing. You don't know how and when it has accumulated.

In their opinions, the musical video films waxed by Nigerian musicians that visit the US present such glamorous visions of the US that everyone would like to be there. So also does news brought home by friends and relatives that visit or live in the US. In most cases, discussants rated media influence above the influence of interpersonal sources of information about the US.

### Trends in the Data

Almost 90% of our respondents want to visit the United States, and more than half want to go as immigrants. Some could abandon their studies if given the opportunity to relocate to the US, even when they have just a few months to complete the studies.

Respondents predominantly view the US in positive lights—prosperous economy; land flowing with milk and honey; a government that cares for the people, and the best and the most beautiful place in the world. It is a place where dreams of comfort and success can be easily realized. This is consistent with the findings of Ambler (2002) regarding Africans' perception of the US. It also echoes young Albanians' description of America in Mai (2004).

There are two leading sources of information about the US: Nigerians who have visited or are based in the US and the media. Nigerians who visit or are based in the US offer predominantly positive information about the US which galvanizes young Nigerians intention to migrate to the US. This corroborates an earlier finding by Togunde and Osagie (2009). These people constitute a source that is first mentioned by discussants. The second is the media.

We saw a predominantly negative image of the US in Nigerian daily newspapers (consistent with the findings by Ojebode, 2009) and a positive one in soft-sell magazines. The dominant image of the US presented by most Nigerian musicians is positive while the one presented in the American films is mixed.

Young Nigerians receive a wide array of information about the US: positive, negative and mixed; true and false, but most of them believe only positive information. This suggests that young Nigerians either ignore negative information about the US or alter the information in a way that makes it consistent with their existing beliefs about the US. The media seems to have greater influence than interpersonal channels.

## Conclusion

Our findings reveal selectivity at work among young people in their treatment of information about the US. Put together, the media portray the US in more negative than positive ways. Yet most of our discussants chose to believe and hold on to the positive image. Back to the selective processes, we would conclude that our discussants had existing positive attitudes to and beliefs about the US, but selected media that convey both positive and negative messages. In other words, they did not select media messages that simply reinforced their existing beliefs and attitudes; but they paid greater attention to such messages that reinforce those attitudes and beliefs. Put simply, there was no evidence of selective exposure. There was however evidence of selective retention as most discussants remember only positive information they had received about the US. There was also evidence of selective perception. Even obviously negative messages were interpreted to be positive.

Negative portrayal of the United States by some of the media is incapable of discouraging migration intentions. Four out of every five Nigerians who thought the US is plagued with crime and pornography still intend to migrate to the US. The dazzle of economic stability (claimed by 70% of our respondents) and prosperity (50%) in the US seems to overshadow the bleak picture presented in some media.

Media portrayal of the US might not have directly caused young people's intention to migrate to the US but it certainly reinforces that intention.

With respect to migration intentions, it appears that the media are not all-powerful but they are not impotent.

## References

Abah Betty "A final bye to meningitis" Tell June 25, 2007, Pg 16
Abah Betty "Stem research and a moral burden" Tell, July 16, 2007, Pg 14
Abah, Betty "Las Vegas: the city of sin" Tell, June 18, 2007, Pg 12
Adesina, O. A (2007) "Checking out": migration, popular culture, and the articulation and formation of class identity" Paper presented to African Migrations Workshop On "Understanding Migration Dynamics in the Continent", Accra, Ghana, September 18th – 21st 2007
Adeyemi, A. "Man attempts to roast wife" Tell, January 15, 2007, Pg 14
Aleem, M "Three-armed wonders" Tell, July 16, 2008, Pg 8
Al-Shaykh, H. (2002). What We Think of America. Granta, 77. Retrieved Feb. 21, 2008, from http://www.granta.com/back-issues/77?usca_p=t.
Ambler, C. (2002). Mass Media and Leisure in Africa. The International Journal of African Historical Studies, 35 (1), 119-36.
Baran, S. J & Davis, D. K (2003) Mass communication theory: foundations, ferment and future Belmont: Thomson Wadsworth
Barrios, S; Bertinelli, L. & Strobl, E (2006) "Climatic change and rural–urban migration: the case of sub-Saharan Africa" Journal of Urban Economics 60; 357–371
Bob, M. "A gift of marijuana" Tell, June 4, 2007, Pg 9
Buruma, I. (2002). What We Think of America. Granta, 77. Retrieved Feb. 21, 2008, from http://www.granta.com/back-issues/77?usca_p=t.
Cameroon', Demographic Research, 16: 413-440.
Chaudhuri, A. (2002). What We Think of America. Granta, 77. Retrieved Feb. 21, 2008, from http://www.granta.com/back-issues/77?usca_p=t.
Cohen, Roger "The Long View from Iraq" The Nation, 22 June 2007, Pg20
De Jong, G., Johnson, A., Richter, K., 1996, 'Determinants of Migration Values and Expectations in Rural Thailand', Asian and Pacific Migration Journal, 5(4): 399-415.
De Jong, G., Richter K., Isarabhakdi P., 1994, 'Gender, Values, and Intentions to Move in Rural Thailand', IMR, 30(3): 748-769.
DeFleur, M. (1970) Theories of mass communication. New York: David McKay
Ekpu, R. (2005) "The press and federalism in Nigeria" in Onwudiwe, E and Rotimi T. Suberu (eds.) Nigerian federalism in crisis: critical perspectives and political options, Ibadan: Programme on Ethnic and Federal Studies, Pg 280-292

# REFERENCES

Ellis, W. E. (1998). New Zealand Perceptions of America: The Teaching of American History/American. The Social Science Journal, 35 (2), 245-51.

Encomiums Weekly "Biola Adegoke off to US", December 4, 2007, Pg 3

Encomiums Weekly "Kanu Nwankwo budgets N100m for father's burial; flies in special casket from America" December 11, 2007, Pg 7

Encomiums Weekly "Saint Obi's wife delivers baby boy in US" December 11, 2007, Pg 4

Encomiums Weekly "Top industrialist, Tunji Sunmonu on holiday" October 9, 2007; Pg A22

Enzensberger, H. M. (2002). What We Think of America. Granta, 77. Retrieved Feb. 21, 2008, from http://www.granta.com/back-issues/77?usca_p=t

Fabiyi, Grace "Surgery not for adults" Tell August 6, 2007, Pg 13

Fleischer, A., 2007. 'Family, Obligations, and Migration: The Role of Kinship in

Folarin, B. (2002). Theories of mass communication: an introductory text. Abeokuta: Link Publications.

Gelderblom, D., 2006, 'Towards a Synthetic Model of Migration', Migration in South and Southern Africa Dynamics and Determinants, edited by Kok, P., Gelderblom, D., Oucho, J., and Zyl, J., Cape Town, South Africa, HSRC Press.

Grieco, E. (2004) "The African Foreign Born in the United States" Migration Policy Institute www.migrationinformation.org/USfocus/display.cfm?ID=250

Griffin, E. A (2003) a new look at communication theory Boston: McGraw Hill

Gruber, R. E. (2002). What Europeans really think of America? The New Leader, 85 (4),15-17.

Guha, R. (2002). What We Think of America. Granta, 77. Retrieved Feb. 21, 2008, from http://www.granta.com/back-issues/77?usca_p=t.

Hamilton Paterson, J. (2002). What We Think of America. Granta, 77. Retrieved Feb. 21, 2008, from http://www.granta.com/back-issues/77?usca_p=t.

Hargreaves, I. (1998). Must Africa always be reported by chaps in cowboy hats? New Statesman, 127 (4414), 46.

Immigrants' Social Network, Irregular Immigration and Access to the Labor

Jackson, P., & Faupin, M. (September 2007). The Long Road to Durban: The United Nations Role in Fighting Racism and Racial Discrimination. UN Chronicle. 44(3), 7-9, 15.

JBHE (1999-2000) "African immigrants in the United States are the nation's most highly educated group" Journal of Blacks in Higher Education (Editorial/opinion); 26:60-61

Khadiagala, G. M. (Winter/Spring 2001). The United States and Africa: beyond the Clinton administration. SAIS Review. 21(1), 259-73.

Ktistof Nicholas "Spineless on Sudan" The Nation, 22 May, 2007, Pg 20

Lazarsfeld, P.; Berelson, B. and Gaudet, H. (1944) the people's choice: how the voter made up his mind in a presidential campaign. New York: Duell, Sloan & Pearce

Lee, E., 1966, 'A Theory of Migration', Demography (3): 47-57.

Mai, N. (2004) 'Looking for a modern life': the role of Italian television in the Albanian migration to Italy Westminster papers in communication and culture 1(1): 3-22

Market', Migraciones, 21: 191-212.

Martinot, S. (Spring 2000). The racialized construction of class in the United States. Social Justice. 27(1), 43-60.

McKenzie, D., Gibsonm, J., & Stillman, S.(2007). A land of milk and honey with streets paved with gold: Do emigrants have over-optimistic expectations about incomes abroad? Retrieved June 17, 2008, from http://www.stanford.edu/group/SITE/archive/SITE_2007/segment_2/mckenzie_ExpectationsFeb07.pdf

Nigeria Tribune "3000th US Soldier Killed in Iraq" January 2, 2007, Pg 43

Nigerian Tribune "'I blame Posh and Co' says mother of girl killed by anorexia" January 1, 2007; Pg 4

Nigerian Tribune "US Government Denies Endorsing Buhari". March 26, 2007, Pg 39

Ojebode, A. (2009) "The portrayal of Europe and America in Nigerian newspapers: the other edge of dependency" Journal of Social Sciences 20(1) 15-21

Okome, M. O (2002) "The Antinomies of Globalization: Causes of Contemporary African Immigration to the United States of America" Irinkerindo: a journal of African migration Issue 1

Oladeinde, Sina "Bush, Saddam and the Hangman's Noose" Nigeria Tribune, January 4, 2007, Pg 7

Olatunji, Dare "Once Upon a Fourth of July" The Nation June 22, 2007, Pg 40

Onwubiko, K. B. C (1986) History of West Africa. Onitsha, Nigeria: African-Fep Publishers

Ovation "Interview with Jumoke", Undated, Pg 35

Pajares, M., 2007, 'Immigrants from a Country of the European Union: Romanian

Patterns and Intentions', Migration in South and Southern Africa Dynamics and Determinants, edited by Kok, P., Gelderblom, D., Oucho, J., and Zyl, J., Cape Town, South Africa, HSRC Press.

Poulton, Edward "Guns are the great American specificity" The Nation June 11, 2007, Pg 21

Schmidley, A. D (2001) Profile of foreign-born population in the US: 2000. Washington, DC: US Government Printing Office

Severin, W. J and Tankard, J. W. (2001) Communication theories: origins, methods, and uses in the mass media. 5th edition. Longman: New York

Takougang, J. (2003) "Contemporary African immigrants to the United States" Irinkerindo: a journal of African migration Issue 2 pp 1-15

Togunde, D. and Osagie, S. (2009). Icons of Progress: Returnees' Effects on Decisions by Nigerians to Migrate to the U.S. International Review of Modern Sociology, Vol. 35. No 1 (spring)

Togunde, D. and Rinkinen, J. (2009). Agents of Change: Gender Differences in Migration Intentions among University Undergraduates in Nigeria. The International Journal of Interdisciplinary Social Sciences, Vol. 4 (2).

The Nation, "16 dead as US troops, Afghan militants clash" March 5, 2007, Pg 58

The Nation, "US Pushes for Kosovo Independence" June 11, 2007, Pg 45

US Census Bureau (2003) "Educational Attainment" Census brief. http://www.census.gov/prod/2003pubs/c2kbr-24.pdf

Wallerstein, I. (1992). America and the World. Theory and Society, 21(1), 1-28.

Waseem, M. (2004) Perceptions about America in Pakistan. Aziya Kenky, 50(2), 34-44.

Wentzel, M., Viljoen, J., and Kok, P., 2006. 'Contemporary South African Migration

Wikipedia "African immigration to the United States" http://en.wikipedia.org/wiki/Africans_in_the_United_States

Williams, Julian "Don't mourn Brown vs. Board of Education" The Nation, July 3, 2007, Pg 21

Wimmer, R. D and Dominick, J. R (2000) Mass Media Research: An Introduction. Belmont: Wadsworth Publishing Company

## Endnotes

[1] In our coding, we discovered that some stories did not carry by-lines. In citing such stories, we cited the paper itself as if it were the author.

[2] *The Nation* fairly regularly maintained a column titled 'Views from Abroad' in which articles culled from non-Nigerian, especially American, newspapers were published. We coded these stories as well since our concern was the image of the US presented in Nigerian papers.

[3] Late Gbenga Adeboye was not a conventional musician. He was a famous comedian, didactic talk artist and a moralist whose talks were interspersed with singing.

[4] 'Urinate there' ('Tò síbè' in Yoruba) is Obesere's euphemism for 'have sex' or literally 'ejaculate into'.

[5] 'Zap' is the slang word taken from, and meaning 'disappear'.

[6] '419' is the Nigerian term for swindling and other forms of Advanced Fee Fraud.

[7] This is a slang expression meaning 24 hours of the day, seven days of the week. That is, all the time.

# Chapter 3
## Imagined America in African Texts and the Desire to Migrate

*Emmanuel Yewah*

**Introduction**

In the introduction to a collection of essays entitled *Remembering Africa*, Elizabeth Mudimbe-Boyi states that "A variety of images of Africa, real or invented, are recorded in studies of literary iconology" (xiv). Most of the works in the field of literary studies she contends, "are concerned with the representation of Africa in its relation to the West. They emphasize the hegemonic gaze and power relations, tradition versus modernity, the colonizer and the colonized" (xiv-xv). For Toyin Falola and Fallou Ngom, "The fictional and often romanticized depiction of wild Africa (...) in traditional travel narratives, tourist accounts, and pictures (...) have engendered in the psyche of global Western media consumers an illusory continent in which "facts are fictionalized, and fiction is 'factualized'" (9). It is indeed true, as African scholars above and other Africanists have asserted, that "Europeans invented a mythical Africa, which soon claimed a place of privilege in the Western imagination" (Adam & McShane). They imagine the continent variously as a "blank darkness" (Miller, 1985), a "subject that has been constructed, invented, and interpreted in writing" (xix), and today as "an artificial entity, invented and conceived by colonialism" (Mayer).

These "inventions of Africa" are what David Mengara calls "the systematic or systemic manufacturing of a continent on the basis of the Aristotelian paradigms of superiority versus inferiority, civilized versus uncivilized among other epithets" (2). Such "manufacturing of [the] continent" has been well documented as evidenced by the sheer amount of critical works on the subject, including *Images of Africa, Images of Empire, Blank Darkness, Artificial Africas, White on Black: Images of Africa and Black, An Enchanting Darkness: The American Vision of Africa* to name but a few. Furthermore, in higher education, this is a subject of inquiry in courses such as *Africa: Myth and Reality* and variations on the same theme which have been designed to critically inquire into the construction of myths about Africa by Western media and at the same time attempt to dismantle those same myths in order to reveal the realities behind them. In contrast, very few studies, if any, have been carried out that attempt, in a systematic and sustained way, to turn Africa's constructive or, indeed, "deconstructive gaze" (Doho, 2005) onto the West. Indeed, works that produce and reproduce *Images of the West* from an African perspective or those that explore America and Americans as linguistic constructs in the African imagination remain rare in spite of Africans on the continent being bombarded daily with filtered images of the West by various Western media.

This absence is all the more remarkable when we consider how listening to the British Broadcasting Corporation (BBC) and Radio France Internationale (RFI), the dominant and influential Western European audio media as well as reading newspapers, and examining photographs all have continued to create and shape the Western image in the African mind. More specifically, listening to the Voice of America (VOA), watching American comedies, music videos as well as Hollywood movies and old discontinued American soap operas, surfing the Internet, interacting with Americans on the continent as Peace Corps Volunteers, tourists, or Fulbright Scholars, and seeing permanent displays on billboards advertising American products such as tobacco that liter many African urban landscapes have contributed even further to creating and sustaining a certain image of America in the minds of virtually any demographic within Africa. Eloise Brière (1999) makes the point quite forcefully and convincingly in her introduction to Julianna Makuchi's (1999) collection of short stories, *Your Madness, not Mine: Stories from Cameroon.* In reference to Yaoundé, the capital city, she alludes to "the scars of Western economic and cultural dumping" such as "billboards of the Marlboro Man [inviting] passersby into the American dream even as Americans are forsaking tobacco" (xvii).

In addition, reading the works and biographies of prominent African returnees notably Kwame Nkrumah and Nnamdi Azikiwe who drew from their indigenous knowledge as well as transferred skills, civil and political consciousness gained abroad in American and British universities to leadership positions in their countries of origin has inspired many of their readers and has awaken in them what Raphael Obotama has described as "the desire to acquire American education, which many Africans find to be pragmatic and intensely scientific" (104).

This study draws from a wide range of literary and cultural texts, memoirs, essays, poetry, short stories, and documentaries. These include *Kwame Nkrumah* (Smertin, 1987), a biography of Kwame Nkrumah, *Consciencism* (Nkrumah, 1964), as well as *America, their America* (JP Clark, 1964), *Why are we so Blest?* (Armah, 1972), *Patron de New York* [One Way] (Dadié, 1964) *Hommes de tous les continents* (Dadié, 1967), "A New York" (Senghor), *Jazz et vin de palme* (Dongala, 1982), *Images of the West* (Vera,, 1996), and the short story "American Lottery" (Makuchi, 1999). These texts deal with various African writers' conceptions of America as a geo-political space with all its contradictions and paradoxes. They also explore Americans as socio-cultural beings whose interactions with the "Other" reveal how they perceive themselves and their country. It also becomes a question of how these Americans project themselves to the outside world. In other words, the present study analyzes those writers' imaginative responses to their encounter with America and Americans or their real or imagined contacts with Americans; contacts that Mary Louise Pratt has explored in another context (the Andeans contact with the more powerful Spanish) in her seminal essay "Arts of the Contact Zone." This concept of the "contact zone" is described variously as: "imaginary spaces where differences and inequalities are sensed, and even recognized" (1); "social spaces where cultures meet, clash, and grapple with each other, often in contexts of highly asymmetrical relation of power, such as colonialism, slavery, or their aftermath ..." (584). Moreover, she views such a zone as a "the space in which peoples [the Andeans and the Spanish] geographically and historically separated come into contact with each other to establish relations, usually involving coercion, radical inequality, and intractable conflict" (527). This study draws from the concept of the "contact zone" to discuss African writers' textual reaction to their encounter as well as examine readers' responses as reading those texts become one among the many factors motivating their readers to perform the act of emigration and displacement.

The guiding question of this essay seeks to understand how the act of reading these texts or watching the various media affects the reader as he or she is enticed into the imaginative world of the writer and how such a reader emerges from that world. As Wolfgang Iser points out, "The literary text activates our faculties, enabling us to recreate the world it presents. The product of this creative activity is what we might call the virtual dimension of the text, which endows it with its reality. The virtual dimension is not the text itself, nor is it the imagination of the reader; it is the coming together of text and imagination" (54). What images of America do these various texts help their readers to construct? How do they go about constructing them? And how do those constructions and those mental images help both to inspire and to shape the African reader's perception of the United States of America – especially recognizing that some of these readers could ultimately immigrate there? In this vein, there are further questions posited such as how do depictions of characters and their interactions generate and nurture readers' desire to want to undertake what Elizabeth and Preston Augustus have called "Voluntary Trans-Atlantic Migration" (221). These questions regarding pre-departure constructions of America will be addressed in the discussion that follows.

**Pre-departure to an Imagined America**

Pre-departure interactions among characters in the "American Lottery", a short story in the Cameroonian critic and writer Makuchi's *Your Madness, not Mine* (1999) reveal both the African character's dreams about and (mis)perception of the United States. The story revolves around Paul, one of the main characters who has won the much sought after American Diversity Visa Lottery. The program, as fully articulated in the introductory chapter to this book and as summarized by Augustus, "awards [55,000] visas [annually] to nationals of a special list of designated countries that are deemed 'under-represented' in the current legal immigration system. The winners of the visa lottery are granted a visa to enter the United States, lawful permanent residence status (the coveted green card), and the recipients eventually qualify for naturalization" (222). Although the program's detractors have decried its contribution to brain drain or its perceived neo-colonialist conception, for winners like Paul, it is a dream-come true. In his specific case, it provides an escape, an exit from Cameroon, his home country where he comes from minority Anglophone population to a country of destination that remains simply an imagined construct. One would expect the decision to pursue immigration to the United States as a lawful permanent resident to be an easy one; however that does not seem to be the case, especially since his friends' critical comments about the United States further complicate the decision process.

In spite of the fact that he does not actively participate in other characters' discussion, he becomes increasingly conflicted by mixed messages from his friends whose unflattering remarks about the United States breed uncertainty. As Linus reminds others, "I was trying to say to my friend [Paul] here that he has every reason to be uneasy about going to America. Actually, he should be afraid of going to America. America is a bad place" (79). Another character reveals how his dream of going to America had been shattered by his brother, a returnee who "bored holes… in his perception of America and the world. He had shattered a dream, a child's dream… He had come back a different person, a stranger: the way he walked; the way he smiled; the way he smiled at people; the way he talked; the way he talked to people; the way he ate; what he ate; when he ate; the way he dressed, what he wore…" (80).

The pertinence of this story lies in the fact that characters' discussions generate various perceptions of America for the reader; perceptions shaped by returnees and different media including movies and soap operas. Incidentally, if Paul were to immigrate to the United States, he would have to transfer survivalist skills and resiliency developed in his country of origin where he hails from a minority Anglophone population in order to cope as a minority in America. As one of the characters warns him, "Paul, you have to be very careful. I don't envy you. You'll go to America, they'll treat you like dirt – no, they'll treat you like doti, yes, exactly; they'll treat you like what they say in Pidgin English, d-o-t-i! and instead of coming back home, you'll remain there like my *brother*, rot, and fertilise their crops" (80). Even as these characters attempt to construct their own imagined America or deconstruct the myth of America, they question the authenticity of the brother's representation of America. How reliable are his stories? What part is truth and what part is fabrication? As someone asks, "Are you sure your brother's telling the truth? ...but your brother's experience might be unique. He could also be paranoid..." (83). Such a psychoanalytic evaluation not only pokes holes in the brother's narrative but helps create a nuanced picture of America for Paul and at the same time in the mind of readers. Their reaction to the brother's lived experience could also be seen simply as a desperate move by desperate candidates for emigration intending to keep their dream alive, be it at the cost of accepting a mystified version of the so-called American dream.

What appears unquestionable in the brother's story is the indirect reference to race relations in the society of encounter where, in the words of Ralph Ellison, he might remain an "invisible man" as African Americans and other African immigrants before him have experienced due to the color of their skin. As textual evidence claims, "In America, white people pretend not to see you, you are invisible to them, or when they do see you, they only see your black skin" (82-3). Ellison is even more emphatic on the invisibility of the Black man in America. As he writes, "I AM AN invisible man...I am a man of substance, of flesh and bone, fiber and liquids – and I might even be said to possess a mind. I am invisible, understand, simply because people refuse to see me. When they approach me they see only my surroundings, themselves, or figments of their imagination – indeed, everything and anything except me" (3). The text skillfully draws the reader into sharing with the characters in the euphoria that comes with winning the United States visa lottery and the subsequent anxiety of leaving home for an unknown world constructed on various characters' stories and their (mis)perceptions. Unfortunately, Paul's anxiety would turn into disappointment as the opportunity to realize his dreams of going to America would be permanently deferred. Indeed, he becomes the innocent victim of two feuding postal women caught in a love triangle. One of these women, wanting to exact revenge on her girl friend and a relative of Paul, had withheld the latter's visa application file at the post office past the deadline for processing.

All this drama helps the reader put together bits and pieces of information from the characters' discussions and exchanges to construct an imagined and nuanced picture of America. Bernard Dadié (1964), the Ivorian writer, in his *Patron de New York* [*One Way: Bernard* Dadié, *Observes America*] seems to have conceptualized such an imagined community prior to his maiden voyage to America just as he had before that constructed his own imagined Europe: "Before me, beyond the ocean, a magical America stretches out" (6). He imagines it to be "a mysterious country where devils easily assume an angel's face" (3), "a marvelous country" (11) where the "American smile has the intoxicating power of the dollar" (11). However, his encounter with the real America creates what Pratt identified earlier as "contact zone" or the social, cultural, and political spaces in which this pre-departure "magic" turns out to be simply a product of his imagination. As Obotama has argued, upon arrival in his new community, the immigrant is dispossessed not only of elements of their past in their country of origin, but also of certain "imaginative perspectives regarding [their] host destination" (106). Such perceptions of dispossession, he contends, "seem rooted in their principles, values, and notions of their new host destination as a virtuous land, and even with the additional possible referential notion of visualizing it as paradise on earth" (106). Within that imaginary zone and in response to his new situation, Dadié, seems to draw from his experiences to construct a rather satirical picture of America. Similarly Yaya, the protagonist of Alasan Mansaray's (1995) *A Haunting Heritage: an African Saga in America* imagines America from Sierra Leone his country of origin as "wonderland" (227) where "every dreamer wants to [go]"; "a country of stunning possibilities, where dreams are fulfilled and lives are lived to the fullest' (53).

The vision of America that emerges from these writers and their characters seems shared by the African Prince in the film *Coming to America* (1988), an American farcical film in which Eddie Murphy plays an African prince who constructs his own fictive America prior to coming there. He leaves Africa, the site of grandeur, a continent steeped in traditions, a land where his status as a member of the royal family has endowed him with certain powers and privileges. Going to America seems to be an escape from the burden imposed on him by traditions and from a palace whose display of wealth and opulence had become his prison-house in that he is forced to live in a world divorced from the realities of his society. Moreover, in his kingdom, his royal status forbids him from interacting freely with ordinary people, from doing any kind of job or, indeed, from working at all, and choosing his own "princess." He is obligated to uphold certain values and has to behave in ways that befit the majesty of his birth and upbringing. With that mindset, he envisions an idealistic America which is the exact opposite of what he has assumed as his land of origin; an America that will set him free from the burden of his past.

Indeed, the fact that Akeem and his sidekick Semmi are robbed upon arrival in Queens has been interpreted by Obotama as an act of dispossession of their material possession, but, more tellingly, as a point of discontinuity from the past. Such a symbolic break provides the prince with the opportunity to reinvent himself assuming a new identity so as to better integrate in his host community. He effects these changes by assuming the role of an ordinary African student, proclaiming his independence from his father's dictates, working in a job as janitor in a fast food restaurant as a "typical immigrant" student in America, and showing courage in a holdup situation by striking the robber to the amazement of his co-workers and customers. He is also shown interacting freely with the "wretched of the earth" such as the homeless, de-emphasizing his royal roots, as well as expressing his hitherto suppressed emotions publicly such as his outburst at a football game. In fact, Akeem envisions an America, whose ideals are captured in another context in these words of *Ian* Buruma,

> [In the U.S] each person is free to choose his own destiny, unfettered by the social chains of whatever old world one had escaped from. Rather than adopting the ready-made identity of another settled tradition, the idea is to start afresh, to make oneself up again and, as far as possible, forget the past. America gives every man a second chance (1).

Akeem's attempt to assimilate in the new society reveals obvious cultural misunderstandings. It also educates the viewer about the transformative nature of the American society and the coping mechanisms to be developed to ease such a transformation for a potential African immigrant. The fact that the actors are African Americans is pertinent in that they may actually be operating within their own imagined Africa; an imagined homeland of opulence, courage, resilience, and hard workers in which they believe they still live and from where they are migrating to an imagined America. Just as this fictional African prince comes to America to seek alternatives to his African traditions, his worldview, etc. so do some African writers turn to America in search for alternatives to the inherited colonialist discursive system and African traditionalist aesthetics. In Francis Higginson's words, they seek "new ways of representing – in realistic fashion – the complexities of the [African] postcolonial quotidian" (381). In the process, the writer establishes "diasporic" connections, indeed, a subject of discussion in the next section namely, a trans-Atlantic bridge between Africa and America.

## Trans-Atlantic Diasporic Bridge

African creative writers such as the Cameroonian Mongo Beti, especially in his later works, have attempted to escape from the prison-house of both the inherited colonialist intellectual tradition of writing and the African traditionalist aesthetics of orality whose proponents include such major figures in African literatures as Léopold Sédar Senghor, Camara Laye, Lamine Diakhaté, Birago Diop, David Diop, etc. All these writers associated with the Négritude or Black consciousness movement - "a cultural and literary renaissance, a rediscovery of black culture forced underground by colonialism, a rising up, a singing of black soul in a black French song" (Diakhaté, 80). The movement has been criticized for its failure to explore dimensions of the African experience in a realistic way and of presenting a rather romanticized picture of the African past. In order to overcome what Harold Bloom has identified as "the anxiety of influence", Beti has effected a "kenosis", or "a movement [of the ephebe or young writer] towards discontinuity from the precursor" (14). Breaking away from those powerful precursors allows him either to chart a new course in his own writing or model his works after those of writers from other traditions. In his case, he chooses the latter option turning to the African Diaspora and, especially, across the Atlantic to America where he would draw inspiration from American, and, more specifically, African American writers. In particular he focuses on Richard Wright and Chester Himes in his choice of genre - the realist novel and his choice of subject - crime fiction, allowing him to create literature independent of the European and African traditions.

Indeed, Higginson's comment on Beti's seminal essay "Afrique noire, littérature rose" vividly illustrates that desire to escape all forms of restrictive bonds be they African or European. He puts it as follows:

> By turning to Wright (and away from France/Laye-as-Lackey), 'Afrique noire, littérature rose' initiates a Black Atlantic handshake, a diasporic bridge between Africa and the United States that anticipates their later narrative strategies. The American rhetorical intervention thus does more than provide a correct model...; it authorizes a nomadic genre, a writing no longer fencing with (and fenced in by) the master, but operating at the mobile crossroads of multiple traditions and trajectories (381).

By turning to crime fiction in his later works "as a logical conclusion to [his] quest for an effective postcolonial aesthetic model" (382), Beti models his writing on that of another African American crime writer, Chester Himes prompting Higginson to observe,

> Once again, an African American author [Chester Himes] serves to project in an exemplary manner, the possibility of an innovative francophone textuality, this time within a postcolonial...aesthetic. Beti's own crime fiction is thus situated within another 'black Atlantic' gesture, a second stylistic and thematic opening to the African diaspora that doubles the early nod to Richard Wright (384).

In constructing such a "diasporic bridge" through his works, Beti not only exposes his reader to an African American and by extension to an "insider's view" of the American experience. But perhaps more importantly, it raises his African reader's consciousness about the possibility of making those connections, imaginatively at first, then by actualizing them through a transatlantic voyage. These later works of Beti, therefore, create new avenues for potential African emigrants, who, hitherto had been conditioned through the colonial and postcolonial experiences in education to seek only one outlet out of Africa, solely aiming for Europe. Equally pertinent in this process of triggering their reader's imagination are other African writers, some of whom have visited the United States and have tapped into their experiences to either present their own (mythic) perception of America to their readers or to imaginatively reconstruct their own image of America.

The current study seeks more specifically to understand the psychology of African reader as potential immigrant to the United States of America and his or her responses to these readings from within that context. What might then be the impact of reading these texts on readers in general and more specifically on the African reader? Simply put, they offer a nuanced and multiple perceptions of America. More importantly, they provide their readers with critical materials for their own interpretation that could lead to the formulation of their own perceptions of America. This multiplicity of perspectives is the product of richness of texts written by American authors including such authors as Faulkner, Hemingway, Mark Twain, etc. and in particular African-American writers who have served to guide the gaze of African authors and readers alike. African-American writers in particular starting with those associated with the Harlem Renaissance have had a great impact on earlier generations of African writers as well as the African reader. Indeed, in *The African Imagination*, Abiola Irele bears testimony to the influence of these writers on African students, "Reading such writers as Langston Hughes, Countee Cullen ....opened up new horizons of thought and awareness of immediate import to our status and existence as colonial subjects. Their example promised nothing less than a form of initiation, in the truest sense of connection, to a wider community of sentiment" (179).

## America and the Shaping of Political and Philosophical Consciousness

The earliest Africans whose works detail their experiences, real or imagined in America include poets/politicians such as Kwame Nkrumah, Nnamdi Azikiwe and Sédar Senghor whose contacts with America brought them face to face with American political and capitalist economic structures, the struggle for civil rights, and allowed them access to the intellectual community of writers, scholars and poets. However, these writers' responses to their encounter with America tend to be individualistic, personal, ambivalent, and contradictory, somewhat dialectical, all reflective of the American society itself.

For some such as Nkrumah and Azikiwe whose contact with the West started in higher education at Lincoln University, Pennsylvania and the University of Pennsylvania, America not only nurtured their intellect and their spiritual education but also shaped their philosophical conscience as well as their political and social thoughts. As Horace Mann Bond contends that both Nkrumah and Azikiwe had to work one as "a porter, a laborer in a steel mill, a boxer and the other "as a welder in a ship-building yard" (136) in order to support themselves as it is customary for students in higher education in America. Working as such, helped to expose them to manual workers as well as raise their consciousness about social injustice. He writes, "I believe this feature [work while in college] of the American educational system of incalculable value, in raising up a leadership that can never be divorced from the common man, that finds identification easy; and it is my further conviction, that the accession of Azikiwe and Nkrumah to leadership among the common people of West Africa owes much to this part of their American education" (136). Of these two prominent Africans, the discussion that follows focuses on Nkrumah whose 'London Years' helped sharpen one of his lasting legacies, his Pan-Africanist drive. That crucial page in his life has been widely acknowledged, documented, discussed, and commented upon by scholars including a well articulated recent piece by Obinna Onwumere that concludes: "Arguably, Kwame Nkrumah is best known as the architect of Pan-Africanism in Africa for the mere purpose of vehemently proposing a single Union of African States as a means to checkmate imperialism and balkanization in Africa.... Emphatically, Kwame Nkrumah's political legacy has left an indelible mark on Africa's political history and it extraordinarily poses, to date, the most intelligible expression of Pan-Africanism" (240).

In America, his studies introduced him to world philosophical systems and provided him with the solid theoretical background that helped him compare his developing system to others, as expounded particularly in his text *Consciencism*. For instance, The London Observer's review on the back cover of the text points out Nkrumah's revisionist interpretation of "Marxism to give it a particular reference to Africa's needs and traditions." And The London Tribune to rejoin, "This is the first book by an African politician that attempts to reinterpret Western philosophy in the context of African change and that proceeds from this to enunciate a 'philosophy' and ideology for decolonization and development ... This book marks the first stage of an attempt to hammer out in detail a form of Socialism appropriate to non-industrial Africa." Nkrumah himself acknowledges the importance of his study of philosophy in America in shaping his world view. As he states,

> The ten years which I spent in the United States of America represent a crucial period in the development of my philosophical conscience. It was at the universities of Lincoln and Pennsylvania that this conscience was first awakened. I was introduced to the great philosophical systems of the past to which the Western universities have given their blessings, arranging and classifying them with the delicate care lavished on museum pieces (2).

It was here also that he sharpened his critical abilities and the independence of mind to question various inherited philosophical traditions, and specifically the concept of universalism in which the powerful had monopoly over the construction and dissemination of new knowledge. Valentin Y Mudimbe further elaborates, "Universalism comes from somewhere, from a locality, from a tradition, from a language, from a philosophy, and poses itself as normality to all other cultures, societies and individualities. And in doing so, what it is promoting is the power, the imperialism of a given local experience" (250). Nkrumah's critical stance on universalism, which he views as a mask of Western hegemony, while aimed at the West seems more directed at his fellow Francophone Africans the likes of Léopold Sédar Senghor who have uncritically embraced the concept of universalism. Listen to him deride his fellow colonial student including Senghor, "He sees these philosophical theories as arid abstractions valuable in academia and meaningless to an African unless translated into tools to tackle the pressing human problems at the time, i.e. colonial domination" (121). Furthermore, he becomes aware through his exposure to other philosophical traditions that "capitalism as a system is incapable of guaranteeing genuine equality and freedom for all" (121) and that Marxist ideology could assist in fighting colonialism. However, as a student of Dialectics, he would capitalize on the synthesis of both systems in an attempt to create a new system that pulls together "the best that capitalism and socialism [have] to offer" (121) and "one based on the traditional communal institutions, on the cooperation and egalitarian principles of distribution which had once characterized them"

(121). Of course, in what could be seen as Nkrumah's experimentation with a mix of socio-political systems or a "mixing of leadership", he failed to translate his ideals into practice as he was unable to advance a platform agreeable to his own people. Such failure ultimately led to his ouster in a military coup allegedly orchestrated by the West.

In addition to American means of intellectual inquiry, Nkrumah drew inspiration from the Civil Rights movement and from prominent African Americans activists and authors such as W.E.B. Dubois and Paul Robeson who helped him "understand the sources of racism in the USA", as well as his "close relationship with Richard Wright, the famous American realist who bravely revealed the ulcers of the 'welfare society' in his novels and newspaper articles" (46). Nkrumah's story is as that of many young Africans who studied in America in the 50s, 60s, and early 70s, some on United Sates government scholarships. He reveals to his reader an America that is intellectually stimulating, that nurtures the mind to independent thinking in spite of its polarized racial and political climate. It remains a country where dreams could potentially come true for the African immigrant reader, especially following the example of Nkrumah who came, saw, learned, and transferred the new knowledge and skills acquired back to Ghana to inspire a whole generation of post colonial African leadership, who like him experimented with various systems including African socialism and the one-party system prevalent in the immediate post-independence era.

## African Writers' Responses to their American Encounter

Nkrumah's reader comes away with an appreciation for his American education opening his mind and exposing him to various world political and philosophical systems. However, for other African writers-scholars including playwrights, poets, journalists, activists, and cultural critics such as John Pepper Clark-Bekederemo and Ayi Kwei Armah who came to the United States in the 60s, the system instead leads to the closing of the mind to intellectual inquiry. They believe that the American education forces foreign students to surrender their cultures to the dominant American culture in their pursuit of new knowledge. In their texts *America, their America* (Clark) and *Why are we so blest?* (Armah), these writers view education and educational institutions or these "contact zones" more as tools of indoctrination and propaganda shaping and advancing Western ideology. Both Clark-Bekederemo and Kwei-Armah contend that rather than serving as spaces to enlighten, generate new ideas, and advance new knowledge, these institutions of learning function more as prison-houses, where education not only serves as a vehicle of alienation and isolation from the immigrant's culture of origin, but, more critically, as a machinery for the production, dissemination, and preservation of Western hegemony. In fact, both writers consider the fellowships they had been offered as visiting fellows in American universities as poisoned chalices with strings attached.

Additionally, these scholarships in turn become tools of enslavement for which they, as beneficiaries, would remain forever beholden to their benefactors. Ironically, these writers' sharp critical perspectives on America grew out of their experiences at the university. What could be a more appropriate space to generate these critical ideas than institutions of higher learning whose founding principles and mission lie in fostering the freedom to think critically and to question ideas, systems, institutions, values, as well as the universities themselves?

Moreover, Clark's interactions with Americans outside of academia seem to reinforce his strong sentiments against his society of destination and its people. He reads in his exchanges with Americans a certain thought process in which individualistic traits including behavior, attitude, opinion, and world view are magnified leading Americans who criticize African immigrant to fault not only the individual African concerned but to implicate his or her country of origin as well as the entire continent. For instance, in *America, their America* this short exchange between Clark and his 'benevolent' host the Colonel, reveals not only the colonel's almost idealistic perception of his own country and his paternalistic attitude, patriotism, inflexibility, intolerance, and ultimately his close-mindedness but it also reveals Clark's own strong personality as an opinionated, ungrateful, independent-thinking maverick with a somewhat pre-conceived view of his community of encounter. Listen to the exchange between these two strong personalities:

Colonel: "You have been a delinquent student, a disgrace to the college and your country."

JP: "I also made it clear that at no time did I regard myself as representing anybody or any country, and therefore whatever disgraceful acts I had done must be visited on me alone as a free and willing agent of myself alone."

Colonel: "Well, we have law and order here, and let me tell you young man, I have seen more life and been to better places than you. We must have law and order; society cannot afford to go on with persons like you."

JP: "Any society should be able to afford a maverick."

Colonel: "No, that would corrupt other citizens who are regular in their conduct."

JP: "Isn't it because they are so regular that you get the mavericks?" (209)

While the exchange reveals intolerance towards dissent and non-conformity in a country that prides itself on the ideals of freedom and liberty, it also highlights another contradiction in that while Clark vigorously asserts his own individuality, which should be an ideal that the Colonel implicitly understands since it is an ideal of the American society, nevertheless the Colonel attempts to strip him of that individuality in order to force him into a desired conformity. Moreover, Clark's defending his individuality as such against the Colonel's attempt to use his acts and behavior to implicate the wider African community or to draw simplistic conclusion on Clark's country and continent goes contrary to the latter's existentialist belief that he alone is responsible for his actions, behavior, and attitude. What could be the possible connection between Clark's critical remarks on American society and its people and the colonel's rather sharp rebuke, "You have been... a disgrace to the college and your country?' Why not simply a disgrace to himself as an individual as he himself retorts "at no time did I regard myself as representing anybody or any country, and therefore whatever disgraceful acts I had done must be visited on me alone as a free and willing agent of myself alone" (209). In a rather subtle way, Clark's encounter with the colonel reminds the reader of mythmaking process, the type of rhetoric that the West has used quite effectively to create and sustain myths about Africa by taking one isolated case and generalizing it such that one individual's act, behavior, attitude, opinion, and worldview has implications not only on that individual per se, but also on his country and by extension on his continent.

As regards the issue of law and order that the colonel vehemently defends, Clark's diagnosis of the American society leads him to claim that the plethora of laws in American system rather than serving to liberate, ironically assumes the role of "controlling, imprisoning, impinging" (209) on people's freedom by turning them into a flock of sheep. In other words, these laws condition citizens, resident "aliens" and even the occasional visitor to the United States to a patterned behavior; to conformity and to view the world through a certain prism as we see in "one way", which incidentally, correspond to the title of the English translation of Bernard B. Dadié's *Patron de New York* in which he engages in a systematic assault on America and its values.

One must take Clark's criticism of America with a grain of salt. On the one hand, he must be given credit for piercing through what E.U. Essien Udom has described as "the fog of official propaganda and stage management into the 'heart of the matter'" (8) to reveal inherent contradictions and, for once, to raise serious questions about American society, its culture, values, and worldview,[thereby] problematizing a society presented to the outside as "an approximation of the ideal." On the other hand, one cannot help but raise these rhetorical questions about Clark's own agenda: is it ideological, philosophical, political, or cultural? Is his text merely an individual's imaginative response to growing American hegemony in the heart of the Cold War in the 60s? Or is it really an unmasking from lived experience in the United States to reveal the realities behind the myth of America as "paradise" as projected to the outside world by various media and other agencies? Does he react to this experience upon his arrival in the States or does he simply build on his own vision and perceptions based on pre-conceived ideas? What could have shaped such pre-conceived and mythic construction? Does his coming to America help to either dispel or reinforce the myth of America? Is the myth so strong that everything he sees, feels, hears, smells or touches gets colored by these myths? Consequently, what impact would his attempt to undo the fabric of American structure have on the reader as potential immigrant?

These questions raised in Clark's *America, their America* provide the reader with critical tools to begin to dismantle widely-held myths about America. Furthermore, given Clark's one-dimensional and extremely skewed portrayal of America with his litany of criticisms throughout the text, the reader might be forced to question the author's intentions and, especially, to ask whether he is indeed a reliable or objective observer of the society of encounter. In pursuing this line of analysis, the reader might contend that the author's knowledge of American society betrays some lack of depth, perhaps because during his brief stay, he remained a stranger to or somehow completely marginalized from the society that he encounters. In fact, Clark seems to have remained confined to a certain frame of mind and space which is to say in the halls of academia. Of course, Clark's reader could imagine this type of marginalization whether willingly or otherwise, as a situation that might await every sojourner into this new society; indeed something to be prepared for prior to departure. In Clark's case, that lack of in-depth understanding of and appreciation for the wider society, the question becomes whether he is really in a position, as an outsider having spent less than a year in the United States prior to "being unceremoniously asked to leave the country" (Owomoyela, 2007), is able to engage in informed, credible, and authoritative commentary on the American society?

The same type of unresolved questions awaits Armah's readers as well although contextualized differently given the pronoun "we" in title of his text in *Why are we so Blest?* which suggests rather deceptively a sense belonging or inclusion as opposed to Clark's text where the possessive adjective "their" in the title *America, their America* seems more exclusive . Both texts use the outsider and insider strategies to achieve similar ends, that is, to undo the fabric of the American construct in order to reveal its inner contradictions and in the process to represent nuanced perceptions of American society. Armah sets up this conflicted dynamic as a way of questioning America's moral values. As he writes, these Anglo-Americans "believe that they have a mission to extend the benefit of their experience even to the most unwilling of the human group. Consequently those who fail to accept the American experience as being valid for all humanity are regarded, at best, as ignorant, at worst, as immoral" (9-10). Armah's interactions with Americans of all races reveal not only his own shortcomings but tangentially raise the important questions of race and race relationships in America.

Armah's text as that of Dadié starts from imagining America as a paradise, a blessed land, perhaps based on how America had traditionally been presented to Africans in their countries of origin through various media and some African returnees. However, such imagined celestial realms turn out to be in reality a place that makes one more aware of one's loneliness and ultimately a society that leads people to self-destruction. As Armah explains, "[M]y life here has had a self-destructive swing all the time, only I haven't thought seriously about it. Loneliness" (268). The only American character in the text allows the reader access to a deep understanding of this notion of loneliness revealing in his notebook how loneliness has become an overwhelming part of the writer's American experience; an experience that he transmits to his reader. As he reports, "these lines transmitted one overwhelming message: loneliness. Not simply loneliness, but isolation so complete, so terrible, I began to feel the words come from my own soul" (268). What the reader and potential immigrant to America might draw from this are the psychological effects of living in a society that by its very nature brings to the conscious state what seems latent in many African societies, the fact that we are born lonely; grow up lonely and die lonely. A society that re-emphasizes our permanent state of solitude which, as the Mexican poet, philosopher Octavio Paz states, "is the profoundest fact of the human condition." And to add, "Man is the only being who knows he is alone... We are condemned to live alone" (195) in spite of the fact that we are surrounded by other people.

Dadié for his part takes up a somewhat different theme in his *Patron de New York* [One Way: Bernard Dadié Observes America] published some fifty years ago as he questions whether love as the most intimate form of human relationships really does exist in American society known for its extreme individualism. As he asks, "Can this America of 'Reader's Digest' be a country of love? Is it possible to love amidst the tumult and the rush, to love deeply when you are constantly chasing time and the main chance? How can you love in a country where each person has his own fan, reading light, and easy chair?" (12). These deep philosophical questions point to the fact that missing these basic connections, the very idea of oneness as a people, as a human family becomes a fallacy in America. It also reveals the superficiality of the structure that permeates all aspects of life there since it does not rest on solid foundation of love.

While in his text discussed earlier Clark employs all the elements of style (i.e. irony, sarcasm, hyperbole, satire, metaphors, journalistic sensationalism, etc.) as well as a rather angry tone to convey his experiences, Dadié injects into his diagnostic a sense of humor about physical realities both animate and inanimate gathered through observation and the nitty-gritty human behavior that he is able to pick up. For instance, he states "Americans are worth nothing unless upright... Americans always walk with chest expanded windward, asserting themselves against advance forces." Indeed, "[t]o be American is to know how to keep cool in all circumstances, especially to be able to get along with the elevator, the key to modern buildings" (23). For Dadié,

> America never sleeps or dozes, especially vigilant about viruses coming from other continents. To enter this country, which sees herself as clean as a new penny, healthy in both body and mind, you must undergo a multitude of tests and examination. But to go out of the country, no more formalities: America considers her maladies [just as her vision] eminently exportable (39).

In spite of the light tone, Dadié's piece is a no less powerful attempt to deconstruct American society and its values than Clark's. As in these remarks from Claude Bouygues' "Foreword" to *One Way*, a translation of Dadié's *Patron de New York* where he accurately observes:

> The keenness of Dadié's observations strikes the reader. He pitilessly exposes all the idiosyncrasies of the American people and their life-style, from the

most benign to the most disturbing, handling them with the candor basic to his personality – mood swings included – using the widest range of tones, from humor, to cynicism, including irony, sarcasm and even admonishment. Thus, he reprimands the Americans for their obsession with abbreviations and acronyms (for example, "X-mas"), suggesting as the root of the obsession, the will to compress both time and space [America of Reader's Digest]. He describes American superstition [forbidding the number 13 in labeling floors and streets] with irony; he is astounded by dating, by funerals, by cars, by the importance of sugar... (vii).

Dadié's reader, seduced by his representations, emerges from that act aware of the complexities of their imagined America. Seduction here should be understood as a narrative strategy whose major proponent, Ross Chambers, has defined as "tactics", "narrative moves", "a way of inhabiting the space of the other without possessing it" or "recruiting the desires of the other [the reader] in the interest of maintaining narrative authority" (214). It is a technique of tapping into the reader's desire in order to lure him/her into inhabiting the space, the text of the writer. In the analysis in the next section of this study, we will explore texts that entice the reader into sharing in African writers' fascination with the real or imagined American landscape or, more precisely, cityscape.

## African Writer and American Cityscape

The American cityscape is a subject of perpetual fascination for many commentators, tourists and, in this context, writers, especially African writers and poets. For example, in an opinion posting entitled "What we think of America", Ian Buruma reminisces about the power of an American urban image and his excitement upon receiving a postcard of Manhattan skyline from his father. "I...have felt [the desire for America] ever since my father sent me a postcard of the Manhattan skyline while on a business trip to America in 1959. There was something about that forest of Babylonian towers, gleaming in the starry night that had the power to excite even the mind of an eight-year-old" (2). African writers seem to share Buruma's fascination for real or imagined American topographies as well. Of significance are the numerous poems about American cities, notably Senghor's 'A New York", Bernard B. Dadié's "Patron de New York" [One Way], "Jesus à New Orleans" and Veronique Tadjo's commentary on Washington D.C.

In the discussion that follows, however, these writers do not simply seek to celebrate the beauty of those topographies or to paint simplistic pictures of those cities, but rather use them metaphorically, as sites of contestation, to draw their readers' attention to the interplay of social, physical, religious, and political spaces. In a collection of poems entitled *Hommes de tous les continents* [Men of all Continents] written in the 60's, Dadié deals with issues varying from dreams and spirituality to more engaged and activist themes as slavery, inequality, and race relations in America. Poems from the collection such as "Harlem' and "Christmas" make critical references to Harlem and South Side Chicago as geopolitical, economic, and social spaces in which hope has given way to hopelessness and where Black people are locked in a cycle of poverty, "là-bas aussi des rêves saignent au pied des buildings" [There also dreams bleed at the foot of big housing projects] (53). Additionally, Harlem, placed within the city of New York, offers a more realistic and macrocosmic picture of the United States as a place of physical contrast as well as wide economic disparity among its people.

Senghor quite aptly captures such contrasting image of New York in his poem "To New York" in which he personifies the city by attributing to it some human qualities. As he exclaims in awe and in utter amazement "New York! At first your beauty confused me, your long-legged girls of gold. I was shy at first by your metal-blue eyes and your frosty smile, ... your sulphurous light and livid towers whose heads thunder back at the sky – Your skyscrapers challenge tornadoes with their muscles of steel and skins of bright, polished rock" (87). In other words, these poets' responses to their encounter with New York force their readers to look beyond the physical structures of Manhattan in order to uncover another American reality represented here by Harlem.

Additionally, textual evidence reveals that the poet uncovers this other reality through exploring Harlem by night. As he recounts, "I have seen them preparing the festival of night in flight from the day. I proclaim the Night more true than the day. That is the pure hour down in the streets when God nurtures life like seeds before memory/And the amphibious bodies strut like radiant suns" (89).

The poems provide another dimension to what has otherwise been a one-dimensional received image of New York from other media. Presenting the other side of the US as exemplified by Harlem provides the reader and potential immigrant with the critical tool to attempt to de-mystify that geopolitical and human space that had been perceived from the outside and that Americans themselves project. Harlem becomes symbolic of America itself in its complexities, its paradoxes, its inequities, its disparities as evidenced by these selected lines from the poem:

Il est un tunnel dans New York.../Harlem

Il est un quartier de briques rouges dans New York

Une ile de naufrages/Harlem!

Un cauchemar dans les rêves/Harlem

Il est une prison dans New York/Un zoo pour touristes/Harlem

Il est un musée de misères dans New York

Un parc pour hommes dits "de couleur"/Harlem

Il est un enfer dans le paradis de New York/ou les flammes d'or savourent du Negre/Harlem! (46-7)

[It is a tunnel in New York.../Harlem

It is a neighborhood of red bricks in New York

An island of marooned people/Harlem!

A nightmare in dreams/Harlem!

It is a prison within New York/A zoo for tourists/Harlem!

It is a museum of misery in New York/ A game reserve for people 'of color"/ Harlem!...

It is hell in the paradise of New York/where golden flames burn black people/ Harlem!]

Here, Harlem with its poor lighting becomes "the tunnel", symbol of grey weather and darkness, the island of marooned, poverty-stricken people within the sea of opulence that is New York, a nightmarish presence within the dream of New York, a blemish in an otherwise clean or masked face of New York. Harlem is also portrayed as a zoo for the curious tourist, a wildlife park reserved for people of color, a hell within New York, and a lieu of repose for the dead. It constitutes a prison for the dispossessed, a museum of misery dominant of other more culturally and historically relevant museums in New York. That description of Harlem stands in sharp contrast to his image of the paradisiacal, vibrant, lively, and brightly-lit Manhattan. Dadié uses such spatial representation through Harlem to raise various questions about the American society itself regarding racial spaces and segregation, the plight of Blacks and their status not only within New York where they seem to have been compressed within the limits of one borough, but within the American society.

For Emmanuel Dongala (1982), the journey to New York through a short story "Mon métro fantôme" [My Ghost Subway] in his collection entitled *Jazz et vin de palme*, focuses on an important fixture of New York – the subway. This first person point of view reflects the same ambivalent, contradictory attitude exhibited by both writers discussed earlier. The narrator experiences life rolling endlessly in circles as he descends into the underground to take the subway; an adventure in itself as it gets increasingly dark as he descends all the deeper, "plus je descends, plus il fait sombre et je dois m'arrêter plusieurs fois pour que mes yeux s'habituent à la nuit des couloirs" [The more I descend, the darker it becomes and I have to stop several times for my eyes to adjust to the darkness of hallways] (129). There, he sees the filth of subway stations littered with cigarette butts everywhere; he observes riders' frozen gaze, the hustle and bustle; he smells the stench of people, the heat and sweat, all of which invoke Dantesque circles of his *Divine Comedy*.

Focusing on the subway and the mass movement of people adds yet another dimension of how the African writer is interested in exposing his or her reader to a multifaceted America. And the train or the metro that rolls on nonstop reflects the fast-paced life of New York and prepares the reader and would-be visitor for this accelerated rhythm as well as the frozen gaze of New Yorkers. In the words of the narrator, "Le train roule, j'ai peur, c'est un train express, un métro fantôme, il ne s'arrête pas, il ne s'arrête pas, il continue à descendre de cercle en cercle, à rouler, à rouler, à rouler..." [The train is rolling, I'm afraid, it is an express train, a ghost metro, it does not stop, it does not stop, it keeps descending in circles, rolling, rolling, rolling...] (132).

For her part the Ivorian poet and playwright, Veronique Tadjo's piece in an anthology on *Images of the West,* sets her short tale "Short diary of an exiled poet in a big city", in another American city – Washington D.C. Tadjo's story deals with an African poet's initial encounter with and response to her first exposure to winter and some of the issues that she, as a sojourner, has to confront. These include questions of identity, loneliness, solitude, and nostalgia. Set in the heart of winter, the story's opening lines remind the reader of an important step of displacement in the process of immigration – the first letter home to family and friends upon arrival in the United States. Of course, her story targets a wider readership. In this letter she writes of the cold, long nights and unbearable darkness, a season that forces one to want to remain both physically and metaphorically inside. As she writes,

> Here we are in the big city of stone which is now so cold. The evening comes fast. At four in the afternoon it is already dark and even the lights come on strangely, throwing a fake brightness. But this darkness which stretches itself to no end is unbearable. Every day it takes you by surprise in the midst of doing something, when you thought you still had time, a little time (15).

Indeed, it is a season during which, as Armah has identified elsewhere, one becomes very much aware of one's loneliness, one's solitude; a time to look back in nostalgia to Africa with its bright sunshine and human warmth; a season to retreat into oneself to explore one's imagination. For Tadjo, that initial introduction to winter and snow in Washington D.C. helps her immerse herself in her writings as they "become your identity, your daily bread, your reason for living.... You lock yourself in your creation and words and bury you, sentences annihilate you and in the solitude of your retreat, you forget the blood and dust of the outside world" (15). The story raises some of the most fundamental issues about American society; that is, crime, violence, poverty, homelessness, and unemployment. Washington D.C. is used metonymically as part of the entity called America. As she writes, "It's a ghetto, this large city of the United States, Washington D.C." (16). Even a traditionally Black college, Howard University becomes part of the ghetto bearing graffiti on bathroom walls. Works discussed in this section draw on some African writers' fascination with American cities to expose readers to a multifaceted America. Moreover, their interest in cities does not lie simply in their aesthetics; they view these cities as spaces in which socio-economic, racial, and religious dynamics take place.

## Conclusion

The African reader of these texts as potential emigrant emerges from his or her readings of various texts discussed in this study with multiple perspectives on America. In fact, the critical approach adopted by some of the writers here not only exposes inherent flaws in the American socio-political, economic, and racial constructions, but more importantly, such undoing helps the reader to construct his or her imagined America prior to departure. Moreover, African writers' imaginative responses to their encounter with their new society reveal a land of many challenges, a land of endless possibilities including the possibility to bury the past and to reinvent oneself. It is also a land where dreams could turn into nightmares as many of the African immigrants could fall and have fallen through the cracks, or have become victims of some of the ills of society including racial profiling leading to death as in the case of Samba Diallo in New York and many others. It is a society portrayed as one of the more promising alternative destinations for potential African immigrant, a society that has and will continue to contribute to shaping intellectual, philosophical, and political consciousness.

## References

Adams Jonathan & Thomas O. McShane. 1992. *The Myth of Wild Africa: Conservation without Illusion*. Berkeley: University of California Press.

Armah, Ayi Kwei. 1972. *Why are we so blest?* Garden City: Doubleday & Company, Inc.

Augustus, Elizabeth & Preston Augustus. 2008. "Voluntary Trans-Atlantic Migration: Nigerians' Attitudes to the American Diversity Visa Lottery Program." *African Minorities in the New World*, ed. Toyin Falola & Niyi Afolabi. New York: Routledge, 221-231.

Beti, Mongo. 1955. "Afrique noire, littérature rose." Paris: *Présence Africaine*, 1-2, 133-145.

Bloom, Harold. 1973. *The Anxiety of Influence*. London: Oxford University Press.

Bond, Mann Horace. 1956. "Reflections, Comparative, on West African Nationalist Movements." Paris: *Présence Africaine*, no. 8-9-10, 133-142.

Bouygues, Claude. 1994. "Foreword." Translation of Bernard Dadié *Patron de New York*. Urbana: University of Illinois Press.

Brière, Eloise. 1999. "Introduction." *Your Madness, not mine: Stories from Cameroon*. Julianna *Makuchi*. Athens: Center for International Studies.

Buruma, Ian. 2006. "What we think of America." http://www.granta.com/extracts/1632; accessed June 1, 2006).

Chambers, Ross. 1984. *Story and Situation: Narrative Seduction and the Power of Fiction*. Minneapolis: University of Minnesota Press.

Clark-Bekederemo, John. 1964. *America, their America*. Heinemann.

Coming to America. 1988. Directed by John Landis. USA: Eddy Murphy Productions.

Dadié, Bernard. 1964. *One Way: Bernard Dadié observes America*. Trans. Jo Patterson (1994). Urbana: University of Illinois Press.

_____. 1967. *Hommes de tous les continents*. Paris: Présence Africaine.

Diakhate, Lamine. 1965. "The Acculturation Process in Negro Africa and its Relations with Négritude." Paris: Présence Africaine, English edition, 4th Quarter, 67-80.

Doho, Gilbert. 2005. "The Illegimate State and Cinematographic Discourse in Cameroon." *Cinema and Social Discourse in Cameroon*, ed. Alexie Tcheuyap. Bayreuth: Bayreuth African Studies 69, 21-37.

Dongala, Emmanuel. 1982. 'Mon métro fantôme' Jazz et vin de palme. Paris: Hatier.

Ellison, Ralph. 1972. *Invisible Man*. New York: Vintage Books.

Essien-Udom, E.U. 1964. "Foreword" to *America, their America*. Heinemann.

Falola, Toyin, and Fallou Ngom, eds. 2010. *Facts, Fiction, and African Creative Imaginations*. New York: Routledge.

Higginson, Francis. 2007. "A decent into crime: explaining Mongo Beti's last two novels." *International Journal of Francophone Studies*, 10 (3), 377-391.

Irele, Abiola. 2001. *The African Imagination: Literature in Africa and the Black Diaspora*. N.Y.: Oxford University Press.

Iser, Wolfgang. 1981. "The Reading Process: a Phenomenological Approach." *Reader-Response Criticism from Formalism to Post-Structuralism*, ed. Jane P. Tompkins. Baltimore: The Johns Hopkins University Press.

Makuchi, Julianna. 1999. "American Lottery." *Your Madness, not mine: Stories from Cameroon*. Athens: Center for International Studies, 75-96.

Mansaray, Alasan. 1995. *A Haunting Heritage: an African Saga in American*. Dallas: Sahara Publishing.

Mayer, Ruth. 1992. *Artificial Africas: Colonial Images in the Times of Globalization*. Hanover: University Press of New England.

Mengara, Daniel. 2001. "Introduction: White Eyes, Dark Reflections." *Images of Africa: Stereotypes & Realities*, ed. Daniel Mengara. Trenton. N.J.: Africa World Press, 1-20.

Mudimbe-Boyi, Elisabeth. 2002. "Introduction." *Remembering Africa*, ed. Elisabeth Mudimbe-Boyi. Porthsmouth: N.H., Heinemann.

Mudimbe, Valentin. 2001. "Africa remains the absolute difference – an interview." *Encounter Images in the Meetings between Africa and Europe*, ed. Mai Palmberg. Uppsala: The Nordic Africa Institute, 248-251.

Nkrumah, Kwame. 1964. *Consciencism: Philosophy and Ideology for Decolonization*. New York: Modern Reader Paperbacks.

Obotama, Raphael. 2008. "Immigrants' Pilgrimage and Imaginations: The Cinematic Portrayals of African Immigrants in Movies." *Trans-Atlantic Migration: the Paradoxes of Exile*, ed. Toyin Falola & Niyi Afolabi. New York & London: Routledge, 97-116.

Onwumere, Obinna. 2008. "Pan-Africanism: the Impact of the Nkrumah Years 1945-1966." *Trans-Atlantic Migration: the Paradoxes of Exile*, ed. Toyin Falola and Niyi Afolabi. New York & London: Routledge, 229-241.

Owomoyela, Oyekan. 2008. *The Columbian Guides to West African Literature in English Since 1945*. New York: Columbia University Press.

Paz, Octavio. 1961. *The Labyrinth of Solitude*. New York: Grove Press.
Pieterse Nederveen, Jan. 1992. *White on Black: Images of Africa and Blacks in Western Popular Culture*. New Haven: Yale University Press.
Pratt, Mary Louise. 1999. "Arts of the Contact Zone." *Ways of Reading*, 5th edition, ed. David Bartholomae and Anthony Petroksky. New York: Bedford/St. Martin's Press.
Senghor, Leopold. 1976. *Selected Poems/Poesies choisies*. Trans. From the French by Craig Williamson. London: Rex Collings.
Smertin, Yuri. 1987. *Kwame Nkrumah*. Trans. From the Russian by Sharon McKee. Moscow: Progress Publishers.
Tadjo, Veronique. 1996. "Short Diary of an Exiled Poet in the Big City." *Images of the West*, ed. Yvonne Vera. Harare: Baobab Books.

# Chapter 4
## The Recent African Immigrant (RAI) as the Radical Other

*Emmanuel D. Babatunde*

"Immigration policy should be generous; it should be fair; it should be flexible. With such policy, we can turn to the world and to our own past, with clean hands and a clear conscience. Such a policy would be but a reaffirmation of old principles. It would be an expression of our agreement with George Washington that, 'the bosom of America is open to receive not only the opulent and respectable stranger, but the oppressed and persecuted of all nations and religions; whom we shall welcome to a participation of all our rights and privileges, if by decency and propriety of conduct they appear to merit the enjoyment.'"

President John Kennedy <u>A Nation of Immigrants</u> (1964 82-83).

"*Every morning in Africa, a gazelle wakes up*
*It knows it must run faster than the fastest lion or it will be killed*
*Every morning a lion wakes up,*
*It knows it must outrun the slowest gazelle or it will starve to death*
*It does not matter whether you are lion or gazelle*
*When the sun comes up, you better start running.*"

Life on the Serengeti (Unknown author).

## Introduction

This paper examines the challenges and resilience of the Recent African Immigrants (RAI) to the United States of America. It explores the role of residual cultural strengths that have accounted for the success of voluntary African Immigrants now considered in research as the most educated group of immigrants to the United States (Bergman 2007, Breland1998, Butcher 1994, Dodoo 1997, Kaba, 2007). The residual force of internalized cultural mores that promote resilience is quite appropriate to balance the steady resonance of quantitatively-driven research that has dominated the discourse on Recent African Immigrants. The section that follows discusses the theoretical framework.

## Theoretical Framework: Rite of Passage and Challenges

If the immigrant is the other in opposition to the norm, the RAI is the 'complete' other in terms of clear differences between the internalized elements of African cultural ethos and those elements of the cultural ethos of the community of encounter. Furthermore, if the African male immigrant suffers from three strikes - race, immigrant status and blackness - and the African woman suffers from four strikes - race, immigration status, blackness and gender - then the African is the complete other. In his comparative study of African immigrants in America, Nii-Amoo Dodoo seemed bewildered to find that his study confirmed that, education, the institution supposedly revered as the leveling factor in wellbeing and upward mobility for all the citizens of the United States, was the one institution that actually proved the treatment of the African as the other. He noted succinctly and I quote extensively to show his disappointment:

> "The most intriguing finding in this study regards the centrality of the role of education in the African disadvantage. Why are African but not Caribbean, immigrants rewarded so poorly for their education, and especially for education obtained abroad? Apparently, foreign qualifications of Africans, presumably gained in their home countries, are not valued as highly as American, or for that matter, Caribbean degrees. Does that mean African degrees are qualitatively inferior, perhaps because they are less transferable (Chiswick 1979)? Or could it be that these degrees are only *considered* inferior? Again, these are questions for which the data do not permit conclusive answers."

However, although education in Africa has fallen upon hard times in recent years, the anecdotal evidence is that this is manifested in an extreme selectivity whereby the few who make it through college are still very highly trained (Domatob 1996). The high School and undergraduate course content, particularly in mathematics and the basic sciences are, across the board, probably more rigorous in these countries than in the United States. The competitiveness of African graduate students in America is also quite telling (Domatob 1997).

The reality at work is the political use of untested information to impose an inferiority complex on the graduates of a competing educational system so that they can accept their inferiority when in competition with graduates of the American educational system. This demonstrates yet another instance of the Weberian notion of power in relation to education. The Weberian concept of power is the ability to impose one's influence on others who are competing against one. The first instance of this ploy was the propaganda unleashed against American education in British colonial countries aimed at presenting American education as inferior. This led to the consequent exclusion of earlier groups of returning American education graduates in the early 1960s from jobs that would have used their needed transferable expertise. The realization that his/her educational achievement is regarded as inferior is a major challenge to the RAI because the understanding was that this educational achievement would serve as the foundation for his thriving in American society.

In order to fully appreciate the challenges that the RAI face as 'the other' in the United States, the life of the immigrants will be slotted into three categories of Arnold van Gennep's research template of rites of passage. He identified three phases that are crucial to rites of passage. The first phase is *preliminality* when the individual is separated from the familiar territory of childhood and adult experiences in his/her community of origin and enters the strange new environment of the community of encounter. The second phase is *liminality* or seclusion when s/he knows that s/he is no longer what s/he used to be but has not become what she wants to become. This period is devoted to learning the rules, expectations, skills, manners and practices of survival in the new environment. The third phase is *postliminality* or integration when s/he becomes a citizen and expects to become ensconced in the society. The usefulness of the rites of passage template to understand the challenges and coping mechanisms of the life of the immigrant lies in the fact that it allows for a disaggregation of the RAI's experiences into phases with their peculiar challenges as well as those specific African cultural elements at work to aid the RAI to be resilient.

The challenges that beset the RAI at the preliminary stage include separation anxiety. Then s/he suddenly becomes aware of the fact that upon arrival in her community of encounter, she would have to find a place to live until s/he can stand on his or her own. The reciprocal network of trusting relationships inherent in the communities of origin and encounter for their autarkic development kicks in to provide a solution to this concern. A classmate of his senior brother from another ethnic group or the cousin of his sister's husband is contacted, at the last minute, and told that a 'brother'/ 'sister' is arriving in the city where she lives and has nowhere to stay. The 'brother'/ 'sister' already ensconced in the community of encounter articulates internalized cultural obligations of reciprocity by meeting the traveler at the port of entry and providing accommodation. Data from qualitative ethnographic research conducted on focused groups of RAI students and faculty at Lincoln University, Pennsylvania identify social capital as the cause of eighty five percent of the first job opportunity for the new arrival.

Hence, the preference of most African traditional societies for non-classificatory kinship terminology in place of specific kinship ones relates to the pragmatic ease with which non-kinship relatives are transformed into kinsfolk with all the rights and privileges conferred. Social capital derived from community bonding is one of the most useful proofs that culture matters in breaking the harshness of the RAI's entry into the community of encounter.

At this seclusion stage, an overwhelming recognition of the tremendous risk s/he has undertaken in leaving familiar environment dawns on the RAI and is exacerbated by the great uncertainty of the outcome of the risky decision. This uncertainty compounds the trauma of the loss of status occasioned by his/her inability to secure a job commensurate with his level of educational achievement. Thus, a RAI who is a medical doctor had a measure of success and status in his community of origin. When upon arrival in the United States, s/he is forced to take minimum wage jobs vending newspapers or making home delivery for fast food chains, the loss of status and the remuneration that come with it is traumatic. Less harrowing is the formerly tenured professor, who upon arrival in his community of encounter becomes an adjunct professor, a job he may lose because his students complain about his accent, his more disciplined approach to teaching and more demanding work ethics, all evaluated to be too harsh and disrespectful of the students – his customers - in his community of encounter. A major source of comfort to the RAI is that things will improve when s/he becomes a citizen.

The postliminality or assimilation into the community of encounter may occur when the immigrant takes American citizenship. All hopes pinned on improved quality of life based on having become an American citizen then produce the first anomaly in the life of the RAI. The opportunities are not coming in spite of the many interviews. The psychological stress this produces is founded on the question, where is the job that is commensurate with educational achievement if education is the criterion for effective integration? Kaba uses the data on Nigerian RAI to highlight this trauma in the life of the RAI. He noted that in1990, out of 158.9 million people in the United States aged 25 and over, 20.3 percent had bachelor's degree or higher and 7.2 percent had graduate degree or higher. For 52,388 Nigerians aged 25 and over, 52.9 percent had bachelor's degree or higher were second only to another African group, Egyptians, with 60.4 percent. The 26.3 percent of Nigerians with graduate degree or higher was the highest rate among all 68 ancestry groups listed (Kaba 2007).

Table 1: Socioeconomic Characteristics: Education

| Areas | U.S. Population | All Immigrants | **African Immigrants** | Asian Immigrants | Europe, Russia, and Canada | Latin, South America and Caribbean |
|---|---|---|---|---|---|---|
| Less than High School | 17.1% | 39.1% | **12.1%** | 21.2% | 23.5% | 57.4% |
| College Degree | 23.1% | 23.3% | **43.8%** | 42.5% | 28.9% | 9.1% |
| Advanced Degree | 2.6% | 4.2% | **8.2%** | 6.8% | 5.8% | 1.9% |

*Source:* United States Census, 2000.

Using data collected from the United States Census, Kaba provided useful information about the levels of educational achievement in the United States. He then compared data on Nigerian and Egyptian levels of educational achievement with those of English, German, French, Scottish-Irish, Dutch, and Swedish descent to highlight the discrepancy in differential remuneration.

Responses to the paradox of RAI's high educational achievement and low remuneration vary from qualitative data collected from different focus groups. These fall into three broad headings. The first category is made up of people who read conspiracy to put down what is African in the national ethos of the community of encounter. They refer to the historical relationship between involuntary African immigrants as a proof and justification of their view. Their solution is to counter this perceived conspiracy by a tunnel vision reactionary socialization process that creates, through ethnic houses of worship and other specific culturally bounded institutions, rigid ethnic centers for the inculcation of the very conservative and change-resistant aspects of the culture of their community of origin.

A second category of response is that adopted by those who take the paradox of educational attainment and low remuneration to imply that the internalized aspects of African culture are a barrier to achievement in their community of encounter. Their intention therefore is to bring their children in what they perceive as the key elements of the culture of their community of encounter. They relent in the inculcation of those values that suggest that the interests of the community are superior to those of the group and encourage practices and values that emphasize the optimum development of the individual complete with a sense of equality that is foreign to relationship in their community of origin. Traditional courtesy of greeting, relating to older members on first name basis, the adoption of a truculent attitude to neutralize the use of seniority by the other as a control lever represent the more superficial instances of this loss of confidence in African cultural practices adopted by this category of people. The more extreme manifestation of this attitude is a refusal of parents to inculcate some of those cultural practices that have assisted their generation to succeed in the face of enormous challenges. Furthermore, the importance of etiquette as a measure of proper upbringing, the skill of learning how to cook some of the nutritionally adequate meals, the importance of eating African food with its high fiber and high vegetable content, the importance of deferring gratification through an inner-worldly asceticism and the usefulness of networking are gradually being eroded as RAI seeks to assimilate in his or her society of encounter.

The third category has adopted a *media via* – the middle road. This group has decided to abstract and blend in their children what they perceive to be good in both cultures. They blend those cultural aspects of the communities of origin and encounter together and incorporate them in the socialization of their children born in the land of encounter. For instance, practices that teach the importance of independence, cooking, thriftiness, and the ability to save for the "rainy day" by deferring instant gratification, are among survival skills into which RAI's children are socialized. The families nurture new experiences and talents that their ethnic culture may not approve. An example is the encouragement of a son to take ballet given the stereotypes associated with boys who take ballet.

## Literature Review

Since this paper focuses on the impact of cultural factors in stimulating resilience in the African immigrant, it is only appropriate to examine briefly the controversy generated by an earlier attempt to focus on cultural factors. Some scholars have correlated the success of foreign-born immigrants to attributes and values brought from their initial cultures, which, after the period of preliminality, translated into success (Chiswick 1971; Butcher, 1994 and Kalmijn 1996). An opposing view to the cultural values carry-over perspective noted that the 1965 Immigration Laws, in facilitating family-based and refugee migrations, opened a Pandora box that unleashed a lower stock of immigrants with tenuous foundations in cultural values and ethics that did not translate to success in America (Borjas 1985). The latter view suggested that the short duration of stay effects of culture on this generation of new immigrants could also translate into faster process of assimilation that in turn can lead to success if assimilation rate is an important variable in attainment of success. Contrary to the prediction of the latter view, RAI have remained the most educated of all immigrant groups to the United States. The suggestion here is that, in spite of predictions of tenuous duration of cultural attributes, the drawback of accent and the perception of over-confidence, Africans are beating the odds to achieve because of the foundation effect of their cultural values, mores and attitudes internalized from their communities of origin and made pragmatic in their communities of encounter. These same immigrants are leaving no stone unturned in the effort to instill these elements of their internalized culture in their children born in America.

One of the first attempts to correlate the immigrants' success in the community of encounter to the values, attributes and hard work ethics internalized by the immigrants in their lands of origin was the provocative book Migrations and Cultures (1996) by Thomas Sowell. It was provocative and ideologically polarizing. It was an interesting study of the immigrant as the 'other', both as a risk taker in his land of origin and an economic middleperson in his community encounter. Sowell's failure to see the characteristics arrogated to six ethnic groups – the Germans(ch.2), the Japanese(ch.3), the Italians(Ch.4), the Overseas Chinese/Indians (ch.5) and the Jews(Ch.6) – as characteristics of resilience exhibited by all immigrants of all ethnicities not the monopoly of any six groups of ethnic immigrants was deliberate and self serving. It was polarizing ideologically because his deliberate selection of these six ethnicities was to serve as the antithesis of a dialectical political struggle in the United States of America. The thesis of this dialectics was the Civil Rights Movement that sought equal rights for all American citizens of all genders, ethnicities and beliefs. The antithesis was the conservative resistance to this much needed change. The synthesis, a compromise of sorts, came in the three landmark Acts that were enacted as a settlement of the Civil Rights struggles. These were Affirmative Rights Act of 1964, the Voting Rights Act and the Immigration Rights Act of 1965 respectively. The conservative political metaphysical given was that these policies on the Civil Rights Acts were unnecessary because America had already gradually integrated groups (Glazer 1987; Takaki 1987). According to Glazer and Sowell, good immigrants would first seek economic rights before all other rights such as political ones were given to them. The Asians brought into California for the Railroads who were tenuously integrated into the economic system without being given the political power was the example often cited. Their political power came eventually. But this assumption is untenable not only because power and privilege concede nothing except through a struggle but more so because the political domain influences the rules that structure participation in the economic domain. To concede the political arena to the powerful in the belief that they will "at the right time" grant the power of full participation to the powerless is tantamount to living in a state of false consciousness.

Two more enduring contributions document the impact of culture on development and personal achievement in the United States. They are the efforts of Lawrence Harrison and Samuel Huntington on the one hand, and Robert Putnam on the other. These twin efforts have reinforced one another sufficiently well to force the perception, in development circles, that contrary to claims that culture does not matter in development, culture actually matters. The former in his body of contributions known as Culture Matters Research Project (CMRP) has, with Samuel Huntington and Peter Berger, given considerable attention to those values and attitudes that nurture progress, success and achievement. Lawrence Harrison noted that the motivation for this effort was "... the notion that values, beliefs, and attitudes are a key but neglected component of development and that the neglect of cultural factors may go a long way towards explaining the agonizing slow progress toward democratic governance, prosperity, and social justice in a great many countries of Africa, Latin America, the Islamic world, and elsewhere. Understanding how culture influences the behavior of individuals and societies, and what forces shape cultural change, can, I believe, accelerate the pace of progress" (2000 xi)

Robert Putnam, in his works on social capital – the reciprocal networks of trusting relationships that exist in a society for the benefit of its development – has reiterated the importance of culture to development. Both efforts have re-introduced a fertile element of the Weberian thesis to reiterate the fact that political and economic changes cannot be fathomed until one understands their relationship to culture (Beger 2000, xvii). In doing these in their different ways, they have assisted researchers to disaggregate culture into its components in other to understand those residual elements of culture that constitute the foundation of resilience in the immigrant. Two questions are pertinent in our quest to understand the root of resilience in the RAI. What are the values and attitudes that serve as the bases for achievement in the African immigrant? What are the instruments and institutions that transmit cultural values, beliefs and attitudes, and how amenable are they to application or modification to promote achievement? A cursory look at the African World view will provide a useful introduction to the prospect of answering these questions.

## African Worldview

There is a tendency in contemporary scholarship to take objection to a presentation of Sub Saharan Africa as if its peoples have things in common that can justify the umbrella approach implied in the generic use of 'African'. Such an approach is deemed mistaken. It is claimed that African societies have a lot of idiosyncratic and particularistic practices that make a sub-continental designation unrealistic. This tendency to see African societies as not having much in common to group them together seems to derive from strategic social engineering intent. This intent is not unrelated to the conviction that African culture is antithetical to modernization following the European/American model of puritanical ethics. The contention is that to make African culture amenable to modernization, it has to be atomized into units, each of which must bargain directly with the puritanical culture of modernization. Presented in this fragmented units, it would have little chance of positioning itself for autarkic modernization comparable to the Asian culturally propelled process. While languages, dialects, rituals, kinship descent types are many and different one from another, the fundamental intensions are similar. The common philosophy behind these rituals and practices provide a coherent 'logic of unity of purpose' behind the practices. These enduring essential traits and trends that run through African cultures provide a sense of psychic unity (Kottak 2008, 280). These residual elements of African culture such as kinship bonding, network of reciprocal trusting relations together with a positive deviance in favor of not failing, gleaned from proverbs, worldview, short stories and songs constitute the foundation of resilience in the African immigrant. Together with internalized values, norms and mores, they imbue the recent African immigrant with an almost fanatic refusal to fail as a function of the positive deviance in favor of succeeding. The intention is to challenge the community of encounter to understand that the meeting of the native born and the African immigrant offers a rich opportunity for learning in diversity for the rejuvenation of the American national ethos.

A brief comparative analysis of the elements of the culture of the community of encounter and those of the community of origin will throw into relief the complex negotiations that the RAI is called to do in becoming a functional member in his or her new community. The extent to which the cultural differences of the community of origin are diametrically opposed to cultural elements in the communities of encounter reiterate the contention at the beginning of this article that posits the African as the complete other. A major difference is emphasis on the optimum development of the individual versus community orientation in the RAI. The next series of elements reflect differences between a very technologically advanced culture and another that is not. Thus while the African has imbibed the expectation to be patient with and dependent on nature, the American seeks to master nature, take control of the environment and use it to his own personal enjoyment and profit.

In Africa, time is measured in patience response to the vagaries of climate, in the United States time is measured in constant activity. Equality is the underlying principle of personal relationship within the American society. The individual's right to privacy within the rule of law is paramount and one is brought up to be independent and sees others in competition with self. The RAI submits to hierarchy that rates those who are older. The elderly are, often in control and deserving of respect. He values protection in the group and would prefer to see his activities in the society as cooperating with rather than competing with them to keep the society running smoothly. American activities are direct, pragmatic, instrumental and informal. They focus on how the present can engineer a more prosperous future. African activities are often indirect. They follow formal rituals attached to a hierarchy sanctioned by the past and hopes that good things will come about for the society through prayer, ritual sacrifices and the manipulation of magic. Effective performance of the African in American cultural milieu demands that s/he learns wholly new ways of behavior, practices and expectations. In spite of these differences, the high achievement of RAI speaks not only to a resilience built on the positive deviance not to fail but also on the ability to negotiate new behavioral and axiological spaces crucial for survival. A brief discussion of the practical values and activities of African work ethics should assist analysis.

## Cosmology and Work Ethics

The outline of African cosmology share common elements even though the stories differ. There is belief in after-life where those who die remain with the Supreme Being. This is the most important and permanent abode that is called several names in different parts of Africa. The earth as the abode of the living is another. It is where one works hard by following the rules of respect, responsibility, reverence, reliability, reason and nurture of the young. Every society has the concept of the 'reasonable' person who epitomizes the quintessential notion of the proper person who is deemed a success in the community. Among the Igbo ethnic group of Nigeria, this human template of success is known as the 'owner of *Ikenga*'. Among the Hausa of West Africa, he is called *Mutumin Kirki*. Among the Yoruba, he is *Omoluwabi*. Among the Barotse, the person is known as the reasonable man (Gluckman 1962). These expectations cut across various African cultures as in the following: a reasonable person is hardworking, enduring in the face of adversity, and is completely devoted to his or her duty of nurturing the young in the ethics and morality of the community of origin; and a reasonable person ought to provide for all the needs of the elders to ensure that they do not lack anything as they prepare to exit to the abode of the ancestors.

A major measure of a responsible adult's life is the extent to which the twin principles of a sense of honor and abhorrence of shame are applicable in his or her life. The usefulness of these "names" resides in reproducing pedagogical elements from African culture in axiological package that guides the behavior of the RAI to thrive. Wise sayings reiterate the need to work together in the community, the need to work hard and not give up, and the obligatory cultural responsibilities of one to those at home. Above all, through the caution for thrift and deferred gratification, that essential requirement for success in the Puritanic ethics referred to earlier as by Berger and Harrison as inner-worldly asceticism, becomes a foundation for resilient behavior. The impact of the pragmatic use of African proverbs to engineer resilient behavior and impact positively on individual efforts for survival as an immigrant will be explored now in relation to childrearing.

## African Proverbs and Childrearing Principles

The argument is that an African immigrant's response to challenges is partly a reflection of the socialized values and norms that are transmitted by parents, families, community as well as other socialization agents such as the media, religion, and the government. Oral tradition through proverbs is one of the mechanism through which cultural values are transmitted from one generation to another. Upon becoming an immigrant, such values later become important resilient tool for overcoming adversity in the society of encounter. Thus the philosophy of African childrearing maybe encapsulated in many proverbs in different parts of Africa. For instance, the Yoruba proverb, *"Omo ko gbon, ani ki oma ku, kini mpa enia bi aigbon"* – A child is utterly stupid and people pray that it should not die, what kills more rapidly than stupidity? - epitomizes key element of the primary African concern. No effort is spared to spoil the child. Etiquette is the first measure of a well-brought up child. From the age of reason, a major internalized force of control is that when one is confronted with an ethical dilemma, the question to ask is "how will my mother and father take this action?" The sense of honor and shame is a powerful residual in the collective consciousness of society.

In the traditional African society, the emphasis on community bonding and respect for elders is reinforced in the school environment. The teacher is a parent away from home who is interested in the wellbeing of the child. S/He is a disciplinarian. If a child misbehaves, the teacher will discipline him and report to his parents why s/he did so. Invariably, the parents then impose more punishment on the child. In doing so, assonance of discipline is reached as the foundation for instilling a rigorous work and behavioral ethics in the child.

A Zimbabwe proverb underscores the importance of training the child to seek for help when in need of one. '*Mwana asinga chemi anofira mumbereko*' – A child who does not cry [when he/she is hungry or sick] will die on its mother's back (Muzorewa 2009). The importance of seeking help when one is needed is drummed forcefully into an African child and is a measure of manhood since it can make the difference between life and death. Hence the Oromo people of the Horn of Africa who live in North Kenya, North Western Somalia and Ethiopia say "*Yoo abban iyyate ollaan namaati birmmata*" – Only when a person shouts or cries out in a loud voice that neighbors rush to help (Tucho 2009). However, if one has cultivated the reputation of always asking for help especially when such help turns into a parasitic life style, traditions frown upon it as laziness. The greatest punishment for a lazy man is to typify him or her as a threat to the survival of his group. No responsible family will give his daughter to marry a lazy man or from a family that has a reputation for laziness. The proverb by the Ngoni peoples of Zambia speaks for the rest of Africa when it notes that "*Munthu wa ulesi asadye*" - Lazy people must not be given free food (Katampi 2009). Thus in the society of encounter, challenges such as unemployment or underemployment, loss of status, prejudice, are not enough barrier to prevent a RAI from being successful in the society of encounter.

## Conclusion

This chapter has explored how various dimensions of African cultural norms and practices have shaped African immigrant's response to coping with challenges in the society of encounter. The Weberian concept of power as the ability to impose one's influence on others who are competing with one is used to understand the immigrants initial challenges of adjustment for survival as the immigrants' experiences are placed in Arnold van Gennep's anthropological research template of rites of passage. Internalized force of residual elements of African culture such as kinship bonding, network of reciprocal trusting relations together with a positive deviance in favor of not failing provide both a cushion and an initial head start for the African immigrant. Given the United States' unqualified success story in embracing individual competition and their struggle in embracing diversity, this paper concludes by suggesting that just as the immigrants learn to survive in their community of encounter, the committee of encounter can benefit from RAI's pre-departure adaptive mechanisms in coping with challenges. As a result as completely "Other" as the African immigrant culture – world view, family values, work ethics, childrearing habits are, they constitute vibrant elements in the diversity pool of cultural resources that communities of encounter can and do benefit from.

## Future research direction

Future research combining quantitative and qualitative methodology is needed to validate or negate the link between residual forces of internalized aspects of culture in the performance of RAI in the United States. Since the avalanche of immigration was set in motion by the Immigration Act began in 1965 the period of forty years provide the timing to gauge the stay effect of the cultural elements carried over from Africa in the behavior of first and second generation of children of RAI. This research is critical in three areas including child-rearing habits, work ethics, and nutrition. Child-rearing habits would attempt to ascertain the presence of old etiquette, values and expectations inculcated to the young in the early stages of the socialization process. Research in work ethics will aim at identifying the continuities in the discipline and resilience in the life of the adult as those born upon arrival in the U.S. would now be nearing forty years of age. The third area of needed research is the continuity or change in the diet of the descendants of RAI particularly as issues of nutrition have become a primary measure of health and wellness in the United States. Since obesity has become an issue of national epidemic, it would be useful to see the frequency of the participation of RAI and their children in this national epidemic. Then whether the perception lingers in the community of encounter or not that Asians and not RAI are the most achieving group of recent immigrants to the United States, data will persuade the enlightened that ideas change slowly in the face of negative media representation of Africa.

## References

Babatunde, E. D. *Culture Shock and Family Dysfunctionality: Case Studies of Some African American Immigrants in Nigeria*. Nwachuku, L. Sudarkasa, N. & Thomas, J. (eds.) *Exploring the African American Experience*. Lincoln University Press, 2006.

Bergman, M. "Earnings Gap Highlighted by Census Bureau Data on Educational Attainment," U. S. Census Bureau. Washington, D. C. Government Printing office 2007.

Borjas, G. "Assimilation, Changes in Cohort Quality, and the Earnings of Immigrants." *Journal of Labor Economics* 3 (Oct.): 463-89, 1985.

Breland, A. M. "A Model for Differential Perceptions of Competence Based on Skin Tone Tone Among African Americans," *Journal of Multicultural Counseling and Development*, 26, (4), 1998.

Butcher, K. "Black Immigrants in the United States: A Comparison with Native Blacks and Other Immigrants," *Industrial and Labor Relations Review*, 47, (2): 265-284, 1994.

Chiswick, B. "The Economic Progress of Immigrants: Some Apparently Universal Patterns." Fellner, W. (ed.) *Contemporary Economic Problems*. The American Enterprise Institute, 1979, pp. 357-399.

Douglas, M. *Purity and Danger*. London: Routledge and Paul Kegan, 1966.

Emeagwali, P. "Brain Drain: Why Nigerians are not Returning Home." Remarks Delivered to the Association of Nigerians in Montgomery, Alabama on October 10, 1999.

Glazer, N. 'The Emergence of An American Ethnic Pattern." Takaki, R. (Ed.). *From Different Shores: Perspectives on Race and Ethnicity in America*. New York: Oxford University Press, 1987.

Gluckman, M. *Barotse Jurisprudence*. Manchester: Manchester University Press, 1972.

Harrison, L. and Huntington, S. (eds.) Culture Matters: How Values Shape Human Progress. New York Basic Books, 2000.

Hobbes, T. *Leviathan*. 1660.

Kaba, A. J. "Educational attainment, Income Levels and Africans in the United States: The Paradox of Nigerian Immigrants." *West Africa Review*, Issue 11, 2007.

Kalmijn, M. "The Socioeconomic Assimilation of Caribbean American Blacks." *Social Forces* 74:911-30, 1996.

Kennedy, E. "The Immigration Act of 1965." *Annals of the American Academy of Political and Social Science*, vol. 367, pp. 137-138.

Kennedy, J. F. *A Nation of Immigrants*. New York and Evanston: Harper and Row, 1964.

Kottak, C. P. *Anthropology: The Exploration of Human Diversity*. Boston: McGraw Hill, 2008.

Luther King Jr., M. Letter from B.

# Chapter 5
## Reproducing African Communities in the US

### Settlement Patterns and Social Organizations

*Bridget Teboh*

## Introduction

The long years of colonialism and white colonial rule, nationalism, neocolonialism, and now globalization with its new modes of consumption imported from the West have forever changed traditional identities and have distorted the notion of an African self. The contemporary mass migration to Europe and the United States further calls into question the meaning of being an African today, and, above all, the location of that identity (Achebe and Teboh, 2007). Is it in ancestral villages, or where Africans work, pray, raise children, and establish social networks (in new communities or locations)? Alternatively, is it in places, one leg here, and another there, part real and part imagined? This chapter seeks to elaborate on African immigrants' social organizations and the reproduction of African communities as well as their implications for African identity and culture. It argues that intellectual discourses on African cultural identity and its spatiality need to be conceptualized in terms of its varied levels of transformation and diversity. As Henry Louis Gates pointed out, the facts of nationality or race "don't exhaust anybody's human complexity" (Gates, 1997: 43). Indeed, if it is true that there is not just "one way to be black" (Awkward, 1995:10) it is also true that there is not just one way to be African. This paper contends that to look at African identity merely in reference to geographical location, without acknowledging other connections such as cultural, economic, spiritual is essentialist.

Multi-positionality and multi-locality is another way of saying that diversity and transformation are two traits of contemporary African community and identity. The question is how does African community in the United States come into being? In answering this question, this paper addresses the concept of place-making and its relationship to African social and cultural practices which reveal African immigrants' sense of community, of belonging, and identity maintenance within three major spheres: African food, annual and monthly meetings (cultural festivals and conventions), and African languages. This chapter highlights the struggles to maintain African culture and identity through a historical lens beginning from slave trade and forced migrations, through voluntary immigrants and early African students of the 1950s. It traces the troubled and complex articulation of Africans in the United States. It is followed by a discussion of settlement patterns of Africans in the United States. The next section recapitulates a socio-economic profile of African immigrants in the United States in order to understand its connection to settlement patterns. Finally, drawing on the experience of Cameroonian immigrants in the United States, a description of some of their practices of community building and (re) creation of identity is examined.

## Methodology

This chapter draws on data collected through archival research, interviews, and oral sources between 2005 and 2007, to explain where and why African immigrants in the United States choose to settle as well as cope in their new communities. Attendance and participation at several annual conventions and African festivals provided an opportunity to interview respondents in four major cities across the United States[1]. These cities were chosen because of the high concentration of Cameroonians and other Africans currently residing there. Additionally, these locations are strategic places where annual national conventions are usually held, thus making access to informants easier. Furthermore, selections of participants in different parts of the United States were meant to capture variations in socio-economic profiles of immigrants in different communities.

Some were also interviewed at their homes after having being identified at monthly cultural/ethnic group meetings (Table 1). At the end, 210 people were successfully interviewed for this study. For some informants who are "asylum-seekers" or "asylees", their real names are being withheld in order to protect their identity[2]. For the other informants they are happy to have their real names used in the discussions and analyses. The University of

Massachusetts, Dartmouth generously provided research support through start-up funds during summer 2005 and 2007.

Table 1: Interview Locations and Number of Respondent

| Interviews | Number |
|---|---|
| **Boston Area** | **Boston Area** |
| Adult Male | 10 |
| Adult Female | 25 |
| Children | 10 |
| Total | 45 |
| **Los Angeles** | **Los Angeles** |
| Adult Male | 20 |
| Adult Female | 20 |
| Children | 15 |
| Total | 55 |
| **Arlington** | **Arlington** |
| Adult Male | 12 |
| Adult Female | 10 |
| Children | 8 |
| Total | 30 |
| **Washington, DC** | **Washington, DC** |
| Adult Male | 15 |
| Adult Female | 10 |
| Children | 10 |
| Total | 35 |
| **New York** | **New York** |
| Adult Male | 18 |
| Adult Female | 15 |
| Children | 12 |
| Total | 45 |
| Grand Total | 210 |

*Source*: Teboh, Field Research Data, 2005-2007.

Of the total respondent (210), 43 are children between ages 4 and 17.[3]

## Africans in the United States: Then and Now

The early history of African immigration in the United States is one of exploitation, resistance, and subversion (Diène 2001). From 1619 when the first Africans arrived in Virginia to 1863 when the Emancipation Proclamation ended the formal market for black slaves, slave traders removed over 450,000 people from the coastal areas of West Africa and relocated them in the swampy areas of the Middle and South Atlantic states to fuel the emerging North American agricultural industry (Carney 2001). The literature on the transatlantic trade shows the efforts made by slave owners to prevent them from recreating their original communities: mothers were separated from their children and husbands from their wives, people from different regions speaking different languages were thrown together to make the construction of a common consciousness if not impossible, definitely more difficult (Endore 1991). Yet, in the slave villages on the plantations, in the homes of their masters where they worked as servants, and all along the networks of the North American colonial economy Africans found a way to recreate their sense of place and identity amidst terror, illness, starvation, and physical and sexual abuses. At times this emerging, insurgent identity was achieved by violent means (James 1963), other times by bringing animals from home/Africa with them on board of ships and rice grains hidden in their hair to be planted in the new world (Carney 2001). They invented new symbolic languages by wearing dresses and headscarves in ways that denoted their mood and consciousness (Wallace Vernon 1993). What is relevant to this discussion however is not simply the capacity of Africans to resist the dehumanization project enacted by their English, Dutch, or French masters, their wives, and their salaried thugs, but, rather, the capacity of African ancestors in the new world to envision a common ground for the making of a new consciousness away from home. This consciousness could be described as eminently inter-tribal, multi-cultural multi-local and hybrid.

The evolution of the slave economy provides a historical canvas from which one could assess the achievements that black people have been able to attain in the United States. The ensuing development of the contemporary African American consciousness constitutes an important aspect of the African identity and its multiple locations. While a discussion of African American identity is an important crucible for the forging of a non-essentialist African identity in the 21st century, it is not the immediate concern in this chapter. The focus remains on the history of contemporary African migration.

Apart from slaves from West Africa, Cape Verdeans form the oldest community of voluntary African immigrants to the United States. They descend from Portuguese, Spanish, and Genoese settlers as well as from other West African groups who were forcibly relocated on these islands to work the sugar cane plantations early in the 15th century. The history of dark skinned Cape Verdean Americans is particularly interesting from a consciousness and/or identity point of view because their identification as "Africans" is a fairly recent phenomenon. Throughout their history in fact, they did not perceive themselves as being different from the light skinned Portuguese. Yet, they were black living in a segregated America. Fearing discrimination by association, the Portuguese excluded the Cape Verdeans from Portuguese institutions in the United States, hence the perceived betrayal and the association of Cape Verdeans with Africa in the 1970s. Students spearheaded early immigration from other parts of Africa during the late 1950s. By 1991, 24,000 African students were officially studying in United States colleges. Before the 1960s, most came to the United States from English speaking countries such as Nigeria, Ghana, and Kenya where they attended predominantly black colleges.

The next wave of immigrants began in earnest after the 1965 Hart-Cellar Immigration Act (Graham et al 1995). This act, spawning from the struggle of the Civil rights movements, changed dramatically the methods by which immigrants were granted residence and work in the United States because it abolished national-origin quotas, a fact that had previously hindered migration from the developing world (Kutler and Stanley 2003; David 1985). The act also entailed a separate quota for refugees. The significance of this bill was that the post 1965 African immigrants came to the United States as skilled workers and professionals attracted by the possibility of higher earnings. Figure 1 shows the dynamics of African immigration in the United States in the post-1965 Immigration Act.

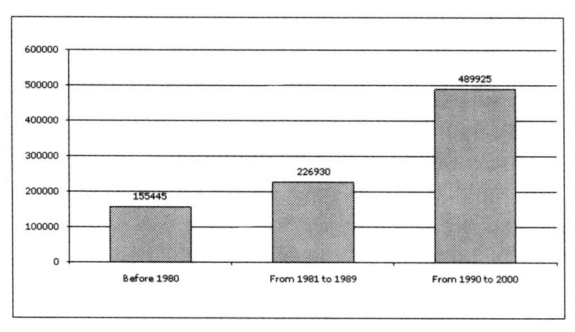

Figure 1: Period of Entry of People Born in Africa in the United States (2000)
Source: United States Census 2000, table FBP-1. Profile of Selected Demographic and Social Characteristic Personal Elaboration.

By 1995, an average of 40,000 (today the number is down to about 14,000) Africans came annually in the United States but non-discriminatory immigration laws explain only part of the wave of African immigration on this side of the Atlantic (Hamilton 1997). Indeed a study by Economic Commission for Africa indicates that skilled African workers abandon their countries at a moment when their national economies need their services (ECA 1986). Among the factors internal to Africa cited in the study it is worth mentioning the decline in real income when prices were constantly rising; lack of merit based promotion practices; political interference; inadequate high education facilities and opportunities; political upheavals and general instability. These factors force professionals and salaried workers to look for gainful employment in countries that pay higher salaries with a certain continuity.

Moving from factors internal to Africa to the articulation of African economies with the wider economic global system, we note the effects of Post-fordism in Europe and the subsequent tightening of immigration laws (Ratnesar 2000; Curtin 1997). If the delocalization and geographical dispersal of the European economy did not slow the *sans papiers*[4] immigration which indeed continues unchecked as we speak, it nonetheless contributed to change the South to North axis of legal immigration, which took a decisive turn East-West toward North America and Canada.

Another external factor at work in Africa since the early 1970s that fueled migration from the continent was the mounting economic pressures including the infamous "structural adjustments" imposed on many African economies by the International Monetary Fund (IMF). These "adjustments," which theoretically were designed to realign the African economies with the so-called "developed" world, further opened the African market to deregulation and liberalization favoring the final penetration of capitalist relations into the remotest hamlet. Faced with insurmountable competition from more developed countries, African economies reacted in two ways. On the one hand, some countries tried to de-link from the capitalist economy by initiating Marxist oriented programs of rural development like Tanzania (Hyden 1980), while other countries in West Africa, for example, preferred to stay linked and devaluated their *franc* in 1994 to gain at least some niches in the global market. Both strategies failed to bring the necessary readjustments, and, while unable to rearticulate the African economy, left the majority of the population with the specter of a life-long unemployment. If to such a dire economic, political, and social climate we add the civil wars that in the early 1980s and 1990s ravaged countries like Sierra Leone, Liberia, Sudan, Somalia and the Ivory Coast, we have a better understanding as to why Africans with the necessary means sought a better life in the United States.

**A Socio-Economic Profile of the Disapora in the U.S.**

Taking for granted that the official Census underestimates the number of Africans living in the United States of America (Grieco 2004), data shows that there were about 881300 people born in Africa legally living in the United States in the year 2000. Of these, about 55% are male and 45% female. The median age is 36 years and their marital status is overwhelmingly married (57%). Families with own children less than 18 years old represent 45% of the total, while married couples with own children younger than 18 represent 45% of the total. Over 44,000 (11%) are women with own children less than 18 years old living alone. Non-family household represents 11.3 % of the total of which 90,195 (11.9%) live alone. Interestingly enough, there are about 19,585 grandparents living with their families and 5,235 of them (25%) declare that they are responsible for their grand children. Of the more than 685,000 people over 25 years old, 592,695 (86%) have a school diploma of which 222, 825 (43%) have a University diploma. These data make the African immigrant the most educated group coming to the United States (Fig.2).

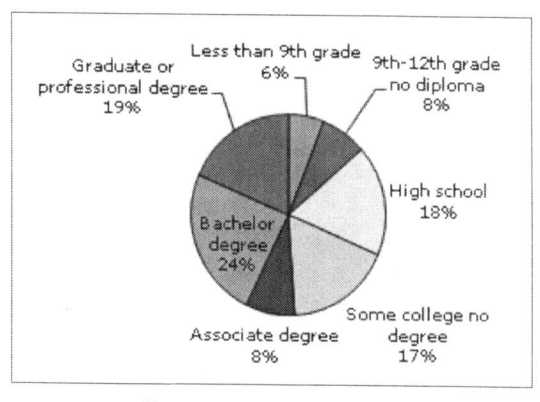

Figure 2: School Attainment

It is important to note that if 58% of African born residents in the United States are black, over 23% declared themselves white, 4.3% Asian and 11.3% of mixed races. The end of apartheid in South Africa and Zimbabwe appears to count for the presence of white Africans.

Taken as a whole, the African subgroups (white, black and "Asian") have average household incomes of about $ 41,000, which places them well above the United States average. Notwithstanding the social mobility and their impressive levels of economic achievements, 35,000 African households out of 395,000, live under the poverty level. Of these families, over 13,000 are households headed by women with no husbands and with children between the ages of five and seventeen. Therefore, the feminization of poverty, a characteristic of the American society in general is pervasive also among African immigrants, especially refugees. It is important to note that these data on school attainment and occupational characteristics of African partly determine African settlement patterns. While most of the educated and professionals prefer to live in suburbs, most less educated and refugees tend to live in cities where access to social services programs, transportation, housing as well as support of kin and friends are easily available, similar to other immigrant groups such as Asians and Hispanics.

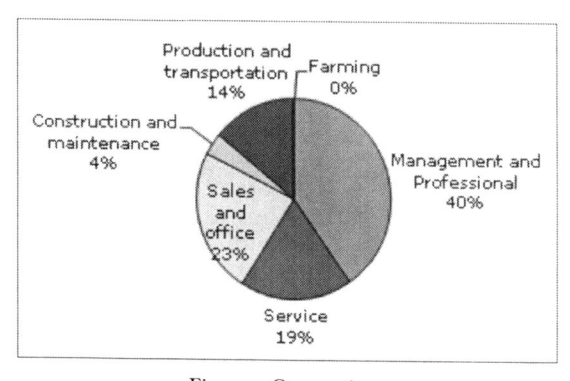

Figure 3: Occupations

## African Culture and Identity in the U.S.

To study the social production of identity and its insertion into a geographically and culturally wider world, the concept of "place-making" is useful for at least two reasons: it captures the importance of locality to people especially in the face of global flows, and it imbues identity with a notion of performance and creativity (Neill, 2004:111-156). Place-making thus involves the double action of developing a consciousness of place and a feeling of belonging (Healey 1997). Without necessarily idealizing identity but looking at it as a social process and acknowledging that individuals are inserted in extended relational webs, we can identify those practices that enable people to endow places with deep meaning. The argument here is that some of these practices relate to African foods, language and meetings/social organizations to celebrate birth, marriage, and even death.

## Food as a Form of Identity

This section begins with an examination of African foods, cultural continuities and discontinuities among new African immigrants in the Diaspora. It focuses especially on Africans in Los Angeles, Washington DC, Boston, Texas, and New York where most of the new immigrants live. It also brings to the forefront of our discourse the question of national identities. How do Africans recreate home, community and identity abroad or outside Africa? What are the tools at their disposal to recreate such communities and identities in different social contexts? What challenges do they face?

In the last two decades, demand for African foods in the US has doubled following an increase not only in the numbers of adult new arrivals but also an increased awareness of African identity and culture among African immigrants. Migration and food are two areas of study which are commanding increasing interest and analysis in contemporary society. Ongoing public and academic debate about the causes and consequences of migration is matched by growing speculation into food related practices and their social, economic and cultural outcomes, complicated by globalization. Most research on food and Africa by scholars has been undertaken in the context of famine or food (in) security in Africa. (Downs, et al.1991; Watson and Caldwell 2005; Hess. 2007). A few exceptions (Timberlake 1986: 42; James C. McCann. 2009), point to the complex and intimate relationship that Africans have with food. Yet the intimate and multidimensional relationship between Africans in the Diaspora and food remains not only under researched.

Food in Africa is life. In the Grassfields of Cameroon among the Moghamo for example food is synonymous with life and the lack of food signifies death[5]. Food is an integral part of all family celebrations and is thus used to create family bonds between parents and their children. That bond is still strong among Cameroonians and other Africans in the United States as my interviews with various groups of Africans revealed. In the Diaspora,

African food is used to create that connection and to identify with ethnic groups and nationalities. In Los Angeles, California, respondents were asked about how often they cooked or ate African food. Overwhelmingly 90% said they cooked or ate African food at least thrice a week. They all said it was more expensive than American food, but they still spent the money on African food. To quote Mami Cathy, "Part of the reason for the high cost of food is that everything is imported from Africa--spices, dried vegetables, stockfish, egusi, etc. all has to be shipped here. What can we do? We love our food and must eat it always. That is who we are."[6] As for George Usongo, he lamented the fact that younger African children love fast food/McDonalds. But added,

> "It is remarkable to see new arrivals get excited about the burger or big Mac for a few weeks. Then when they've eaten it to their heart's content, they go back to *foofoo* and/or *achu*. As a tool of community creation, our food becomes important. It takes on new meaning as it defines us."[7]

Culture therefore expresses itself through food. Another respondent, a more recent arrival (she came to the USA in 2005) emphasized the need to continue to feed her children with African food to keep them grounded in their culture. To quote Anna Njei:

> "I buy palm oil and crayfish from Madam Obichie every time... I make sure my children continue to eat Cameroonian food before they get lost in the American fast food system. I do this every time so that we do not forget these rituals and traditions."[8]

Since the 1990s there has been an increase in the number of African markets, African food stores[9] and African restaurants[10] in major cities in the United States of America. According to the *Star Telegram*, Arlington's Saturday paper, there are approximately 25 African restaurants in the Dallas-Fort Worth area of Texas. Food is thus not just lunch or dinner; it is a conduit for cultural expression, history, and nationalism in the Diaspora among African immigrants. In every African country there are special dishes that have become the symbol of the nation. They feature on the menu of all national celebrations and festivals, and for non-Africans these foods represent the nations and therefore transcend ethnic differences as they are eaten by all citizens of the said nations in the Diaspora. For Cameroon, *Achu, ndole, eru*, roasted fish and *miyondo or dodo* have attained that status.[11] Through food, changes and continuities can be depicted. According to Edith Takere, parents have a great task because:

> "They have the burden of finding the balance and helping their children maintain their culture and identity out here, while making sure they adapt properly to their new environment-new schools, new food, and new accent."[12]

Hence, at national and provincial level (or ethnic group level), food, *njangis*, traditional dances, African dresses, annual conventions, monthly meetings, travel back and forth between overseas, African churches, etc. are all part of that umbilical cord that connects Africans in the Diaspora to continental Africa. They perform those activities diligently and make sure that at each event, meeting or gathering, they have traditional African dishes, which are often prepared by women. At annual conventions and meetings African dishes are mandatory. As time goes by, the art of cooking and eating within African immigrant groups sometimes become altered through contact with other groups, as well as in the context of the availability of different foodstuffs. Thus we see culture albeit in a modified form – modified by the context, by conditions impacted by living elsewhere other than in Africa. As these processes play themselves out, avenues are thus created for continuity or change. For example, a popular and time -consuming Cameroonian (Bamenda) dish, *Achu,* where cocoyams are first boiled, peeled, and then pounded into a smooth, seedless dough, is now a "flour" blended in the USA, which now takes less time to prepare.[13]

For African migrants, food therefore has a major role in maintaining kin, social and cultural linkages to other villages and cities in Africa. It does contribute to building new communities/groups based on cultural or social identity brought from Africa or based on new ties forged in one's new home. The diverse tastes of African cuisine in the United States comprise a body of historically gendered knowledge practiced and perfected in households across the continent. Apparently, immigrants are not alone in this matter. Talking about Columbus's 16th century journey eastwards in search of spices and gold, the cultural revolutions that ensued and their far-reaching effects worldwide, Schwartz had this to say: "The changes in the global menu don't simply mean better eating—the new foods altered the fates of nations and strengthened a growing sense of national identity". Schwartz 1991: 59. This research reveals that African culinary practices are integral to the understanding of their history and they constitute lively and living records of change and adaptation at a new destination.

### African Social Organization in the Diaspora

Social organization in the Diaspora is dependent on 'familiar' practices from the homeland-Africa as discussed above. These practices include but are not limited to monthly and annual meetings/festivals. I focus here on *njangis*.[14] In Africa, the *njangi* popularly known as money-go-rounds because of their unique rotating feature is a widespread self-help social and economic group that often meets once a month. They are called by different names in different places, but they all have the same simple self help and rotating feature. They are *tontines* in Francophone West Africa, esusu in Nigeria, and *Osusu* in Ghana and Sierra Leone.[15] Emerging literature on njangis now distinguish between the rotating clubs –ROSCAS and the non rotating clubs-ASCRAS. Ardener in her pioneer work on ROSCAs in Africa defines them as follows (Ardener 1964): ROSCAs are associations in which members regularly contribute to a fund that is given in whole or in part to each contributor in turn. Unlike ROSCAs, ASCRAs are microcredit clubs which do not rotate. Sometimes known as Accumulating Savings and Credit Associations, these tend to be more businesslike. The majority gets startup funds and help from NGOs which expect loans to be made and repaid. They are often too involved with banks and these NGOs end up distancing themselves from their members.

The above definition of ROSCAs captures the essence of *njangis* or money-go-round. The premise is simple – and in particular its rotating feature – has made it an incredibly resilient and flexible tool of empowerment for people across all classes and genders. Several hundreds of thousands of African immigrants have benefitted from *njaggis*. They really are life-savers for most people. To quote Epo,

> "More than ever, today I depend on my *njangi* groups for support and networking. When I first arrived from Germany to New York I knew few people. The group members became close friends. The money from the three *njangis* is the main source of funding for my Licence Vocational Nurse training (LVN)."[17]

Just how do *njangis* function? How important are they for African immigrants? Why are they so popular? Research findings reveal that 95% of all adults interviewed in the United States belonged to one or more *njangis*. Picks rotate among members in turn. It sounds simple. First, the members (say 10 in all) form a group and elect officials. Then, they choose an amount of the monthly dues-say $10, and select numbers which determine the order of their pick. Each month for ten months, these 10 people meet and contribute $10 each. The total of $100 is given to the first person and later to each in turn every month. Members feel a sense of belonging with the community or group. They eat, work and play together. The larger group of Cameroonian friends forms an important social network for them, and really are their "social capital". They provide money to its members for all kinds of necessities: medical bills, start-up funds for small income-generating projects, school fees, books, construction of homes and purchase of building materials, etc. Today, *njangis* are very important in the context of immigration as they constitute local forms of self-help and credit which have been transported to the Diaspora by immigrants.[18] Africans living in the United States and Europe reproduce these forms of self-help cooperatives. Most newcomers face challenges and have to struggle before settling in their new environment. *Njangis* are the first places that new African immigrants go to for help. An asylum-seeker recounted how he came to New York in winter and was rescued by the *njangi* group:

> "I left Bafut in the Northwest Province of Cameroon in November 2001. It was my first time to venture out of the country. I had no idea that it was winter in New York. When the plane finally landed after what seems to be an endless flight, I was confronted by harsh reality. There I was, waiting for my cousin's husband to pick me up, in the snow, without a winter coat! I had on my nice suit, but it was nothing compared to the biting old outside. He arrived, took me home and the next day, we went to the Mankon (ethnic group in Northwest Cameroon) monthly meeting where I was introduced to everyone. I got help and advice from members. I felt at home. I joined the group and later took money from the *njangi* to buy a winter coat."[19]

On arrival, the first thing immigrants do is to seek and join existing national or ethnic social groups and *njangi* groups in their city, or create one with other Africans. These groups are important loan providers for such necessary things as winter jacket and boots purchase, car purchase, rental deposit, and education fees. Group members also help by explaining cultural differences and proper behavior. Additionally, *njangis* provide a space for members to network, eat African/Cameroonian food and assert themselves and their identity. They are the mainstay of Africans' social organization in the United States and the Diaspora. The preferred languages used in such village and ethnic groups are African languages, to maintain unity, a sense of belonging and foster identity.

### African Languages in the Diaspora: An Expression of Identity

Africa is host to 2000 of the 6000 world languages. Lupke (2008) notes that in this context, "it seems paradoxical that African linguistics has not assumed a leading role in establishing the research agenda for documentation of endangered languages... and that there is almost no activism in favor of their maintenance by speakers." During the colonial era in Africa, European languages were imposed on Africans. As a result, Africans now have to joggle constantly between their indigenous languages and western languages.[20] This situation left indigenous languages at a disadvantage since they were not used in public schools and colleges or in the workplace. Focusing on the effects of globalization processes on the vitality of languages in two West African cities-Maiduguri in Nigeria, and Banfora in Burkina Faso, Gudun, et al. argue that "the contrast between language and social institutions is most obvious in colonial and post colonial world of Africa, characterized as it was by the import of European institutions which were of qualitatively new nature and which led to the establishment of a hierarchy of African languages in Africa."[21]

African languages reflect the diversity that is an integral part of Africa and its people. While most scholars and researchers have recently engaged in African languages discourse their voices are varied. Some see African languages as endangered languages due to the impact of European languages on Africa (Webb and Kembo-Sure 2000; Lupke 2008); others have looked at the syntax and grammar as a way to incorporate these languages in the mainstream European mode of use (Heine and Nurse 2002, Konig 2008). Many others have taken up the challenge of introducing African languages and linguistics covering typology, structure and sociolinguistics to a non-African audience, (Nurse and Philippsen 2006). Makoni (2003) examines the range of similarity and difference between Black speech communities in Africa and the Diaspora and the impact of imperialism and enslavement on language. Others embrace the main discourses in the field of African languages and linguistics and argue for the absolute necessity of developing African languages as a condition of socio-economic development (Chia 2006; Djite 2008). However, few have taken on the transnational uses of African languages and their impact on Africans in the Diaspora. Vigouroux and Mufwere (2008) discuss the effects of globalization on languages in Africa.

In contrast to previous studies, these authors examine whether or not globalization is affecting African languages in the same ways and at the same rate in different countries. The marginality of African languages has received very little attention to date despite the fact that many of them are spoken by millions as a first or second language. Exceptions include Swahili, Hausa, and a handful of other *linguae francae*.

In Cameroon for instance, a country that was colonized by the Germans (1884-1919), and then mandated to the British and the French at one time, English and French became the official languages at independence in 1960. Cameroonian languages were relegated to individual homes and ethnic groups. The 21st century Cameroon saw an upsurge in globalization[22] "the process of closer interaction of human activities across a range of spheres, including the economic, social, political and cultural, experienced along three dimensions: spatial, temporal and cognitive."[23] Integral to this process is the movement of Cameroonians and other Africans out of Africa and into a new social context, overseas. With that movement across the oceans came a re-engagement with issues of African consciousness and a war against cultural imperialism[24] waged at various levels, in different immigrant communities.

In Cameroon as in the rest of Sub-Saharan Africa, there has been an upsurge of efforts to preserve their cultural heritage and to cater to the growing tourist industry as a means of solving the poverty crisis.[25] Among Cameroonians in the Diaspora, efforts are being made by many ethnic groups to preserve their cultural legacy through an emphasis on Cameroonian local languages. Case in point, Moghamo, Mungaka, Nso, Bayangi, Bawkeri, Douala, Ewondo, Bassa, etc. are actively used at home, at monthly meetings and during annual conventions. Parents are encouraged to teach these languages to their children, as there is evidence that most children could not speak the Cameroonian languages. This is becoming a major concern among Africans living outside Africa.[26] How should African cultural heritage be preserved? Batibo (2005) has examined the nature and extent of the problem of languages decline in Africa.[27] In his work he traces the aims, causes and circumstances of language endangerment, the processes and extent of language shift and extinction, and consequences of language loss to the continents rich linguistic and cultural heritage. Findings from this study corroborate results of scholars who are concerned about language marginalization (Chia 2006; Vigoureux and Mufwere 2008). Interestingly, this section has demonstrated how globalization is affecting African languages in the Diaspora and how Africans use African languages to strengthen national identity in their new settlements. Therefore, representing African cultural heritage among Africans is an innovative approach to the study of immigration from Africa and other developing regions to the United States and Europe, and this deserves the attention of further research.

## Conclusion

In the words of Usongo (2005) "The fact that we now live outside Africa does not stop us from maintaining our culture, speaking our African languages, and holding fast onto our identity. We dance and sing and dress up. Who are we without our culture?"[28] In this study the relationship between food and the culture, history and national identity of Africans at home and in the Diaspora has been clearly articulated. Place-making, cultural (re)creation and performance are crucial to African immigrants' sense of belonging and identity. Immigrants go where they have friends and relatives. Later they find jobs. The concept of identification is central to this process. Thus, from a seemingly fractured and multiple identities in multiple places (due to the different countries and ethnic groups in Africa), and from globalization of African culture, an identity emerges and its diversity and transformation persists. Ultimately we get glimpses of cultural creation and survival strategies in African communities in the Diaspora. African immigrants settled in diverse locales across the United States, and employed in various fields, still hold fast to some elements of their cultural heritage. Although highly urban as a whole, African immigrants have not clustered only in select metropolises. The community has its highest representations in Washington, D.C. and New York, there are a far more geographically dispersed community than, for example, their West Indian counterparts who really have enclaves. Between 1990 and 2000, the largest influx of African immigrants was reported in Minneapolis/St. Paul, where the population increased 629 percent. Overall, migration from Africa increased 170 percent during that period, with Nigeria, Ethiopia, and Ghana, in that order, having the largest communities in the United States. With such high numbers of Africans removed from "home", the need for cultural connectivity is more urgent, and is closely linked to identity formation.

As I conclude a few recurring concerns put forth by different informants come to mind. For example, is it true that African culture in the Diaspora is dwindling? What factors can lead to such "dwindling"? Given the urgency and importance of mass migration from Africa, these questions merit future research. If Cameroonians like other Africans in the Diaspora must survive away from "home," how do they deal with loneliness or handle being on the fringe of two cultures? African culture is important in the Diaspora. What is challenging is how to keep it alive in a foreign land or in a new community while adapting to the host nation or new environment.

## References

Awkward, M., 1995. *Negotiating Difference: Race, Gender, and the Politics of Positionality*, (Chicago: University of Chicago Press).

Batibo, H.M. *Languages Decline and Death in Africa: Causes, Consequences and Challenges.* 2005. UK. MultilingualMatters.

*Berlitz African Phrase Book.* 2004. USA, Berlitz Publishing CO.

Bhabha, Homi. 1994. *The location of Culture*. London: Routledge.
Bilger, Veronika/Kraler, Albert (Hrsg.) 2005. "African Migrations – Historical Perspectives and Con-temporary dynamics." In *Stichproben* (Wien; Sonderheft), 5, 8.
Bridget Teboh and Nwando Achebe, "Dialoguing Women: Challenges of Being African and Conducting Research on African Women and Gender." In *Africa After Gender?:An Interdisciplinary Reader* (Editors), S. Meischer, Takyiwa Manu and C. Cole (Bloomington: Indiana University Press, 2007) 91-113.
Cabral Amilcar. 1980. "National liberation and culture". In *Unity and Struggle*, 139-154. Translated by M. Wolfers. London: Heinemann.
Carney, J., 2001. *Black Rice* (Cambridge: Harvard University Press).
Chia, Emmanuel N. (Ed.) 2006. *African languages and the development of African communities*. Senegal, CODESRIA.
Curtin, P. 1887: "Africans and Global Patterns of Migration," in Wang Gungwu(ed.) *Global history and Migration* (Boulder: Westview Press), 63-94.
David M., 1985. *Still The Golden Door: The Third World Comes To America* (New York: Columbia University Press).
Diène, D. (Ed.) 2001. *From Chains to Bonds: The African Slave Trade Revisited* (Oxford, New York: Berghan Books).
Dijk, Rijk A. van/Foeken, Dick/Bruijn, Mirjam de (Hrsg.) 2001. *Mobile Africa: Changing Patterns of Movement in Africa and Beyond*, (Leiden: Brill).
Djite, Raulin G. 2008. *The Socio-linguistics of Development in Africa*. UK Multilingual Matters.
Dr. Hess, p. 9. "Food Security in Africa: the impact of Agricultural Development: A hearing before the Subcommittee on Africa and Global Health of the committee on foreign affairs House of Representatives." July 18, 2007.
ECA 2006. *International migration and development – Implications for Africa* New York, United Nations Economic Commission for Africa. <www.uneca.org>, 24.10.2006.
ECA 1986. "Measures to facilitate the return and reintegration of highly skilled migrants into African countries," *International Migration* (24) 1:197-212.
Endore, G., 1991: *Babouk*, (Monthly Review Press).
Fanon Frantz. 1961/1967. *The Wretched of the Earth*. Translated by Constance Farrington. Harmondsworth; Penguin.
Friederike Lupke. 2008. (ELAP, SOAS). "At the Margin-African Endangered Languages in the context of global endangerment discourses."
Gates Jr., H.L., 1997. "Parable of the talents," in H.L. Gates Jr. and Cornell West,*The Future of the Race*, (New York: Vintage Books).
Graham Jr., Otis L., 1995. "Tracing Liberal Woes to '65 Immigration Act," in *Christian Science Monitor*; v 88, n 23, 19-23.

Grieco, E.: "The African Foreign Born in the United States" *Migration Policy Institute* http://www.migrationinformation.org/USfocus.

Gudun, Michel, Owens, Jonathan, and von Roncador, Manfred (Eds.) *Language in African Urban Contexts: A Contribution to the Study of Indirect Globalization.* 2007. Germany: Lit Verlag.

Hamilton, K.A. 1997: "Europe, Africa, and International Migration: An Uncomfortable Triangle of Interests," in *New Community*, 23,4, pp.549-570.

Harris, Katherine J. 2003. *Pan African Language Systems: Ebonics and African Oral Heritage.* UK: Karnak House.

Healey, P. 1997. *Collaborative Planning: Shaping Places in FragmentedSocieties*, July 03, 2000 VOL. 155 NO. 25. (Basingstoke: Mcmillan).

Heine, Bernd and Nurse, Derek (Eds.) 2000. *African languages: An Introduction.* UK Cambridge University Press.

James C. McCann. 2009. *Stirring The Pot*, Ohio University Press. Series "Africa in World History," eds. Joe Miller and David Robinson.

James L. Watson and Melissa L. Caldwell, eds. 2005. The *cultural politics of food and eating*; a Reader (Blackwell).

J. O'Brien and E. Gruenbaum, 1991. "A Social History of Food, Famine, and Gender in Twentieth Century Sudan." 183-4, In *The political Economy of African Famine*. Eds. R.E. Downs, D. Kerner, and S. Reyna. (Gordon and Breach Science Publishers: Amsterdam), 117-185.

John Schwartz, 1991. "The Great Food Migration", in *Newsweek* (Special Issue, Fall/Winter , pp.58-62).

Kenji Yoshida and John Mack, *Preserving the Cultural Heritage of Africa: Crisis or R enaissance?* (James Currey Publishers: March 2007).

Kohnert Dirk. 2006. "On the benefit of African immigration to Europe. Turn in the EU immigration policy?" *http://mpra.ub.uni-muenchen.de/1064/*

Kohnert, Dirk. 2006. "Cultures of Innovation of the African Poor – Common roots,shared traits, joint prospects?" *On the articulation of multiple modernities in African societies and Black Diasporas in Latin America*, (Hamburg: GIGA)Working Paper, No. 25.

Konig, Christa, *Case in Africa*. 2008. UK Oxford University Press.

Kutler and Stanley. 2003. "Immigration Act of 1965," in *Dictionary of AmericanHistory*, Third Edition; New York, Charles Scribner's Sons, v 4, p. 230.

Lee, K. 2000. "Globalization and Health Policy: A Review of the Literature and Proposed Research Agenda" in *Health Development in the New Global Economy*. PAHO: Washington.

Makoni, Sinfree B. (Ed.) Black Linguistics: Language, Society and Politics in Africa and the Americas. 2003 UK, Routledge.

Nurse, Derek and Philippson, Gerard (Eds.) 2006. *The Bantu Languages*. UK Routledge.

Nana Wilson-Tagoe. 2007. "Representing Culture and Identity: African Women Writers and National Cultures," in Catherine M. Cole, Takyiwaa Manuh, and Stephan F. Meischer, eds. *Africa After Gender?* Bloomington and Indianapolis: Indiana UP.

Neill, W.J.V. 2004. *Urban Planning and Cultural Identity* (New York: Routledge), 111-156.

Ngugi, Wa Thiongo. 1986. *Decolonizing the Mind: The Politics of Language in African Literature*, (Heinemann).

———. 1993. *Moving the Centre: The Struggle for Cultural Freedoms.*

Ogundipe-Leslie, Molara. 1994. *Recreating Ourselves: African Women and Critical Transformations.* Trenton, N.J.: Africa World Press.

Ratnesar, R. 2000. "Knocking on Europe's Door," in *TIME EUROPE.*

Said, Edward. 1985. "An Ideology of Difference." *Critical Inquiry* 12, no.1:38-58.

Timberlake, L. 1986. *Africa in Crisis.* (Earthscan: Philadelphia).

United Nations, *UN Report* 2005.

Vigouroux, Cecile and Mufwere, Salikoko S. (Eds.) *Globalization and Language Vitality: Perspectives From Black Africa.* 2008. UK Continuum.

Wallace Vernon, A., 1993. *African Americans At Mars Bluff, South Carolina* (Baton Rouge: Louisiana University Press).

Webb, Vic and Kembo-Sure (Eds.) 2000. *African Voices: An Introduction to Languages and linguistics of Africa.* South Africa: Oxford UP.

Westermann, Dietrich, *Practical Phonetics for Students of African Languages.* 1990. UK: Kegan Paul International.

Wright, D. 2004. *The World and a Very small Place in Africa.* (ME Sharpe), 217-220.

## Endnotes

[1] These cities were chosen because of the high concentration of Cameroonians and Africans currently residing there, or simply as strategic places where annual national conventions are usually held—thus making access to informants easier. Their selection in different parts of the US was meant to capture the socio-economic impact of differences of various immigrants in different communities and how they adapt.

[2] It is an open secret that several governments in Africa do not tolerate free speech by their citizens. The possible real and imagined danger that awaits some of my informants if identity is revealed could not be ignored.

[3] I included younger children that were present at Annual National Conventions in Washington DC and New York, and also because they obviously could speak. Some of them were born in the US and had interesting opinions about African culture and food. The remaining children were interviewed in their homes their parents present and at monthly meetings where their parents brought them (a few kicking and screaming "no pepper!").

[4] In Francophone Africa some immigrants enter France and Belgium illegally. They are commonly known as les sans papiers or the "undocumented."

[5] Ma Wumunjong, phone interview by author, August 10, 2005, Batibo, Northwest Province, Cameroon.

[6] Mami Cathy, mother of three, interview by auther, July 10, 2007, Los Angeles, California.

[7] George Usongo, former civil servant, father of five, Interview by author, July 10, 2007, Los Angeles, California.

[8] Anna Njei, mother of three, Interview by author, July 12, 2007, Los Angeles, California.

[9] See for example, Asafo Market, Africana, Safari African Markets (Arlington, Texas); Madam Obichie (Los Angeles).

[10] See for instance, Lagos Cafe (Los Angeles), African Kitchen, African Village restaurant, Wazobia restaurant, (Arlington, Texas). For fabric stores and African wear, see, Angelyes International (Arlington, Texas).

[11] Achu is made of tarot tuber, ndole is a bitter vegetable (bitterleaf) cooked with fresh peanuts, miyondo is fermented cassava (yuca), and dodo is common name for fried ripe plantains (Americans call them bananas).

[12] Edith Takere, single mother of two, Interview by author, July 14, 2007, Los Angeles, California.

[13] Grace Ndam, single mother of one, Restaurant Owner/Manager, Interview by author, January 08, 2007.

[14] These are indigenous rotating savings and credit clubs or associations found all over Africa. For a discussion of njanggis see, Bridget Teboh, 2007, "Money-Go-Rounds: Navigating a Hostile Gendered Economic Environment in the Grassfields [Cameroon]. "Gendering African History: In Honor of E.A. Alpers and Christopher Ehret" paper presented at African Studies Association (ASA)'s 50th Annual Meeting, on 21st Century Africa: Evolving Conceptions of Human Rights at The Sheraton Hotel and Towers, New York, NY, October 18-21, 2007.

[15] Bridget Teboh,1995, "Women and the Njanggi Phenomenon in Cameroon." Paper presented at the (AAA), African Activist Association, 3rd Annual Young Scholars Conference at UCLA, April 7-8, 1995.

[16] Shirley Ardener and Sandra Burman, eds. 1995. Money-Go-Rounds: The Importance of ROSCAs for Women. Berg: Oxford/Washington, DC.

[17] Epo K. student and husband, interview by author, August 10, 2007, New York

[18] Bridget Teboh, "Women and the Njanggi Phenomenon in Cameroon, " Unpublished Paper.

[19] Che Benedict, Retired teacher , interview by author, July 19, 2007, New York, NY.

[20] English, French, German, Portuguese, were imposed during colonization and at independence the new nation-states decided to keep these languages as medium of instruction in schools as well as the workplace.

[21] Gudun, et al (Eds.) 2007 Language in African Urban Contexts: A Contribution to the Study of Indirect Globalization. 2007. Germany: Lit Verlag.

[22] Globalization is probably best defined in terms of easy access to movement of trade items and people between nations and world regions.

[23] Lee, K. "Globalization and Health Policy: A Review of the Literature and Proposed Research Agenda," in Health Development in the New Global Economy. PAHO: Washington (2000).

[24] See, Ngugi Wa Thiongo, Decolonizing the Mind: The Politics of Language in African Literature, 1986 (Heinemann); Ngugi, Moving the Centre: The Struggle for Cultural Freedoms (1993); Edward Said (1985).

[25] Countries in Eastern Africa such as Kenya, Tanzania and Uganda, and Western Africa such as Ghana, Senegal, Benin, Nigeria have all seen an upsurge in their tourism activities.

[26] For more information see, Kenji Yoshida and John Mack, Preserving the Cultural Heritage of Africa: Crisis or Renaissance? (James Currey Publishers: March 2007).

[27] Batibo, H.M. Languages Decline and Death in Africa: Causes, Consequences and Challenges. 2005. UK. MultilingualMatters.

[28] George Usongo. President, Ngie Cultural and Development Association, Southern California, Los Angeles, Interview by author, Los Angeles, California, 15 January 2005.

# Chapter 6
## African Émigrés in the UNITED STATES

### Negotiating Ethnic Identities, Majority-Minority Statuses, and Negative Media Co-Representation

*Anthony A. Olorunnisola*

## Introduction

Discourses of migrations, particularly those focused on *acculturation* and *intercultural adaptation*,[1] often take off from the perspective of the *host country* and *host culture*. As such, assessments of immigrants' acculturation and/or adaptation are carried out with the overriding goal of measuring their competencies or lack thereof; relative to the expectations of the host country and culture. This chapter departs from that tradition by locating African émigrés' pre-migration *identity* at the core of an evaluation that includes why they immigrate to countries like the United States. and whether or not they tend to *assimilate* or merely *integrate*. Jandt (2007: 310) informs that

> assimilation results from giving up one's original cultural identity and moving into full participation in the new culture. The person identifies with the country and not an ethnic group ... integration is maintaining important parts of one's original culture as well as becoming an integral part of the new culture."

A number of factors inform our preference to de-marginalize African émigrés' experiences in the United States. Primarily, this author's assessment – informed in part by more than 20-years' participant observation – is that African émigrés possibly integrate better than they assimilate into the UNITED STATES sub-cultures. Secondly, a synthesis of secondary and interdisciplinary[2] findings throw up factors that appear to better position Africans on the integration side of the acculturation divide in the United States. than on the assimilation side.

There are a number of benefits to an approach that locates African émigrés' identity at the core of their immigration experiences in the United States. In general, examination of the issue of identity as a strong dimension of acculturation and adaptation experiences of immigrants into the United States is long overdue. Many stakeholders, including immigration and acculturation scholars, are likely to benefit from the trajectory of this chapter's discourse of the African dimension and the follow-up investigation of other nationalities that this approach may generate.

With a constant rise in the desire of Africans to relocate to the United States (see Togunde & Osagie, 2009), interested persons at the pre-migration stage may benefit from the broader scope of this chapter's discourse. Such readers should expand their horizon beyond anticipated opportunities (educational, economic, and/or political) to include consideration of such issues as the prospective role of identity in their respective adjustments to the host nation. Some of the issues raised in this chapter may be of use as pre-departure orientation and as post-entry education. While the chapter does not offer how-to-survive strategies, readers in foregoing categories stand to gain a better appreciation for a road traveled by others who hardly speak in these terms about the quality of their sojourn in the United Sates.

The focus of this chapter should benefit African émigrés who are already sojourners in the American cultural milieu. This category of readers will include ethnic[3] or racial majority and minority group members who are by categorization minorities in the New World (see Falola & Afolabi, 2008). As a matter of course, African émigrés often seek clearer understanding of what may be a new or renewed minority identity in the host country against the background of majority-minority ethnic and racial contestations in their respective home countries as well as such other complexities of displacement. Those among African immigrants who may have questioned the road either taken or not taken may find some clarity through the issues raised and discussed in the remainder of this chapter.

The cumulative import of this chapter's approach and discourse should be of interest to scholars of acculturation, intercultural adaptation and other aspects of migration studies who seek to understand the location of African immigrants and other nationalities who, though classified as minorities by the system, may exhibit traits that may be consistent or inconsistent with received knowledge about minority groups. This category of readers is invited to undergo co-reflection over a dimension of the migration process that has hitherto been largely ignored by scholars across disciplines interested in human migration. By reviewing this abandoned side of the coin, we are not creating something out of nothing; we are simply drawing attention to a process that has proceeded in spite of its neglect in academic investigations.

Though previous studies have tended to exclude considerations of identity as a unique feature of immigrant acculturation, there has been cursory reference to its indirect role. In defining key factors that facilitate the adaptation process, Kim (2005) identifies the individual's own background at the tail end of such other factors as intrapersonal communication; interpersonal communication; mass communication and; the new environment. Much earlier, Berry, Kim, and Boski (1987) find that two factors tend to influence immigrant acculturation; one is the value that the immigrant places on maintaining his/her original culture. The second factor is the value given to maintaining relationships with other groups in one's new culture. Nonetheless, little to no attention has been paid to the assessment of immigrants' adaptation with their pre-migration identity at the center of such evaluation.

Lesser attention has been paid to the status of Africans as minorities in the United States. In a recent co-edited volume, Falola and Afolabi (2008) examine the location of African minorities in the New World stating that new African immigrants have come to represent a significant force in the configuration of the American polity and identity in the last 40 years. Chapters in the volume focus on African immigrants' accomplishments in the academic, business and scientific arena and the demographic shift that the population now represents. Among others, the co-editors suggest a conceptual shift in how we describe the connection between Africa and the New World. "By its very connection to the "old African Diaspora," the notion of a "New African Diaspora" marks a clear indication of a historical progression reconnecting continental Africa with the New World without the stigma of slavery," (p.1).

Co-editors also recognize identity as a core and stable dimension of how well an African immigrant might conform to the new culture. In their words:

> Migration brings about the hyphenated self, that is, the old self versus the newly formed or emerging self. Such a state of flux and of trauma brings about a psychological crisis of identity and of consciousness. On the one hand, the immigrant is still clinging to the old identity; in this case, the African, while at the same time, he/she is obligated to assimilate cultural values and social conditionings of the United States that make integration more feasible. Ultimately, the levels of flexibility, conformism, and resistance determine whether assimilation will happen or if a compromise will be reached. The impact of migration on cultural change and ethnic identity may then be theorized as a permanent state of crisis, negotiation if not confusion (Falola & Afolabi, 2008: 4-5).

Foregoing attempt to track identity fluxes in the African immigrants' experience resonate in two ways. First, the immigrant is under pressure to adapt to the new cultural environment. Second, there is not a temporary but a sojourn-long push and pull between the "old identity" and the "emerging self". What is unclear in the co-editors' explication is whether or not the "old identity" is indeed old in cases where émigrés retain dual-citizenships, are transnational in their engagements or resist the new culture.

Contributing authors to Falola and Afolabi's volume miss the opportunity to consider pre-migration identities on a broader base and along majority-minority dimensions. By moving pre-departure identities and experiences from the margins of immigration studies, this chapter considers African majority/minority personalities one of the carry-over progressions that are pertinent to the African experience in the New World. Though chapters in Falola & Afolabi's volume skirt around push- and pull-factors (see e.g., Augustus, 2008: 233-245) none attend in a substantive manner to the pre-departure majority-minority contestations that are often characteristic of relations between African ethnic and racial groups.

It is public record that occurrences such as the genocide in Rwanda and ongoing event of similar magnitude in the Sudan are themselves prelude and perhaps contributing factors to the migration of Africans. We suspect that the selfsame factors would influence the cultural adaptation of Africans to host nations like the United States. We assume that the foundation of acculturation and/or cultural adaptation of African immigrants to the United States will have to be erected on top of carry-over identity and ethnic group contestations. More specifically, the Hausa and Ogoni (Nigeria) as well as Hutu and Tutsi (Rwanda) men and women who migrate to the United States will have to process group relations in the "New World" on the bases of their respective home country experiences. A significant dimension of this chapter is devoted to establishing the latter as a factor in African émigré experience.

Analyses presented in this chapter include the abiding cultural, relational and mass mediated gulfs between recent African émigrés and African-Americans.[4] We argue, foundationally, that the subject of African immigration in the United States cannot be discussed with any finality if it either ignores the role of African-Americans or excludes impacts of one group on the other or omits a treatment of the legacies that one group bequeaths to the other. Legacies bequeathed by African-Americans to African émigrés include the polarity of Whiteness and Blackness that is a part of the American inter-racial terrain and such other incidentals as decades-long majority-minority contestations. Both (African émigrés and African-Americans) have also endured several decades of negative co-representation by Western- and mainstream-media respectively. As a part of the offers of this chapter, we posit that the stability of the African identity collaborates with the pre-existence of an African-American population in the United States to pose contextual challenges to the extent to which the African émigré can be assimilated into the American cultural space.

## Impacts of African Émigres' Pre-Departure Identities

The African world is partly understood in light of complex historical, cultural, economic and social-political processes governed mostly by differential opportunities afforded to majority and minority ethnic and/or racial groups. Relative to majority groups in most African countries, minority groups are numerically smaller as a segment of the population. With the exception of countries like South Africa under apartheid and Zimbabwe as Rhodesia[5] where groups constituting the majority were politically and economically disenfranchised, minority groups do not constitute as powerful a voting block in the African context. In socioeconomic terms, minority groups are subordinated to majority ethnic groups in terms of language, nationality, religion and/or culture. In this dimension as well, South Africa and Rhodesia provided the exception and add to the complexity of the extent to which we can offer general assessments of how home-country cultures pose questions to host-country cultures and impose demands on African émigrés' adjustments. In his effort to clarify the issue Feagin (1984: 10) informed that a minority group would typically display five characteristics: (a) subsist on the receiving end of discrimination and subordination; (b) exhibit physical and/or cultural traits that set them apart and which are disapproved by the dominant group; (c) share a sense of collective identity and common burdens (d) have their status determined by socially-shared rules about who belongs and who does not and; (e) marry within the group.

The relatively smaller numerical strength of minority groups, their inability to influence change in the body politic, as well as their subordination by majority groups have often led to multiple contestations. Protestations by the minority against the majority are viewed as militant, often draw charges of treasonable felony, and, at times, lead to warfare. Recent examples of such contestations include ongoing (May, 2009) violent confrontation between Nigeria's military and elements of the Movement for the survival of the Ogoni People (MOSOP) in the Niger Delta. Ongoing civil war in the Sudan and the 1995 genocidal attack against the Tutsis of Rwanda (see Olorunnisola, 1995) provide examples of majority-minority contestations that are steeped in ethnic particularism.

The Afrikaner population in South Africa under apartheid provides many exceptions to the conditions of the minority as envisioned by Feagin (1984). However, its political status in years following the termination of apartheid relative to the newfound status of Black South Africans would have brought the group in line with characteristics drawn by Feagin (1984). The exception is that the significant amount of economic power located in the Afrikaner group is stupendously higher than is typically found among minority groups on the African continent. Given that the Afrikaner population in South Africa represents an infinitesimally minute segment of a buoyant minority, it should be safe to argue that foregoing majority-minority contestations and the search by minority populations for more accommodating havens often motivate emigration from African countries. Many Africans depart in search of political asylum and others who are forcefully displaced by warfare become refugees. Falola and Afolabi (2008: 8) note that

> ... the most recent immigrants to the United States are those affected by interethnic civil wars, such as many Eritreans, Somalis, Sudanese, and Liberians, among others, as well as those affected by political persecution and ethnic cleansing such as the Ogonis of Nigeria, members of Nigeria's democratic opposition, civil society, and intellectuals (mainly during the Abacha dictatorship), the Somali Bantu, the Rwandan Tutsis ... many others ... especially skilled professionals, are pushed by factors of economics and existential satisfaction to emigrate ....

Across the board, the inability of national governments to accommodate the disparate aspirations of majority and minority ethnic and racial groups has contributed to increased affiliation to the primordial group in many African states. As such ethnic and tribal loyalties tend to be stronger than attachment to the nation state. When they have not led to migration, ethnic conflicts have resulted in secessionist attempts (see Olorunnisola, 1995). Foregoing predilections for ethnic particularism that cause national disunity informs the dimension of our argument that the primary identity of Africans is located at the primordial level. Secondly, Africans have typically endured many years of distrust of the nation state. We doubt that there is as yet a structure in the African experience for the translocation of trust from the cultural ethnic group to the formalized and impersonal state. Gudykunst (2004: 77) notes that

> (o)ur social identities can be based on our memberships in demographic categories (e.g., nationality, ethnicity, gender, age, social class) the roles we play (e.g., student, professor, parent), our membership in formal or informal organizations (e.g., political parties, social clubs), our associations or vocations (e.g., scientist, artist, gardener), or our memberships in stigmatized groups (e.g., homeless, people with AIDS). The degree to which we assert our social identities varies from situation to situation, but the general degree to which we identify with particular groups appears to remain relatively stable over time.

Among others, Gudykunst's assertion that "the degree to which we identify with particular groups appears to remain relatively stable over time" is consistent with our argument that the social identities of the African from the pre-emigration to the post-migration phases may remain stably connected to the primordial affiliation. What is of particular interest from here on is the extent to which said 'identity stability' impacts the quality of acculturation and/or cultural adaptation of African émigrés who in their respective home countries are majority and minority persons but in the United States are categorized as minorities.

This is possibly a good juncture to explore the likelihood that differences between majority and minority persons may be less significant than suggested. Quoting Kraust & Higgins (1984, p. 114) Gudykunst (2004) shares that majority members may face challenges when interacting with minority members and implies that there are significant communicative differences between the two groups. As such majority speakers feel the conscious need to make adjustments when speaking with minority audiences. Yet, the "(a)djustments majority speakers make when speaking to minority members often give the impression that the speaker is patronizing and distant and, in turn, affect the recipients' behavior and conversational style." There are important implications in the foregoing quote for how we make sense of majority-minority communicative interactions and differentials: (1) ongoing contestations between the two groups appear to creep into everyday engagement and create conversational anxieties on both sides; (2) conscious adjustments have to be made when majority persons speak with minority persons to ensure that recipients do not misconstrue speakers' intentions; (3) majority and minority persons are in associational respects strangers, with varying perspectives on issues, who need to tread carefully in each others' company and be sensitive in conversations; (4) minority members respond defensively when they perceive that majority speakers are patronizing. These real and/or perceived behavioral patterns have the capability of reducing the effectiveness of communication between majority and minority persons (see Gudykunst, 2004: 266).

If majority and minority persons of African descent exhibit foregoing differences, what impacts are these traits likely to have on their post-immigration interaction? Bastian's (1999) ethnographic study of Internet use by Nigerians in the Diaspora demonstrates that the emergent culture of interaction observed in cyberspace is not peculiar to the context. Rather offline behaviors are transported online; an indication that the Internet enabled context had no dramatic influence on the traits that were observed. For instance, Nigerian politics dominates online discussions among Nigerians as it does offline deliberations. Notably also, discussions of controversial and sensitive aspects of Nigeria's political history, such as the 1966-1970 civil war; the annulment of the 1993 presidential elections, among others, motivated the creation of five fractional online networks. Oduduwa (the listserve to which the Yorubas – a majority ethnic group – subscribe) was not accessible to Nigerians who are non-Yorubas. Oduduwa was created in response to the discomfort of other Nigerians with the dominance of Yoruba-speaking participants on Naijanet (a network to which Nigerians of all ethnic groups belonged). As well, the creation of ANA-net (an online network created by members of the Association of Nigerians Abroad, an activist group) was motivated by the fission between Naijanetters who were interested in sanctions against the military government for annulling the 1993 presidential elections and subscribers who were uncomfortable with that level of activism.

By the same token, Igbo-net (to which Igbo-speaking Nigerians subscribed) was created after a heated debate over the secession of Biafra from Nigeria and the resultant 1966-1970 Nigerian civil war. Similarly, Rivnet grew out of discussions of the aftermath of the Nigerian civil war. The controversy over property abandoned during the civil war and the rights of Rivers State's indigenes to regain usage of such properties did not go down well with members of Naijanet from the affected areas. Rivnet was especially active during the detention and eventual execution of Ken Saro-Wiwa and the Ogoni ten by the Abacha regime in 1995. The bone of contention was the maltreatment of peoples in the oil-producing areas by the Nigerian government and the Shell Oil Company (see also, Olorunnisola, 2000; 2006). Evidently, these online fissions amount to post-migration cliquing (see Weimann, 1989) which follows pre-migration ethnic lines of demarcation.

Foregoing scenario is, however, informative in multiple ways. Firstly, Nigerian émigrés have exported a national characteristic – "political jaw-jaw" – imbibed in the pre-migration phase to foreign geographical locations. Secondly, sensitive aspects of Nigeria's political history – many of which constitute unbridgeable gulfs between majority and minority ethnic groups in Nigeria – continue to divide Nigerian émigrés along ethnic fault lines. There is an across-the-board implication for the foregoing scenario in Gudykunst's (2004) explication of the space between strangers whose unfamiliarity may particularly be driven by majority-minority categorizations; it is that there is always the undertone of conflict in the relationship.[6] Bastian's study shows that there is no geographical or technological limit to the possibility of majority-minority persons' conflict.

Speaking of the incidence of conflict in majority-minority relations, Gudykunst (2004: 277-278) suggests that

> (t)wo of the important factors influencing how we manage conflict are our cultures and our ethnicities. All members of the same culture and ethnic group do not handle conflict in the same way, but there are relatively clear patterns across cultures and ethnic groups. The cultures in which we are raised influence our view of conflict. Our cultures influence the assumptions we make about conflict and the styles we use when we try to manage conflict).

Ting-Toomey et al (2000; cited in Gudykunst 2004: 284) informs that

> One of the major factors that influence members of different ethnic groups' approach to managing conflict is the strength of their cultural and ethnic identities. European Americans, Latino(a) Americans, and Asian Americans who strongly identify with the United States culture, for example, use an integrating style more than European Americans, Latino(a) Americans, and Asian Americans who weakly identify with the United States culture. Latino(a) Americans who strongly identify with their ethnic group tend to use an emotionally expressive conflict style more than Latino(a) Americans who weakly identify with their ethnic group. African Americans who identify strongly with the United States culture tend to use a compromising style more than African Americans who weakly identify with the United Sates culture. African Americans who strongly identify with their ethnic group tend to use an integrating style more than African Americans who weakly identify with their ethnic group.

Between Gudykunst and Ting-Toomey et al's explications and though there is room for individual differences, we see a line of association drawn from ethnicities, conflict resolution styles to the extent of acculturation to the host culture. Fundamentally, the role of ethnicity is dual; it is the primary point of association and the possible point of departure.

## Contextual Dimension of Cultural Identity and Affinity

E.B. Tylor (1871/1889 – see Jackson, 1999)[7] who is credited with being the first scholar to define culture as a concept may have also been the first to insinuate that culture has to be connected to membership in a specific society. Edward T. Hall (1989: 85) provides additional clarity when he deposed that "one of the functions of culture is to provide a highly selective screen between man and the outside world. In its many forms, culture therefore designates what we pay attention to and what we ignore." Hall adds that there are rules governing culturally-influenced perception and blindness. "These are: the subject or activity, the situation, one's status in a social system, past experience, and culture. The patterns governing juggling these five dimensions are learned early in life....," (Hall, 1989: 87). By progression, Hall adds context to his explication of culture when he suggests that "what one pays attention to or does not ... is largely a matter of context ... I have observed that meaning and context are inextricably bound with each other," (Hall, 1989: 90). The progressive exploration of context culminates in Hall's presentation of two ends of a communicative continuum; one end enables high-context (HC) communication and the other produces low-context (LC) communication between parties in communication.

In his words,

> High context communication or message is one in which most of the information is either in the physical context or internalized in the person, while very little is in the coded, explicit, transmitted part of the message. A low context communication is just the opposite; i.e., the mass of the information is vested in the explicit code. Twins who have grown up together can and do communicate more economically (HC) than two lawyers in a courtroom during trial (LC) or a child trying to explain to his mother why he got in a fight, (Hall, 1989: 91).

If Hall's explication of the intersection between culture, selective screen, context, and meaning is accurate, there are a number of theoretical derivations that we can make based on our discussion so far. Using majority and minority persons as communicants, we propose some possible HC and LC scenarios as follows:

Majority communication with Majority (HC)

Minority communication with Minority (HC)

Powerful Minority communication with powerful Majority (HC)

Powerless Majority communication with powerless Minority (HC)

Majority communication with Minority (LC)

Minority communication with Majority (LC)

Our proposal of foregoing majority and minority persons' HC vs. LC communicative scenarios draws from cumulative indication, informed by extant studies (see, e.g., Feagin, 1984; Weiman, 1989; Olorunnisola, 1995; Bastian, 1999) that majority and minority groups are experientially polarized and do not tend to share the caliber of cultural and contextual affinity that Hall (1989) associates with communicative economy. There is also power differential that leaves majority and minority groups along the powerful vs. powerless continuum. As such their communicative engagements will throw up the possibilities represented in our sample scenarios. Our references to powerful minorities and powerless majorities here and elsewhere in the chapter draw from atypical instances in the former Rhodesia (now Zimbabwe) and in South Africa during apartheid where majority-minority factors were turned on their heads.

We, however, took the liberty to raise a few speculative questions that may lead others to explore these issues further. For instance, is it possible for majority persons from two varying nation states to enjoy causal connection (e.g., familiarity with contending with minority persons and their issues)? On the other hand, is it possible for minority persons from two varying nation states to enjoy causal connection (e.g., familiarity with the antecedents of majority persons and all the vagaries of political and socio-economic suppression)? Lastly can majority persons (immigrants and host persons) and minority persons (immigrants and host persons) enjoy communicative functionality at HC level as Hall suggests?

We are aware that the scenarios presented earlier do not, by any means, represent fait accompli. Other eventualities would lead majority and minority persons to exhibit scenarios that may be inconsistent with those that we presented. For instance, the possibility of High Context level of communication may elude minority persons/groups when they have been pawns in divide-and-rule strategy by the majority in power or when one group is perceived as reaping benefits of rights won from majority groups without sowing the time and blood that is often the price.

Adaptation to a new country and cultural space will undoubtedly throw up communicative and conflict situations that the immigrant has to manage. We can safely surmise from foregoing discussion that the repertoire of communicative and conflict management skill sets that are influenced by identity, culture, and contextual factors will have to be tapped by the immigrant. We can further assume that African immigrants will have to pull from the familiar when engaged in intra- and inter-group communicative and conflict situations. Gudykunst (2004) appears to imply, however, that these stances are not sacrosanct. As individuals continue to adapt to the United States culture, traits that rub off may include a shift in the manner of conflict (and communicative) management. There is, however, no set pattern; some will identify with the United States culture, others will not. Some will retain strong resolution approaches that are consistent with their ethnic groups, others will not. Jandt (2007) adds that no immigrant, as long as livelihood needs are to be met in a new country, can escape acculturation. He (Jandt) also allows that individuals do differ as to the degree to which they become acculturated. If Gudykunst (2004) and Jandt (2007) are accurate in their propositions, how do African émigrés' experiences play out over their sojourn in the United States? Do they adapt to United States cultures while retaining the African root? If they do the latter, then integration[8] which Jandt (2007: 310) describes as "a continuity of culture," while engaging functionally with the new culture may be a better descriptor. As a means to exploring the multiple challenges posed by their identity and host-country factors, it does, however, interest us to explore the extent to which African émigrés can, solely on the bases of their own willingness, tend toward complete assimilation[9] into the United States subcultures.

## Racialized Nature of Majority-Minority Relations in the United States

Evidence abounds that countries in the global North, including the United States of America, are among destinations of choice for African émigrés (see Togunde & Osagie, 2009); in particular those who are either seeking political asylum or are refugees (see Falola & Afolabi, 2008). When African émigrés enter the shores of the United States of America, they primarily arrive as carriers of Cameroonian, Nigerian, Rwandan, or South African passports; legal documents certifying their respective citizenships. To all socio-cultural intents and purposes, however, we argue that African émigrés enter the United States more specifically as Ogonis or Hausas (of Nigeria); as Hutus or Tutsis (of Rwanda); as Afrikaners or Zulus (of South Africa). As Tshiyembe (2000) does, foregoing addresses the identity duality that Africans depart their respective countries with – on the one hand an affiliation with "the legal nation" – the "state" and connection to "the sociological nation" – the "ethnic group" that is more deep-rooted.[10] To these, we add the layer of majority (Hausas; Hutus; Zulus) and minority (Ogonis; Tutsis; Afrikaners) identifications that are arguably a significant part of the metaphorical immigrant suitcase that Africans arrive with and, depending on whether they adjust competently or not, may not unpack while sojourning in the United States

As African émigrés pass through the immigration gates at popular ports of entry in Baltimore, Los Angeles, and New York, most of them step into an ongoing majority-minority relations and conversation of a kind different from that with which they are familiar. This is given that race is at the core of the majority-minority categorizations and contestation in the United States as it is in only a few African nations. As Jackson (1999:31) informs:

> ...the United States has historically presented insufficient resolutions to a very severe social disease – racism. Despite efforts ranging from Reconstruction to Gunnar Myrdal's "melting pot theory," racial, economic, social, and political inequality persists in the United States

A part of that history of racism led to racial disturbances that were visited upon many American cities in the 1960s. Coincidentally and according to immigration records provided by the United States Bureau of Census (see Table 1 and Table 2 below) African migration started to develop an upsurge thereafter. The racial disturbances to which we refer motivated the inauguration of a National Advisory Commission on Civil Disorder (otherwise called the Kerner Commission) in August 1967. In its report tendered in March 1968, "the commission chided White America for creating, maintaining, and condoning societal conditions that precipitated the disturbances," (see Stroman, Merritt, & Matabane, 1989-90).

Table 1[11]: African Refugees/Asylees by Selected Country of Birth

|  | 71-80 | 81-90 | 91-00 | 01-07 |
|---|---|---|---|---|
| AFRICA | 2,991 | 22,149 | 51,469 | 136,587 |
| Ethiopia | 1,307 | 18,542 | 17,829 | 20,768 |
| Ghana | 3 | 135 | 430 | 1,141 |
| Nigeria | 6 | 14 | 442 | 2,722 |
| Kenya | 4 | 87 | 1.438 | 7.648 |
| Liberia | 2 | 109 | 3,836 | 15,386 |
| Rwanda | 0 | 3 | 389 | 1,469 |
| Somalia | 6 | 70 | 16,737 | 32.585 |
| South Africa | 14 | 285 | 194 | 140 |
| Sudan | 4 | 739 | 5,174 | 17,458 |
| Zimbabwe | 3 | 24 | 32 | 496 |

Table 2[12]: Africans with Legal Permanent Residence by selected African Countries

|  | 71-80 | 81-90 | 91-00 | 01-07 |
|---|---|---|---|---|
| AFRICA | 91,500 | 192.293 | 382,520 | 526.127 |
| Ethiopia | N/A | 27,214 | 49,258 | 67,087 |
| Ghana | N/A | 14,876 | 35,607 | 41.486 |
| Nigeria | 8,800 | 35,343 | 67,232 | 70,108 |
| Kenya | N/A | 7,853 | 13,989 | 35.400 |
| Liberia | N/A | 8,058 | 15,979 | 25,534 |
| Rwanda | N/A | N/A | 614 | 1,772 |
| Somalia | N/A | N/A | 20,149 | 35,457 |
| South Africa | 11,500 | 15,690 | 22,626 | 24,256 |
| Sudan | N/A | N/A | 12,599 | 23,330 |
| Zimbabwe | N/A | N/A | 2,760 | 4.974 |

We argue on the basis of foregoing that recent African émigrés from such countries as South Africa and former Rhodesia (now Zimbabwe) will possibly be more familiar with racial matters than fellow émigrés from Nigeria and Rwanda who are more familiar with ethnic majority-minority contestations. United States Bureau of Census describing populations of African immigrants to whom asylum, refugee, and permanent residency statuses have been granted in the 37 years that culminated in 2007 show far more immigrants from the combination of Nigeria, Ethiopia, Ghana, Liberia and

Somalia respectively than there have been from South Africa and Zimbabwe (see Table 1 and Table 2 below; see also Togunde & Osagie, 2009).

United States Bureau of Census statistics further strengthens our argument that the inconsistency between ethnic and racial bases for majority/minority contestations in African countries versus the United States will pose a potential source of adaptation anxiety for most African emigrants to the United States Not only does the migration trends imply that African émigrés will exhibit a within-group inconsistent response to the United States' struggle with race relations, it also suggests that many may experience the caliber of "alienation" that Chen and Starosta (1998) describe in their treatment of immigrants' emotional and affective responses. In their correlate explication of symptoms of "culture shock", Chen and Starosta (1998: 251) suggest that "(s)ocial difficulties tend to increase when the differences between the host culture and the sojourner's culture become greater". Future research assessments of the substantive variances between adaptation and/or acculturation patterns of African émigrés who relocated from countries with ethnic versus racial majority-minority compositions and contestations should be informative.

In the American socio-economic, cultural and political terrain, issues of the status of minority populations have evolved over the last four centuries. Conversations have resolved such issues as the emancipation of slaves and the enfranchisement of women and minority groups among other civil rights issues. There are such unresolved issues as affirmative action about which contestations continue and on which civil society groups and the mass media outlets that cover the debates are divided into camps of proponents and opponents. Over time and across disciplinary boundaries many others have examined the affirmative action debate as it affects the ability of the American society to ensure employment for all "without regard to ... race, creed, color, or national origin," (see, e.g., Gamson & Modigliani, 1987; Wise, 1988; Braun, 1995; Entman, 1997; Arriola & Cole, 2001; Moy, Domke & Stamm, 2001; Clawson, Strine & Waltenburg, 2003). Suffice it to say that the affirmative action debate has and will remain one of those public debates that provide subtext for the racialization of the American body politic. Given that many African émigrés count economics as one of the reasons for migration, we suggest that they are directly affected by and should be interested parties in this ongoing debate. Empirical review of African émigrés' position on affirmative action should be informative. African émigrés from South Africa should be willing to share comparisons between United States affirmative action policy and South Africa's Black Economic Empowerment program introduced in the years following the termination of apartheid. Nigerians in the pool may find reason to compare affirmative action with the Quota system employed in Nigeria.

## African Émigrés' Collective Re-Categorization in the United States as Minorities

Haven examined the racialized context of the American terrain into which they are embraced, it is appropriate, in view of earlier discussion of pre-migration identities, to turn attention to the re-categorization of African émigrés to the United States as a collective minority group. We suspect that re-categorization poses a significant challenge to the acculturation experience of African émigrés. The process as a factor and its likely socio-cultural, economic, psychological, and communicative implications has received insufficient attention by interdisciplinary scholars who ponder the question of migration.

In his attempt to address the issue of re-categorization, Gudykunst (2004) informs that the action is typically directed at out-group members. Citing Brewer & Gaertner (2001: 459), he clarifies that the goal of re-categorization is "to structure ... inclusiveness in ways that reduce inter-group bias and conflict." In other words and following in-group identity model, re-categorization converts individuals with "two separate identities" into one "common inclusive identity," (Gudykunst, 2004: 154):

> To illustrate, members of two different ethnic groups might find that they share a common religious identity or start to think of themselves as "Americans" (Gaertner & Dovidio, 2000) or share a common organizational identity (Huo, Smith, Tyler, & Lind, 1996). The cognitive processes that lead to in-group favoritism when individuals perceive they are members of different groups is "redirected to benefit the former outgroup members" when a common identity is formed (Brewer & Gaertner, 2001: 459).

Because Gudykunst and others did not have African émigrés and African-Americans in mind, the challenge that we take on in subsequent paragraphs is to explore the way in which their explication of the process of re-categorization (evidently a noble goal) can be applied to the connection between recent African émigrés and a pre-existent African-American population. We know that in the process of completing immigration papers to legalize their presence, majority of recent African émigrés check their identity as Black – an action that locates them in the same racial and minority category as the pre-existent African-American population. A number of complex issues are set off by this connection that are worthy of careful examination.

First, the re-categorization of recent African émigrés as Black immigrants in the American terrain completes a historical continuum that embraces the arrival of Africans in America as slaves in the 1600s[13] at one end and the recent entry of African émigrés at the other. Kposowa (1998: 17-18) clarifies that the "involuntary nature of their" entry via slavery was why they "were not considered immigrants by the White population ... however ... racial prejudice may have been a more accurate motive."

Second, the re-categorization of African émigrés as Blacks underscores the existence of a hierarchical order between the four centuries-old (c. 410-years) presence of African-Americans in the United States and the more recent phenomenon of African immigration in the less-than 40 years spanning 1971 and 2009 (see Table 1 and Table 2 above). This hierarchical order suggests that the possible extent of African émigrés' immersion into the United States culture cannot be discussed with any finality if it either ignores the role of African-Americans or excludes impacts of one group on the other or omits an assessment of the legacies that one group bequeaths to the other. In other words, the location of the African-Americans' sojourn in the United States is the threshold against which African émigrés can measure the extent to which they will be embraced by other racial groups in the United States body politic. If the latter statement reads like an identification of a location of the proverbial glass ceiling, the reverse is also true. Minority versus majority contestations that have been resolved should be available to the benefit of African émigrés. Examples include such civil rights victories as the enfranchisement of Black voters, the desegregation of public school systems and the enactment of an affirmative action policy that guarantees non-discriminatory employment opportunities for all races among others. The recurrent debate over affirmative action is a part of decades-long majority-minority contestations that African-Americans pass along.

Legacies bequeathed by African-Americans to African émigrés include the polarity between Whiteness and Blackness. Earlier in this chapter, we cited Jackson's (1999) suggestion that racism, which he describes as "a very severe social disease" is unresolved. In the same book he alludes to the notion that

> (b)eing White is often considered synonymous with what it means to be American. This sets up an I-Other dichotomy between White Americans and "other" Americans – a relationship that leads to several forms of exclusion, including but not limited to socioeconomic imparity, (Jackson, 1999: 31).[14]

The proposed cultural positioning of Whiteness as synonymous with being American represents by now an age-long hurdle that African-Americans and other ethnic groups[15] in the United States have contended with. The fact that Whiteness is a physically insurmountable obstacle for Blacks has not removed it as a yardstick for measuring social acceptance because the issue proceeds beyond disparate skin colors. Frantz Fanon (1967: 110) compounds the problem when he states that the "Black man ... must be Black in relation to the White man." Fanon also appears to suggest the only way out of the paradox when he states that as "long as the Black man is among his own, he will have no occasions, except in minor internal conflicts, to experience his being through others (p. 109).

Upon arrival, the African émigré is historically and hierarchically positioned behind African-Americans in the unattainable task of becoming fully American which, to all intents and purposes, is achievable only by attaining Whiteness. With this obstacle, we argue that it would be impossible for the African émigré to become fully assimilated into the American cultural landscape in the way that Jackson (1999); Gudykunst (2004) and Jandt (2007) envisioned assimilation. In his own explication, Jandt (2007) provided a ray of hope when he suggests that assimilation is a long-term and sometimes multigenerational process. If this is accurate, then it is fair to suggest that assimilation has to exclude first-generation African émigrés; their great-grandchildren may, however, have a better opportunity at becoming fully assimilated.

However, if we choose to explore the broader continuum of the African presence in the United States, a good question to ponder is whether or not African-Americans are fully assimilated into the American cultural landscape after 410 years. This is a question that African and African-American scholars as well as interested others in African migration should ponder. We can, however, proceed for now by suggesting that the stability of the African identity over the term of migration would have to collaborate with the pre-existence of an African-American population in the United States to pose contextual obstacles to the extent to which the African émigré can become fully assimilated into the American cultural landscape.

Now that Africa has become a steady contributor to human immigration into the United States of America (see Tables 1 and 2 above), it is valid to ask what values the continent and its émigrés offer the African-American population. Jackson (1999) suggests that the most valuable bequeath of Africa to the African-American population is both geographical and cultural. When the hyphen "African" replaced "Black" in their identifier in the 1980s, the Black-American population received both land-referent and cultural identity from Africa. By so doing, African-Americans fulfilled E.B. Tylor's (1871/1889) prerequisite that culture has to be connected to membership in a specific society; met Abrahams' (1970) suggestion of need for culture to be connected to a land mass and Levine's (1977) specification of the need for a land-referent. With the addition of African as hyphen, Cordell (2008) indicates that African-Americans and Africans became co-ethnics. Prior to that name-change and among Americans sharing the minority[16] and hyphenated statuses, only the group formerly known as Black-Americans lacked a land-referent.[17]

Additional justification for the adopted cultural referent came with Molefi Asante's (1987) argument that African slaves brought cultural continuities with them to America. It is at least academically valuable to question the extent to which contemporary African-American worldviews exhibit African cultural continuities. Are there by now more or less discontinuities than continuities? Such areas of discontinuity, where they exist would have been fed primarily by two realities among many. The African continent is no longer what it was: after its engagement, by omission or commission, in the enslavement of some of its peoples; after extensive encounter with colonialism and; after decades of post-colonial interactions with the West and the adoption of a myriad of socio-political and economic ideologies that many consider a part of cultural imperialism (see Thiong'O, 1993). Secondly, multiple generations of African-Americans have been more exposed to the American end of their hyphenated identity than to the African dimension. Gates (1994: xii) in his memoir jovially reports his father's response to Gates' own ambivalence about being an integrated African-American: "Your black ass ... is integrated already."

At the same time, it appears as if African émigrés in the United States are adapting to social aspects of life via educational achievement and engagements in the professions more than in the cultural domain where other nationalities appear to have found enclaves. Agbali (2008a; 2008b) focuses on African immigrants' importation of religion and spirituality to St. Louis, Missouri. Addressing the issue of religious (or denominational) enclaves, Agbali (2008b) states as follows:

> Like the St. Louis Chinese, the concept of cultural community aptly references the African immigrants given their diffusion throughout the metro areas while still uniquely engaging diverse cultural institutions such as churches, mosques, and other cultural centers catering to African immigrants, (p. 141).

Agbali's account points out a few issues that are pertinent to ongoing discussion in that he profiles African émigrés' spiritual interaction (limited or lack thereof) with America as something that they are doing to and not taking from America. While this depiction may suggest the absence of assimilation into mainstream religious organizations in the United States, it also does suggest the likelihood of integration as earlier defined and to a similarity with the African-American community's religiosity and denominational independence. There may also be a similarity in spiritual objective between the African émigrés and the African-American community's need to use spirituality as a means of escape from difficulties of life in exile and from the tyranny of slavery respectively. As Agbali (2008a) reports: "(T)he Ogoni refugees resettled in St. Louis area engaged the forum of prayers ... for their survival from tyranny and bestial death during the military dictatorship that dislodged them," (p. 145).

Altogether significant, however, is the absence in Agbali's (2008a; 2008b) and Cordell's (2008) report of any appreciable relationship between African émigrés and their co-ethnics in the African-American community.[18] The foregoing evidence suggests that each group separately brought religious (cultural) continuity to the United States With shared land-referent, Mbiti's (1992) suggestion that the African is religious through and through may have gained indirect support. The same evidence also underscores the notion that the two are among multiple out-groups that co-exist in the United States Perhaps the re-categorization that Gudykunst (2004) and others suggest as well as the shared geo-cultural and ethnic roots provide incentive for both to explore the possibility or otherwise of increased in-group associations with Africa, as confluence, than there currently is. Exploration of the latter is outside of the purview of the current chapter but is one that is worthy of further assessment by others. Interested researchers may wonder why there is little or no interaction at the institutional level outside of outfits like Randall Robinson-led Trans-Africa[19] and at the personal level outside of scattered inter-marriages. Between such institutional and personal engagements is a gulf signifying unoccupied space for consistent political (policy), socio-economic and cultural interactions –

the kind that builds affinity and potentially leads to Hall's (1989) notion of High Context (HC) communication. The extent to which negative media co-representation of Africa and the African-American community may have contributed to the lukewarm relationship between the two groups will be explored later in this chapter.

Because it serves our central goal, we consider it valuable to explore the extent to which the relationship between African émigrés and African-Americans in the United States cultural landscape can communicatively occur at a High Context (HC) level. At least theoretically, it appears safer to suggest that interaction will be at the Low Context (LC) level a la Hall. We anchor our rational on the varied historical trajectories of the two groups from the era of slavery to the contemporary immigration stage. This leads us to suggest that communicative context, as Hall conceived of it, is indeed more about communicants' experiential affinities than it is about sharing geo-cultural roots, being co-ethnics, occupying the same geographical space in contemporary United States or simply being minorities. Though generations of African slaves and new African émigrés share roots in Africa and now co-habit the United States, it appears that ongoing but extensively divergent experiences will continue to steer their sojourn in different experiential and cultural directions. The latter will also suggest that communicative interactions will veer more toward the low context end of Hall's (1989) continuum. Foregoing provides bases for the claim that we make here that African émigrés' acculturation in the United States may not pull significantly toward the direction of the African-American worldview. This is partly because of African émigrés' ongoing direct interaction with Africa. The cultural disconnection will also proceed in spite of the hierarchical order of arrival that benefits African Americans. Our assertion does not foreclose deliberate effort to bring Africa's children under the same cultural roof.

## Negative Media Co-Representation of Africans and African-Americans

Many decades of empirical evidences signify that media representations of Africa and of African-Americans have been and remain overwhelmingly negative. In addition to sharing roots in mother-Africa, African émigrés and their African-American siblings have endured negative co-representation by Western- and mainstream-media respectively. We consider the exploration of this phenomenon relevant to ongoing attempt to gauge the adaptation of African émigrés in the United States In particular, we find exploration of mass mediation of the African continent and African-Americans valuable to earlier suggestion that there is low context (LC) communicative relationship between African émigrés and African-Americans and to a large extent between African-Americans and Africa. If our assumption of a gulf in communicative and cultural relationships is accurate, we further speculate that the mass media would remain the single most frequent domain through which the two sides engage in indirect communication and contact. Therefore, the quality and/or quantity of media representations become pertinent as a way of substantiating our assumption and speculation. We are also interested in the extent to which what is read, heard, or seen on the pages of newspapers, via radio, and on television in the United States may influence inter-group relations and create illusions in the minds of African émigrés and African-Americans about Africa and Africans.

## Western media representations of Africa

It is well established that Black Africa is virtually not covered media in the West (see Cohen, 1995). When covered, nearly three-quarters of the news focuses on trouble spots (such as South Africa, Rhodesia; now Zimbabwe), the Portuguese colonies (see Tiffen, 1976) and the 1966-1970 Nigerian civil war and the Rwandan genocide[20] (see, Olorunnisola, 1995). Ironically, the Rwandan genocide was aided and abetted by virulently anti-Tutsi Radio-Television Mille Collines which was controlled by the Hutu-led national government. The Rwandan ethnic cleansing showed the mass media in double articulation. First there is media complicity made possible by control mechanism which favored one of the ethnic groups in contention. Second is the role of the Rwandan media and of the Western media – as multipliers of the crisis and, by extension, 'reinforcers' of Africa's reputation as a continent given to the unusual, the absurd, and the repugnant.

The relatively small quantity of information that emanates from Africa tends to ignore important developmental events and to distort the reality it presents (Schramm, 1964). The news items also tend to be ill-informed and superficial (Rosemblum, 1979: 203) and laced heavily with undue emphasis on turmoil, natural disasters, assassinations, wars, and the more bizarre aspects of life. Altogether news about the African continent tends to be "qualitatively misrepresentative, under-representative, distorting, angling and slanting" while "full of ethnocentric bias" (Nwosu, 1983: 29). Along the years, therefore, "the Western mass media have had largely adverse coverage of Africa that capitalized on its real and imagined weaknesses...," (Melzer, 1988: 54).

Contemporary Western news media do not appear to have shifted far away from previous representations of Africa as a place where coups, drought, disease, pestilence, and a host of other human tragedies occur.[21] Africa remains location of human suffering with many dimensions (Hawk, 1992; Quist-Adade, 2000). Referring to foreign news covered by the United States media, Gans (2004: 36) aver as follows:

> Wars, civil wars, coup d'état, and revolutions are reported from countries large and small; smaller countries, especially in Latin America or Africa, generally break into the news only under such conditions...conflicts producing racial violence between whites and blacks, as in ... South Africa.

In his attempt to provide justification for the way that American news media cover foreign news in general Gans explains that they "often limit themselves only to the most dramatic overseas events" (p. 37). In addition a persistently negative image that is undiluted by direct personal experience[22] will leave negative impressions on the respective minds of the segment of American audiences that is more directly concerned about the African continent.

## American mainstream media representation of African-Americans

American mainstream media representation of the African American community has a lot in common with western media coverage of Africa. Scholars have observed a trend that has transited over 70 years from under-representation to stereotypic representations. Entman (1992) noted that Life Magazine did not give much visibility to Blacks between 1937 and 1972. In their assessment of television coverage of African Americans, Stroman, Merritt, & Matabane (1989/90: 46) note that in "...the 1950s and 1960s, African-Americans were most likely to be cast as maids and handymen. There was so much discrepancy between media portrayal of Black and White America in the 1960s that the Kerner Commission's report, in part, cited the media as one of the institutions responsible for creating a "schism between Black and White Americans" (Stroman, Merritt, & Matabane, 1989/90). On the strength of its observation, the Kerner Commission recommended a drastic shift in the depiction of African-Americans:

> Television should develop programming which integrates Negroes into all aspects of televised presentations.... In addition to news-related programming, we think that Negroes should appear more frequently in dramatic and comedy series, (Report of the National Advisory Commission on Civil Disorders; cited in Stroman, Merritt and Matabane, 1989/90: 45).

Things appeared to change slightly after the Kerner Commission tendered its report "... at the beginning of the 1970s, African Americans were frequently featured in high-status professions and in glamorous roles...," (Stromann, Merritt, & Matabane, 1989/90: 46).

However, in an earlier study that Stroman (1986) conducted to examine African-American family shows between 1969 and 1982, she found most to be single-parent families headed by females depicted as poor. In contradistinction, the Cosby Show, which aired between September 20, 1984 and April 30, 1992, focused on the life of the Huxtables – an upper middle class African-American family living in Brooklyn, New York. There is ample evidence (see Gates, 1992; Inniss and Feagin, 1995; Jhally & Lewis, 1992; Lewis, 1992) that the Cosby Show did not go down well with African-American viewers who were not pleased with a seemingly well-assimilated Black family led by two professionals (a medical doctor and a lawyer) whose reality was not perceived as reflecting the realities that most African-Americans experience. Some African-American viewers described the Huxtable family as "being White people in Black face" (Innis & Feagin, 1995: p. 700) and considered the depiction a false image. The underlying response is that media depiction of African-Americans had oscillated to a place where it bore no resemblance to the reality of their circumstances (see Jhally & Lewis, 1992). Wood's (2003) report that Blacks were seen in one of two extreme ways – either good, the rare token, or bad, the more common – summed the development up nicely. The dichotomy between the good and the bad is adjudged to reflect that between the house Negro and the field Negro during slavery.

Entman (1992) noted that TV news tended to associate blacks as a collective threat and burden to society and in that mode, "news subjects ... trigger stored information processing categories and associated negative affective responses," (Entman, 1992: p. 345).

Grose (2006) provides an answer to a question that is logical; that is, where does the African-American need to go to find respectable coverage when he/she deposed that minority press outlets are more likely to cover Latino, African-American and Asian American legislators' activities. Though Grose did not elaborate, it is safe to assume that minority legislators did not receive complementary coverage of their activities in the mainstream media.

## Cumulative Impacts of Negative Media Co-Representation

Littlefield (2008) would consider foregoing coverage trend a part of media complicity in sustaining a hegemonic social structure. In her view, the media are the "primary agent of socialization in which participants are seduced, educated, and transformed by ideas concerning race, gender, and class on a global level, and these ideas often support a White supremacist capitalist patriarchy," (p.676). Could Africa and the African-American community be dealing with the same hegemonic structure? Is there any ideological or structural connection between operators of mainstream media and owners of transnational news agencies? Is it more likely that there is uniformity in the definition of news and a predilection for the negative on both ends of the national-transnational news operations?

The fundamental challenge in all of this, however, is how to validly suggest that these alleged under-representations, misrepresentations, and gross exaggerations of the African and African-American conditions by the mass media convert into, influence or lead audiences (including African émigrés, African-Americans and White viewers) to cultivate certain responses. Gerbner[23] and his colleagues spent many years on cultivation research. A synthesis of their findings is that heavy dosage of negative media message has to coincide with heavy viewer exposure for cultivation of media representation (or under-representation, or stereotypic depictions) to validly occur.

In his assessment of the complexity of foreign news, Louw (2009:153) suggests as follows:

> ...the way foreign places are reported by the media can have significant impacts. For example, because United States power underpins the New World Order, the processes whereby Americans "make sense of distant places" now have real consequences for non-Americans. To a great extent, Americans

form impressions of distant places, issues and events from their news media. These impressions often translate into electoral pressure on United States politicians to act in certain ways toward distant populations.

Louw omitted to add that the way distant places are covered also has impacts on the way Americans see, think of, and conceive of those places. For instance, places where there are many human and natural disasters may receive relief as a result of electoral pressure; but so much negative news also tends to leave unattractive impressions on the minds of the very same electorates. As such the same event that was a pull for sympathy could also be a push away from direct engagements that include travel and foreign direct investment by African émigrés and African-Americans among others. For African émigrés, disillusionment may also set in for those with plans to relocate in the near- or long-term.

There is a dangerous implication for the African and African-American communities in foregoing developments given the notion of non-existent inter-group relations which leaves mass mediation as the avenue of contact. Besides, research has suggested that in general minority members are more frequent media users than Whites (see Albarran & Umphrey, 1993; Roberts, Foehr, Rideout, & Brodie, 1999) and they are more likely to consider content of media as realistic (Greenberg & Brand, 1994). In addition, minority images conveyed via the media have been found to contribute to public opinions on racial policies (see Pan and Kosicki, 1996; Sniderman, Brody & Tetlock, 1991; Tan, Fujioka, & Tan, 2000). In particular, Tan et al suggest that negative media portrayal of African-Americans (perceived by White viewers) is related to White viewers' negative perception of Blacks in general and that the negative impression converted into their opposition to such policies as affirmative action.

Two among other disincentives can be deduced from our review of media coverage and their implications for audiences that include the portrayed communities. On the one hand, persistent negative news about Africa and the complementary reliance on news outlets to keep up with home news (see Bastian, 1999; Olorunnisola, 2000; 2006) can breed the perception of failed states and feed the reluctance of African émigrés to return to their respective home countries while they are still professionally active. The development has possibly contributed to a concept called 'brain drain' – the systemic suction of African professionals to the United States and other countries in the West (see Okeke, 2008; Togunde & Osagie, 2009).

On the other hand, negative media coverage of African-Americans may contribute to the unwillingness of the African émigrés to appropriate (or be assimilated into) the African-American worldview and the preference to be culturally distant from African-Americans. Cordell (2008) reports this trend as evident in his study of Nigerian immigrants in Dallas/Fort Worth, Texas. Waters (2001: 195) found similar reluctance among the West Indian population in New York. Her report on the trend is cogent:

> One finds cultural distancing from black Americans among immigrants we interviewed. They argued that West Indians have strong work ethic ... and value ... education, and lack pathological behaviors .... West Indians make a case for

inclusion in American society based on being different from Black Americans .... Cultural distancing ... leaves intact and reinforces stereotypes of blacks as inferior, thus harming other group members.

A part of cultural distancing which Cordel (2008) and Waters (2001) miss in their analyses but which this author is aware of via casual conversations with immigrants (Africans especially) on the subject matter is the deliberate effort to raise children without exposing them to what is perceived as missing from the African-American experience – absence of footedness in contemporary African culture. As suggested elsewhere, further empirical studies is needed to explore the myriad of questions that have been raised about the interaction (or lack thereof) between African émigrés and the African-American community in the United States

Moreover, divisive framing perpetuated about such a sensitive issue as the affirmative action debate by mainstream and black press as Black versus White contestation (see Entman, 1997; Clawson & Wattenburg, 2003; Early, 2006) adds to minority persons' (including African émigrés) disillusionment about issues that are considered important to and underscore society's admittance of historical inequalities. In this instance, media role may be perceived as over-representative of the majority opinion on the issue: the notion that racial discrimination in employment and educational opportunities no longer exists; and as such, that affirmative action is no longer needed to forestall non-existent discriminatory practices.

We suggest that negative media co-representation of Africa and African-Americans has created cultural distancing on both sides. This phenomenon can only exacerbate Low Context communication between the two groups (see Hall, 1989). Our analysis will, however, be inaccurate if we were to leave the impression that the mass media are the sole reason for the lukewarm interaction between Africans and African-Americans. It is more accurate to state that factors that lead to Low Context communication between the groups collaborate with the overly negative media representation of the communities to increase cultural distancing. With infinitesimally minute non-mediated opportunities to close the gap exacerbated by media under-representation, to rectify misrepresentation, and to supplement stereotypic images with personal contacts, the experiential gulf can only grow wider.

## In Conclusion – An Exercise in De-Marginalization

A central argument that resonates throughout this chapter is that the African émigré's pre-departure identity – as member of an ethnic as well as majority or minority group – bears important relevance to and influences post-migration categorization, adaptation and/or acculturation, and constitutes limits to the possibility of his/her assimilation either into the African-American subculture or the White-American worldviews. We supported foregoing argument, in part, by drawing extensively from interdisciplinary secondary sources in our attempt to show how the African identity collaborates with contextual factors that include: (1) racialized nature of majority-minority relations in the United States – a factor that presents unfamiliarity and communicative inconsistencies for majority of Africans; (2) the categorization of the African émigré with African-Americans as a minority group, and the bequeath of contradistinction with Whiteness which, among other factors, poses insurmountable obstacles to both groups' ability to progress toward cultural assimilation; (3) the complicity of western and mainstream media in the negative portrayal of Africa and the African-American community and how this may have exacerbated mutual cultural-distancing and the reluctance of the African émigré to return home while still professionally active.

Altogether, we posit that African émigrés tend to integrate into the American multicultural terrain while being able to maintain their uniqueness. Complete assimilation appears beyond reach for reasons that go beyond the willingness of the African émigré to engage in primary culture abandonment.

In the process of developing our central argument, we stated among others that there is a majority and minority mindset, demonstrable in communicative patterns, conflict resolution approaches and possible engagement with host others while sojourning. In the body of the chapter and in the endnotes, we generated many questions, answered some, and left others in their rhetorical state so that future researchers may pursue them as attempts to understand migration, cultural adaptation and the prospects of cultural assimilation for Black Africans continue.

Our attempt to view migration and acculturation as complete processes that are influenced by such life-long factors as identity provided a broader base from which we were able to introduce pre-departure factors as influential on post-entry (dis)orientations. The approach taken in this chapter is atypical. Migration and adaptation studies tend to focus more on factors that create the movement of migrants and the ways in which those migrants adapt or are maladapted to the cultures of the host countries. The inability of immigrants to adapt is more often viewed as incompetence and is hardly weighed as the result of inconsistencies between one cultural orientation and others. There is, as a result, a dearth of studies that investigate the extent to which contextual factors in the host-country can contribute to the inability of the immigrant to acculturate, adapt and/or become fully assimilated.

By placing the pre-departure identity and cultural orientation of African émigrés at the center of our consideration of how they fare as immigrants in the United States, we moved the typical location of the immigrant from the conceptual, theoretical, and methodological margins. We believe that this de-marginalization is crucial to a better understanding of African immigrants in the United States The approach has potential to improve the construction of cultural independence and cultural interdependence in a globalized world. Though our arguments are not infallible, we hope that the approach taken and the factors examined will modestly contribute to the manner in which migration experiences (Africans' and others') are investigated.

# References

Abrahams, R. (1970). *Positively Black*. Englewood Cliffs, NJ: Prentice Hall.

Agbali, A.A. (2008a). 'African Immigrants' Experiences in Urban America: Religion and the Construction of Social Identity in St. Louis.' In T. Falola and N. Afolabi (Eds.). *African Minorities in the New World* (pp. 51-104). New York: Routledge.

Agbali, A.A. (2008b). 'Ethnography of Religion and Spirituality among St. Louisan African Immigrants.' In T. Falola and N. Afolabi (Eds.). *African Minorities in the New World* (pp. 105-151). New York: Routledge.

Albarran, A.B., & Umphrey, D. (1993). "An examination of television motivations and program preferences by Hispanics, Blacks, and Whites." *Journal of Broadcasting & Electronic Media*, 37, 95-103.

Anonymous (accessed June 11, 2009). Sub-Saharan Africa. Santa Clara University Markkula Center for Applied Ethics. www.scu.edu/ethics-center

Arriola, K.R. & Cole, E.R. (2001). "Framing the affirmative action debate: Attitudes toward out-group members and White identity." *Journal of Applied Social Psychology*, 31 (12), p. 2462-2483.

Asante, M.K. (1987) *The Africentric Idea*. Philadelphia, PA: Temple University Press.

Asante, M.K. (1990). *Kemet, Africentricity and Knowledge*. Trenton, NJ: African World Press.

Augustus, O. (2008). 'Managing the Migration of Health-Care Workers toward the Transfer of Knowledge, Skill and Professionalism.' In Falola, T. & Afolabi, N. (Eds.). *African Minorities in the New World* (pp. 233-245). New York: Routledge.

Bastian, M.L. (1999). Nationalism in a Virtual Space: Immigrant Nigerians on the Internet. West Africa Review, 1, 1: Retrieved May 2009: http://www.icaap.org/iuicode

Berry, J.W., Kim, U., & Boski, P (1987). "Psychological acculturation of immigrants." *International and Intercultural Communication Annual*, 11, 62-89.

Braun, C.M. (1995). "Affirmative action and the glass ceiling." *The Black Scholar*, 25 (3), 7-15.

Brewer, M., & Gaertner, S. (2001). Toward reduction of prejudice. In R. Brown & S. Gaertner (Eds.). *Intergroup Processes*. Oxford, UK: Blackwell.

Casey, M.W. (2007). *The Rhetoric of Sir Garfield Todd: Christian Imagination and the dream of an African Democracy*. Waco, Texas: Baylor University Press.

Chen, G. & Starosta, W.J. (1998). *Foundations of Intercultural Communication*. Boston, MA: Alyn and Bacon.

Clawson, R. & Waltenburg, E. (2003). "Support for a Supreme Court affirmative action decision: A story in Black and White." *American Politics Research*, 31, 251-279.

Clawson, R., Strine, H.N., & Waltenburg, E. (2003). "Framing Supreme Court decisions: The mainstream versus the Black press." *Journal of Black Studies*, 33, 784-800.

Cohen, Y. (1995). "Foreign Press corps as an indicator of international news interest." *Gazette: The International Journal for Mass Communication Studies*, 56, 2: 89-100.

Coover, G.E. (2001). "Television and Social Identity: Race representation as "White" accommodation." *Journal of Broadcasting & Electronic Media*, 45, 413-431.

Cordell, D.D. (2008). 'Paradoxes of Immigrant Incorporation: High Achievement and Perceptions of Discrimination by Nigerians in Dallas/Forth Worth, Texas (USA).' In Falola, T. & Afolabi, N. (Eds.). *Trans-Atlantic Migration: The Paradoxes of Exile* (pp.13-28). New York, NY: Routledge.

Early, M. (2006). War of the Words: The role of the News Media in the Affirmative Action Debate. Unpublished M.A. Thesis, Penn State University.

Entman, R.M. (1992). "Blacks in the News: TV, Modern Racism and Cultural Change." *Journalism Quarterly*, 69, 2, 341-361.

Entman, R.M. (1997). "Manufacturing discord: Media in the affirmative action debate." *The Harvard International Journal of Press/Politics*, 2 (4), 32-51.

Falola, T. & Afolabi, (2008) *African Minorities in the New World*. NY: Routledge.

Fanon, F. (1967). *Black Skin White Masks*. New York: Grove Press.

Feagin, J.R. (1984). *Racial and Ethnic Relations*. NY: Prentice-Hall.

Gaertner, S., & Dovidio, J. (2000). *Reducing Intergroup Bias*. Philadelphia: Psychological Press.

Gamson, W.A. & Modigliani, A. (1987). "The changing culture of affirmative action research." *Political Sociology*, 3, 137-177.

Gans, Herbert J. (2004). *Deciding what's News: A study of CBS evening news, NBC Nightly News, Newsweek, and Time (25th Anniversary Edition)*. Evanston Illinois: Northwestern University Press.

Gates, JR, H.L. (1992) TV's Black World turn – But stays unreal. In Anderson, M. & Collins, P.H. (Eds.). *Race, Class and Gender: An Anthology* (pp. 76-87). Belmont, CA: Wadsworth.

Gates, JR., H.L. (1994) *Colored People: A Memoir*. NY: Alfred A. Knopf.

Gerbner, G., Gross, L., Eleey, M.F., Jackson-Beeck, M., Jeffries-Fox, S., & N. Signorielli (1977). "Violence profile no. 8: The highlights." *Journal of Communication* 27 (2), 177-180.

Gerbner, G., Gross, L., Signorielli, N., & Morgan, M. (1980). "Aging with Television: Images on Television drama and conceptions of social reality." *Journal of Communication*, 30, 37-47.

# REFERENCES

Gerbner, G., Gross, L., Morgan, M., & Signorielli, N. (1982). "Charting the mainstream: Television's contribution to political orientations." *Journal of Communication*, 32 (2), 100-126.

Greenberg, B.S., & Brand, J.E. (1994). 'Minorities and the Mass Media: 1970's-1990s.' In J. Bryant and D. Zillman (Eds.). *Media Effects: Advances in Theory and Research* (pp. 273-314). Hillsdale, NJ: Lawrence Erlbaum Associates, Inc.

Grose, C.R. (2006). 'Bridging the Divide: Inter-Ethnic Cooperation; Minority Media Outlets and Coverage of Latino, African American, and Asian-American Members of Congress.' *Harvard International Journal of Press/Politics*, 11, (4), 115-130).

Gudykunst, William B. (2004). *Bridging Differences: Effective Intergroup Communication, 4th Edition*. Thousand Oaks, CA: Sage Publications.

Hall, E.T. (1989). *Beyond Culture*. NY: Anchor Books (Doubleday).

Hawk, B.G. (1992). *Africa's Media Image*. NY: Praeger.

Huo, Y., Smith, H., Tyler, T., & Lind, E. (1996). "Superordinate Identification, Subgroup Identification, and Justice Concerns." *Psychological Science*, 7, 40-45.

Inniss, L.B., & Feagin, J.R. (1995). "The Cosby Show: The view from the Black middle class." *Journal of Black Studies*, 25, 692-711.

Jackson II, R.L. *The Negotiation of Cultural Identity: Perceptions of European Americans and African Americans*. Westport, CN: Praeger

Jandt, F.E. (2007). *An Introduction to Intercultural Communication: Identities in a Global Community, 5th Edition*. Thousand Oaks, CA: Sage Publications.

Jhally, S., & Lewis, J. (1992). *Enlightened Racism: The Cosby Show: Audiences and the myth of the American dream*. Boulder, CO: Westview.

Kim, Y.Y. (2005). "Inquiry in Intercultural and Development Communication." *Journal of Communication*, 55, 554-577.

Kposowa, A.J. (1998). *The Impact of Immigration on the United States Economy*. Lanham, MD: University Press of America.

Levine, L. (1977). *Black Culture and Black Consciousness*. NY: Oxford Press.

Lewis, J. (1991). *The Ideological Octopus: An Exploration of Television and its Audience*. New York: Routledge.

Littlefield, M.B. (2008). "The Media as a System of Racialization: Exploring Images of African American Women and the New Racism." *American Behavioral Scientist*, 51 (5), 675-685.

Louw, P.E. (2009). 'Reporting Foreign Places.' In De Beer, A.S. & Merrill, J.C. (Eds.). *Global Journalism: Topical Issues and Media Systems* (pp. 153-164). Boston, MA: Pearson.

Mastro, D. (2003). "A social identity approach to understanding the impact of television messages." *Communication Monographs*, 70, 98-113.

Mbiti, J.S. (1992). *African Religions and Philosophy*. London: Heinemann.

Melzer, V. (1988). "Africa through Racist Spectacles." *African Events*, 2, 54.

Moy, P., Domke, D., & Stamm, K. (2001). "The spiral of silence and public opinion on affirmative action." *Journalism and Mass Communication Quarterly*, 78, 7-25.

Okeke, G.S.M. (2008). "The Uprooted Emigrant": The Impact of Brain Drain, Brain Gain, and Brian Circulation on Africa's Development. In Falola, T. and Afolabi, N. (Eds.). *Trans-Atlantic Migration: The Paradoxes of Exile* (pp. 119-139). New York, NY: Routlege.

Olorunnisola, A.A. (1985). The Pan-African News Agency: Analysis of the content matter of selected wire copies. Unpublished Master's Thesis. Ibadan: The University of Ibadan.

Olorunnisola, A.A. (1995). "When tribal wars are mass mediated: Re-evaluating the policy of 'non-interference'." *Gazette: The International Journal for Mass Communication Studies*, 56: 123-138.

Olorunnisola, A.A. (2000). "African Media, Information Providers and Emigrants as Collaborative Nodes in Virtual Social Networks." *African Sociological Review*, vol 4, 2: 46-71.

Olorunnisola, A.A. (2006). *African media, information providers and emigrants as collaborative nodes in virtual social and knowledge networks.* University of Ibadan: 30th Postgraduate School Interdisciplinary Research Discourse.

Pan, Z., & Kosicki, G.M. (1996). "Assessing new media influences on the formation of Whites' racial policy preferences." *Communication Research*, 23, 147-178.

Quist-Adade, C. (2000). In the shadows of the Kremlin: Africa's media image from communism to post-communism. In Malek, A., & Kavoori, A.P. (Eds.). *The Global Dynamics of News: Studies in International News Coverage and News Agenda* (pp. 169-176). Stamford, CN: Ablex Publishing Corporation.

Richburg, K.B. (1997). Out of America: A Black Man Confronts Africa. New York, NY: Basic Books.

Roberts, D.F., Foehr, U.G., Rideout, V.J., & Brodie, M. (1999). *Kids and Media at the new Millennium*. Menlo Park, CA: Henry J. Kaiser Family Foundation.

Rosemblum, M. (1979). *"Coups and Earthquakes:" Reporting the World for America*. New York: Harper and Row. 203.

Schramm, W. (1964). *Mass Media and National Development*. Stanford, CA: Stanford University Press.

Schulman, S. (2005). *The Impact of Immigration on African Americans*. New Brunswick: Transaction.

Sniderman, P.M., Brody, R.A., & Tetlock, P.E. (1991). *Reasoning and Choice: Explorations in Political Psychology*. Cambridge, England: Cambridge University Press.

Stebbins, R. (1992). *Sociology: The Study of Society*. NY: Harper and Row.

Stroman, C.A. (1986). *Black Families and the Mass Media*. Washington, DC: Howard University Institute of Urban Affairs and Research.

Stroman, C.A., Merritt, B.D., & Matabane, P.W. (1989-1990). "Twenty years after Kerner: The portrayal of African Americans on prime-time television." *The Howard Journal of Communications*, Winter, pp. 44-56.

Tan, A.S., Fujioka, Y., Tan, G. (2000). "Television Use, Stereotypes of African Americans and Opinions on Affirmative Action: An Affective Model of Policy Reasoning." *Communication Monographs*, 67, 362-371.

Thiong'o, N. W. (1993). *Moving the Center: The Struggle for Cultural Freedoms*. Portsmouth, NH: Heinemann.

Tiffen, R. (1976). "Australian Press Coverage of the Third World." *Australian and New Zealand Journal of Sociology*, 12.

Ting-Toomey, S., Yee-Jung, K., Shapiro, R., Garcia, W., Wright, T., & Oetzel, J. (2000). "Ethnic identity salience and conflict styles in four ethnic groups." *International Journal of Intercultural Relations*, 23, 47-81.

Togunde, D. R. & Osagie, S. O. (2009). "Icons of Progress: Returnees' effect on decisions by Nigerians to migrate to the UNITED STATES" *International Review of Modern Sociology*, vol. 35, No. 1 (spring).

Tshiyembe, M. (2000). Inventing the Multination: Would a United States of Africa Work? http://mondediplo.com/2000/09/12africa Accessed on June 11, 2009.

Tylor, E.B. (1871/1889). *Primitive Culture: Research into the Development of Mythology, Philosophy, Religion, Language, Art, and Custom*. NY: Holt.

UNITED STATES Bureau of Census http://www.census.gov/compendia/statab/tables/09s0049.xls Accessed June 06, 2009

UNITED STATES Bureau of Census http://www.census.gov/compendia/statab/tables/09s0050.xls Accessed June 06, 2009

Waters, M.C. (2001). Growing up West Indian and African: Gender and Class differences in the Second Generation. In Nancy Forner (Ed). *Islands in the City: Wets Indian Migration to New York*, (pp. 193-214). Los Angeles, CA: University of California Press.

Weimann, G. (1989). 'Social Networks and Communication.' In Asante, M.K. & Gudykunst, W.B. (Eds.). *Handbook of International and Intercultural Communication* (pp. 186-203). Newbury Park, CA: Sage Publications.

Wise, T. (1988). "Is sisterhood conditional? White women and the rollback of affirmative action." *National Women's Studies Association Journal*, 10 (3), 1 – 26.

Wood, J.F. (2003). 'House Negro versus field Negro: The inscribed image of race in television news presentations of African-American identity.' In R.R. Means Coleman (Ed.), *Say it loud!* (pp. 95-114). New York: Routledge.

## Endnotes

[1] The terms acculturation and adaptation are used interchangeably in this chapter to refer to the process during which an immigrant, regardless of country and culture of origin, adapts, learns, copes with "the norms and values of the new host culture" (Jandt, 2007: 309). Unlike others who lump the terms together, we consider assimilation as a higher-level of engagement with the host culture that is premised on primary culture abandonment. Some explications of assimilation are very definitive. In Jackson's (1999) view assimilation is a "process of erasing the boundary between one group and another", (p. 18). Other authors (see, e.g., Jandt, 2007: 310) consider assimilation as the abandonment of the immigrant's "original cultural identity and moving into full participation in the new culture. The person identifies with the country and not an ethnic group," (see also W.B. Gudykunst, 2004). We endorse Jackson and Jandt's view. More significantly, we consider assimilation, as defined, a near-impossibility for the African émigré on account of the factors discussed throughout the length of this chapter; among others.

[2] Most of the literature on migration, migrants and attendant issues is dispersed amongst disciplines such as political science, psychology, sociology, demography, and international/intercultural communications.

[3] Stebbins (1992) suggests that present conceptions of the word ethnic are understood in ways similar to the etymology of the word, traced to the Greek "ethnikos", meaning a foreign group or nationality within a society. Earlier, Asante (1990) expounds on the description of ethnic groups when he describes them as displaced peoples noting that Eurocentric writers omitted Europeans from discussions of ethnicity; an indication that the word is a referent reserved only for non-Europeans.

[4] The suggestion has been made that "new African immigrants" may negatively impact the "economic security of African Americans." Falola and Afolabi (2008: 6) quote Steven Schulman (2005) as suggesting that "the debate about the impact of immigration on African Americans is fundamentally empirical, but it has broad political ramifications. Immigration advocates often say that "we are a nation of immigrants." However, African Americans are descendants of slaves, not immigrants. Immigration may increase ethnic diversity, but it does so at the expense of African Americans.... (p. x)." Though not intended, Schulman provides this chapter with a way to distinguish between African émigrés (whose ranks may include those who are now naturalized Americans) and African Americans. In this chapter "African émigrés" are first generation immigrants from Africa regardless of date of arrival or cause of emigration. "African-Americans", in the words of Schulman, are "descendants of slaves" whose arrival on the shores of America had nothing to do with voluntary emigration/immigration.

[5] In a December 7, 1979 commencement address given at the University of Otago, New Zealand, Sir Garfield Todd provided useful background to the institution of racism in former Rhodesia when he stated as follows: "Racism is real and this evil expresses itself in many ways.... In Rhodesia a similar madness seized us Whites and became government policy. Although we are fewer than 5% of the population we severed our colonial ties with Britain by the Unilateral Declaration of Independence and then we highjacked our five million protesting black fellow citizens. We defied world opinion and declared that we had launched Rhodesia on a thousand years of White rule. That declaration for a thousand years ... has been overwhelmed and destroyed in seven years of bloody war in which probably as many as 30,000 people have lost their lives.... A quarter of a million of our people have fled to neighboring countries and now live in destitute in refugee camps," (cited in M.W. Casey, 2007: 315) Foregoing excerpt indicates that the line between majority and minority contestation for power and migration is often a direct one. This in part suggests that it

is insufficient to discuss the minority status of African émigrés without linking their adaptation process to their antecedents.

[6] These issues raise a relevant question to which future research work should be devoted: How do pre-migration majority-minority ethnic/racial relationships intersect with post-immigration experiences? How do African émigrés and Americans who are either in majority or in minority racial groups interact?

[7] E.B. Tylor (1871/1889: 3) defines culture as "that complex whole, which includes knowledge, beliefs, art, law, morals, customs, and any other capabilities and habits acquired by man as a member of society."

[8] In the same discussion, Jandt (2007: 310) suggests that "biculturalism and pluralism ... describe integration. The person feels as loyal to the country as to any ethnic group. Integration is supported by the dual-nationality trend, which allows expatriates from immigrant-sending nations to retain rights as nationals while taking on citizenship status in the United States ... In a seeming paradox, new UNITED STATES citizens must formally renounce allegiances to foreign governments as part of the naturalization process, but the UNITED STATES law still permits citizens to possess other nationalities." Chen and Starosta (1998) endorse a broad definition of biculturalism; a development that they describe as "duality ... ability to accommodate ... both the original and the host culture.... Such flexibility provides ... new skills to value cultural contrasts, to integrate new and existing beliefs and rules," (p. 171).

[9] Jandt's (2007: 310) suggestion that "assimilation results from giving up one's original cultural identity and moving into full participation in the new culture" is also helpful. By "full participation" he clarifies that the "person identifies with the country and not an ethnic group." The latter possibility raises a critical question: To what extent does identity (ethnic or racial) play a role in African émigrés' post-immigration engagement in the UNITED STATES? In addition, what impact does the absence of trust for the African nation-state have on the ability of African émigrés to trust and be loyal to the UNITED STATES government?

[10] Tshiyembe notes that the "sociological nation is founded on shared traits (language, blood ties, religion and a common history) .... But the post-colonial state merely notes its existence, having no historical or administrative memory of the people and countries ... simply because colonialism willed it so. Others have argued that the post-colonial "nation state" has not been able to transplant the primordial "ethnic nation" as a base for citizens' affiliation and loyalty (see Bastian, 1999; Olorunnisola, 2000; 2006).

[11] Sourced from the UNITED STATES Bureau of Census at http://www.gov/compendia/statab/tables/09s0050.xls Accessed June 06, 2009

[12] Sourced from the UNITED STATES Bureau of Census at http://www.census.gov/compendia/statab/tables/09s0049.xls Accessed June 06, 2009

[13] Agbali (2008a: 51) reports that the "first recorded immigration of Africans into the United States occurred in August 1619, in Jamestown, Virginia, when a Dutch Man O' War ship exchanged for food their cargo of twenty Africans for service as indentured servants." Kposowa (1998: 17-18) added that "millions of Africans migrated, albeit involuntarily between 1650 and 1800. Thus African Americans rank among the earliest settlers in the United States. There is evidence that Africans were in America at least one year before the Mayflower landed the Pilgrim Fathers at Plymouth Rock."

[14] More recently, Littlefield (2008: 675-676) appears to agree with Jackson when she states that "American pluralism enforced the Anglo conformity that excludes all groups outside the norm and realm of Whiteness. This binary distinction among

races created a hierarchy in which Anglo perceptions about race and ethnicity dominated the social structure, and other non-White groups were placed in the "other" category, which translates into inferior social status.

[15]Though Stebbins (1992) admits that White ethnic groups exist (White ethnic populations consist of Irish, Polish, Italian, German and Mediterranean peoples) he informs that the term "ethnic is reserved as a descriptor for non-White, foreign and heathen groups (see Jackson, 1999, p. 31). More recently, Coover (2001) and Mastro (2003) also report that Whites put no significance on their ethnicity.

[16]Other minority groups in America include the Asian-, Chinese-, German-, Irish-, and Italian-Americans.

[17]Abrahams (1970) argues that any critical definition of culture must include a connection to a land mass that represents the origin of the culture. Levine (1977) adds that the absence of a land-referent strengthens the suggestion that Blacks had neither culture nor cultural identity.

[18]It is useful to mention that the noted absence of extensive relationship is not a phenomenon that is unique to the African and African-American communities. Similar occurrences may be noticed between Asian émigrés and the Asian-American communities and so on. Though this may read as an anti-melting pot comment, America does appear to engender cultural diversity more than it does cultural hybridization.

[19]Randall Robinson, an African-American, is founder and president of Trans-Africa; a UNITED STATES-based organization that has consistently spearheaded movement to influence UNITED STATES policies on Africa.

[20]Hutu genocide of 500,000 Tutsis in Rwanda was one of the most terrible debacles of the 20th century.

[21]The civil war in Dafur, Sudan, Africa's largest country geographically, which has been described as the "world's worst humanitarian crisis" pits government-backed Arab Muslim mounted militias, the Janjaweed, against predominantly black Muslims," (see Markkula Center for Applied Ethics' website).

[22]Keith Richburg's direct personal experience with African countries provides a ceiling of sorts to this recommendation. As Washington Post's bureau chief, Richburg traversed Africa's trouble spots, from Rwanda to Zaire, reporting about the wars, famine, mass murders and official malfeasance. Any romanticized notion that this African-American correspondent might have had about Africa disappeared with his experience. His book, Out of America: A Black Man Confronts Africa, first published in 1997, details his confusion and, among others, gratitude for slavery that brought his ancestors to America. In the process of sorting his deeply-scared sense of being, he denounced his African-ness. Many critics were appalled by Richburg's confrontation. Our position is to acknowledge the extremity of the events that he witnessed; to grant him the right to his felt response; and to simply express the academic doubt that Richburg can express gratitude for slavery and expunge his African-ness at the same time.

[23]See for example, G. Gerbner, L. Gross, M.F. Eleey, M. Jackson-Beeck, S. Jeffries-Fox, and N. Signorielli (1977); see also, G. Gerbner, L. Gross, N. Signorielli, and M. Morgan, (1980); see also, G. Gerbner, L. Gross, M. Morgan, and N. Signorielli (1982).

# Chapter 7
## Emigration and the Social Value of Remittances in Nigeria

*Ayokunle Olumuyiwa Omobowale*[*,1],
*Mofeyisara Oluwatoyin Omobowale*[2] *and*
*Olawale Olufolahan Ajani*[3]

## Introduction

Human migration from one geographical location to another has a historical underpinning. Evidence from anthropological records indicates that such movement has led to the development of social structures. During the colonial period, Africans also traveled to the metropolis to acquire further education and enhance their technical skills. Over time and due to rapid social change, reasons for human migration from less developed to developed societies has become elaborate, though in a somewhat regulated manner because of border controls (Adesina and Adebayo 2009, Akanle 2009). One major aspect of migration is remittance which has been defined as "that quantity of currency that migrants earn abroad and then send home to their families and communities" (Orozco 2002:43). While the means of sending remittances may be formal or informal, its meaning has been expanded over time to include material goods (Osili 2007, Hermandez-Coss and Bun 2006).

Since the 1980s when most African nations adopted the Structural Adjustment Programs (SAP) imposed by the International Monetary Fund (IMF), the importance of remittances has attracted the attention of scholars (Mohan and Zack-Williams 2002). This came about as unemployment grew in SAP nations and their currencies also lost value leading to the search for new and creative ways to improve their standard of living. However, the SAP had unintended consequences. It has led to further impoverishment rather than development. In Nigeria for instance, SAP was introduced by General Babangida's Administration in 1986. By the 1990s Nigeria's economy was in serious decline to the extent that about 70 per cent of the population was living for less than $1 per day. To further buttress this assertion, table 1 shows the impact of SAP-induced inflation on the real purchasing power of low, medium, and high level civil servants between 1979 and 2003.

Table 1: Real Take Home Remuneration in Public Service in Naira

| Year | Grade Level 01 | Grade Level 08 | Grade Level 15 |
| --- | --- | --- | --- |
| 1979-1983 | 244.00 | 737.22 | 1,947.70 |
| 1984-1988 | 164.29 | 427.64 | 1,064.06 |
| 1989-1993 | 149.23 | 272.64 | 576.14 |
| 1994-1998 | 82.10 | 198.20 | 369.70 |
| 1999-2003 | 139.40 | 340.30 | 728.90 |

Source: National Bureau of Statistics (2006: Chapter 13)

The data above shows that the real take home pay for public workers in Nigeria declined dramatically from N244 to N82.1, N737.22 to N272.64 and N1,947.70 to N369.7 for Grade levels 01, 08 and 15 respectively, between 1979 and 2003. It should be noted that real take-home pay grossly depreciated, especially as from the post-1986 era, signaling the effect of SAP on wages in spite of salary increases granted to workers. This simply meant that the volume of bills taken as wages only increased while their real purchasing value actually declined. Given the precipitous decline in the value of wages in Nigeria, emigration becomes the logical alternative to remedy the poor standard of living. Those who are fortunate to emigrate are exposed to greater opportunities not only to improve their own socio-economic wellbeing but to send part of their earnings to extended families and friends.

Between 1980 and 1991, McComic and Wahba (2000) reported that estimated global remittances through formal channels increased from US$43.3 billion to US$71.1 billion. More specifically, Haas (2006) submitted that remittances sent to developing nations by emigrants based in developed countries increased from $31.1 billion in 1990 to $76.8 billion in 2000. By 2005, it had further increased to $167 billion which now doubles the value of Official Development Assistance to Third World nations (Haas 2006).

Scholars have however, identified the merits and demerits of emigration and remittances. Orozco (2002) has argued that remittances to developing countries have directly or indirectly helped alleviate poverty and improve the economy of recipient countries. For instance, particularly he has noted that remittances contributed significantly in rescuing Latin American economies during the period of depression and decline in production and export. A similar finding by Hass (2007), Mohan and Zack-Williams (2002), and Mc Cormic and Wahba (2000) has been reported to show how remittances have enhanced the economies of many countries and contributed to alleviating poverty worldwide. On the contrary, remittances could lead to growth of economic inequality among families as those who do not have relatives abroad may not benefit from remittance flow (Mohan and Zack-Williams 2002). Nevertheless, it is usually expected that emigrants will remit goods for family and friends' benefits. Those who fail to send remittances may be seen as greedy and errant members of a familial network system and thus ostracized. The ongoing interaction between an emigrant and relatives at home serves as an essential component of the network theory of migration, which posits that the exchange of information between an emigrant and his/her relatives at the area of origin becomes a stimulating factor for further migration from the areas of origin. An in-depth discussion of the motivation for migration, however, is beyond the scope of this paper.

In this chapter, we examine the social value of remittances by drawing on the essential elements of African family structure and organization. The goal is to articulate the cultural foundation that propels the African emigrant to send remittances. Unlike previous studies on remittances, this perspective provides a unique approach to grounding remittances within the framework of African family structure.

## Theoretical Background

In examining the socio-cultural relevance of remittances in the African context, cognizance must be given to the importance of the extended family structure. Underlying the African family organization is the notion of familism or collectivism; a notion that differs substantially from the Euro-American definition where the nuclear family and individualization of members takes precedence over the extended family (Coontz, 2000). For the Africans, the extended family network includes the nuclear family members as well as uncles, aunties, cousins, in-laws, other kits and kins and friends and associates who are recognized as part of the familial networks. As a result, in most African societies, uncles and aunties may be seen as parents; cousins as siblings, and friends as brethrens - who all participate in a social network aimed at ensuring the wellbeing of every member (Balogun and Olutayo 2005-2006, Sofola 1973).

In addition to mutual responsibilities of members towards one another through a network of relationships, the extended family organization in Africa emphasizes the need to strengthen the sense of cohesion and a sense of belonging of members. Consequently, contribution of each member to the common good of the family institution becomes very important. It is not uncommon for family members to contribute financial resources to support aspiring emigrants. In this case, migration destination choice becomes a household decision taken for the common good and welfare of the family. This perspective is reinforced by new household economic theory of migration. Given the difficulty in securing visas to developed countries such as the United States, a successful applicant who has been given permission to travel abroad is celebrated. Such a celebration has two components. One, it indicates a collective effort that has been rewarded. Second, it raises hope in the family that their investment will pay off in the form of remittances. The emigrant is reminded prior to departure not to forget family who in one way or the other has been instrumental to his/her success in leaving an area of origin. If for one reason or the other the emigrant fails to send remittances s/he would be viewed as having abandoned his/her family, roots, and those who made him/her what s/he has become. Thus, individual success in the African context at the area of destination translates into family or community success. The community's expectations sometimes lead some emigrants to embark on some form of socio-economic development in their community as an appreciation of the role of kin, and as a link to his/her heritage.

Furthermore, members promote communal participation in family events and ceremonies such as naming, funerals, inheritance and succession. In most cases, support network is created for needy members of the family such as the elderly, widows, orphans, and the disabled. An African that grows up within this culture who emphasizes interdependence and multi-dimensional network of relationships that bind various relatives together is more likely to remember the obligations that s/he has been socialized to fulfill as an emigrant or as a sojourner in a foreign land. Using the Yoruba of southwestern Nigeria as an example, a family member who travels abroad is expected to bring back gifts. In particular, the one who emigrates to an area with better socio-economic opportunities has an even greater obligation to ensure that distance does not create severance of ties with his/her family in the country of origin. Part of the strategy to continue the bond that has been created before departure takes the form of frequent contacts through telephone, mails, or return visits. In an attempt to ensure that the welfare of family members at home is not imperiled, it is expected of an emigrant to send remittances. In a study carried by Hermandez-Coss and Bun, (2006: 3) on remittance out-flow from Nigerians resident in the United Kingdom, respondents emphasized

> the importance of being able to stay in touch with their families and improve the economic situation by sending remittances. The Nigerian culture in general requires the more fortunate to provide for the less fortunate...since there are limited formal welfare systems in Nigeria, senders often feel obligated to provide for immediate family members, as well as extended family, friends, and orphans.

As evidence, Nigerians living abroad sent home $5.4 billion in 2006 alone (Joseph 2007), which represents about 65 per cent of remittances coming to sub-Saharan Africa (Hermandez-Coss and Bun 2006).

In recognition of the financial support that is received by family members in the country of origin, the Yorubas would use a phrase such as *"omoluabi to ranti ile"* (that is, a responsible person who remembers home) to describe an individual that sends remittances. These remittances also show the sender as a successful person who must have benefited from this Yoruba prayer:

*Olodumare je ki a ko ere oko dele*

*Ki a rajo kabo, ki a ma r'ajo gbe s'ajo*

*Ka ma pada l'owo ofo*

May the Almighty God grant the grace to come back home

with the proceeds from the land of sojourn

May we return from our sojourn, may we not perish in

the land of sojourn

May we not return empty handed.

The prayer quote above shows that as emigrants strive to be successful in the land of sojourn, an important part of their cultural background that expects them to support their extended family resonates with them even in the midst of immediate challenges. As a result, remittances sent home become symbols of their presence even though they are physically absent. An African emigrant, therefore, sees the land of sojourn as a land of work. S/he sees "home" not as a place of residence; rather "home" is the place of origin where s/he was raised and socialized. Hence, his/her allegiance and commitment go to the family back at home. In that way, remittances reinforce the emotional bond that exists in the organizational structure of the African family. In the section that follows, we discuss the source of data and methods of analysis.

## Source of Data and Method of Analysis

In this paper, we employed a qualitative methodological approach. Data were collected from both secondary and primary sources. Secondary data were collected through a review of literature while primary data were garnered through interviews conducted both in the United States of America (USA)[4] and Nigeria. It was particularly difficult to secure primary data from Nigerians resident abroad because of the distance between the researchers and potential respondents in the USA. Consequently, the research instrument was sent to a close relation in the USA who assisted in conducting interviews with only five Nigerians (3 males and 2 females) resident in the USA. All responses from interviews in the USA were received between December 2007 and January 2008 via e-mail. In an attempt to enlarge our sample size and to increase the depth of our analysis, we decided in January 2009 to interview 12 new respondents – 6 males and 6 females - (through a snowballing sampling technique) who had relations sending remittances. At the end, a total of 17 interviews were conducted with the aid of 2 sets of specially designed questionnaire guides. We then utilized a descriptive analytical technique to present results.

## Findings on Remittances and Human Development

As earlier articulated, the goal of this chapter is to provide an empirical analysis of the socio-cultural value of remittances in Africa drawing on data collected from both emigrants and their relatives. The socio-cultural organization of African family that expects an emigrant to assist family members at home is captured by a Nigerian resident in the USA who relayed his experience with remittances thus:

> The nature of the assistance that I have given and continue to give falls into two classes-financial and non financial. I do send money via Western Union to Nigeria for the payment of school fees of both my relatives and in-laws. I have sent a laptop computer for the use and improvement of the skills of my loved ones in school. It is my opinion that the remittances have been well used as I have contributed to the graduation at university level of one in-law while I am also currently helping out two others. I have been rewarded by their continued excellence in school as well as phone calls and gift items from Nigeria. A sister in-law graduated this last term with a bachelor's degree in Accounting from the University of Benin while another one is a final year law student at Abia State University. I am both proud and honored to play a part in their education. Finally, I support both my mother and mother in-law who are widows and extended family members who are in business as well.

Yet another interviewee stated thus:

> The assistance I have given to my siblings and loved ones are in form of financial help and provision of equipment. I have sent money home to help my brothers and I have also bought them a desktop computer. I think it has enhanced and improved greatly their learning process and capacity building. The monetary assistance has been a great benefit to all my brothers. School fees are getting paid on time and books are also being bought to enhance their studies. To top it all, the computer back home has improved their access to educational materials online and two of my brothers have completed PhDs while two others are in the process of completing theirs too.

Furthermore, another emigrant stated,

> The type of assistance I have made is financial. It was meant to help a relation complete medical school because his parents could not afford his school fees anymore. The assistance being sent home will not only benefit the recipient in completing his degree but his younger ones as well when he gets a job. I receive progress reports on his grades at school and he gets into less trouble now that he is engaged with studies. From every indication this will be a success story because not only is he in his final year but he is one of the best in his class and he is already guaranteed a job once he is done.

The preceding quotations confirm that remittances are not sent just to show off new found wealth in the land of sojourn. They are usually meant for human development and capacity building. Though the sender and recipient are miles apart, to maintain the existing social bond, African emigrants are obligated to send money home. These aspects of African culture are hereby validated. What follows is sense of relief and fulfillment for the senders knowing quite well that they are contributing to human capital at the area of origin.

Remittances received keep emigrants in mind. At the same time, the expression of appreciation by the receiver motivates further remittance-flow, thereby strengthening the social bond and contact between the emigrant and his/her kin in the country of origin. The assertion above was corroborated by an interviewee thus:

> ...there is a very big value attached to what is sent from abroad especially because the livelihood of parents at old age may be dependent on what is sent. The sender should however also relate responsibly with the parents by calling besides the money sent so that their joy may be full. Those living abroad should also be encouraged to return home someday. Ajo o dabi ile (a place of sojourn is unlike home).

In addition, we find that remittances enhance the prestige of family members in their communities as they go to receive USA Dollars from financial institutions such as MoneyGram and/or Western Union outlets or through unofficial channels, they exude a sense of the privilege few.

As another interviewee opined:

> That a person's close sibling stays abroad boosts the family social status. Especially if the person is the type that remembers home, the family's economic standard will be improved.

Furthermore, the non material component of remittances, that is, goods such as clothing, shoes, and computers become symbolic gestures that make recipients happy, connected, and valued. Clearly, remittances carry positive psychological impact on recipients. Moreover, senders are perceived as fortunate with clear advantages that make their family and friends look up to them. In the words of one interviewee,

> If you have somebody abroad, you have access to opportunities much faster than those who do not have relations abroad. You have more access to cash and technology. Their lifestyles and ideologies tend to impact their relations at home as the relations view those abroad as the ideal. Economic hardships make things difficult here in Nigeria but with a relation abroad, a lot of things could be made easier.

The findings further reveal that recipients place greater emphasis on their perception of the quality and durability of goods received from abroad as compared to those made in Nigeria. Recipients wear name brands sent from abroad; they stand out tall as the imported foreign goods give the impression of comfort, affluence, and care from kits and kin residing in the United States. The following statement from another interviewee bears evidence to the assertion:

> I have received gifts from friends and siblings abroad. What they have sent were usually better than the goods that may be procured in Nigeria. This is because what they use abroad is of better quality and value than what we have here. For example, American butter and tea will be better appreciated here. I remember that when my sister came with American tea, I appreciated it so much. I have received assistance financially. I have also received clothes, shoes

and many other goods. I consider the goods durable. You cannot compare it with a made in Nigeria product.

## Conclusion

Beyond the economic value that remittances convey, this chapter has shown that it is imbued with social values, which enhance social cohesion irrespective of the thousands of miles that separate emigrants from loved ones. Given that African emigrants are often motivated to travel to developed countries in order to gain access to socio-economic opportunities in the countries of destination, this chapter confirms that the African family structure that emphasizes interdependence, togetherness, sharing, maintaining family ties and cohesiveness serve as bases for remittance-flow. The analysis in this chapter reveals that remittances solidify social bonding and keep the meaning and essence of African family alive. Thus, this study elucidates the socio-cultural value of remittances as they serve as a unifying tool that connects the senders with their families and communities of origin.

## References

Adesina, O.C. and Adebayo, A.G. (2009) "Introduction: Globalization and Transnational Migrations: An Overview in Adebayo, A.G. and Adesina, O.C. (eds.) *Globalization and Transnational Migrations: Africa and Africans in the Contemporary Global System* (Newcastle upon Tyne) pp. 2-13.

Akanle, O. (2009) "Immigration Cultism and the Nigerian Migrants: Tidal Dynamism in the Age of Globalization" in Adebayo, A.G. and Adesina, O.C. (eds.) *Globalization and Transnational Migrations: Africa and Africans in the Contemporary Global System* (Newcastle upon Tyne) pp. 181-200.

Agarwal, M. and Sengupta, D. (1999) "Structural Adjustment in Latin America: Policies and Perfomance" *Economic and Political Weekly* Vol. 34 No. 44 pp. 3129-3136.

Angell, A. and Graham, C. (1995) "Can Social Sector reform Make Adjustment Sustainable and Equitable? Lessons from Chile and Venezuela" *Journal of Latin American Studies* Vol. 27 No. 1 pp. 189-219.

Balogun, S.K. and Olutayo, A.O. (2005/2006) "Globalization and the African Family System" *Psychopathologie* Vol. 33 No. 1 pp. 77-91.

Beetsma, R. and Debrun, X. (2004) "Reconciling Stability and Growth: Smart Pacts and Structural Reforms" *IMF Staff Papers* Vol. 51 No. 3 pp. 431-456.

Blau, P. (1964) *Exchange and Power in Social Relations.* (New York : John Wiley and Sons Limited).

# REFERENCES

Briggs, J. and Yeboah, I. (2001) "Structural Adjustment and the Contemporary Sub-Saharan African City" *Area* Vol. 33 No. 1 pp. 18-26.

Coontz, S. (2000) "Historical Perspectives on Family Studies" *Journal of Marriage and the Family* Vol. 62 No. 2 pp. 283-297.

Dollar, D. and Svenson, J. (2000) "What Explains the Success or Failure of Structural Adjustment Programmes?" *The Economic Journal* Vol. 110 No. 446 pp. 894-917.

Eckstein, S. (2004) "Dollarization and its Discontents: Remittances and the Making of Cuba in the Post-Soviet Era" *Comparative Politics* Vol. 36 No. 3 pp. 313-330.

Faust, J. (2004) "Latin America, Chile and East Asia: Policy-Networks and Successful Diversification" *Journal of Latin American Studies* Vol. 36 No. 4 pp. 743-770.

Florio, M. (2002) "Economists, Privatization in Russia and the waning of the 'washinton Consensus'" *Review of International Political Economy* Vol. 9 no. 2 pp. 359-400.

Folson, G. (1991) "Structural Adjustment in Ghana" in B. Turok (ed) *Alternative Strategies for Africa: Debt and Democracy* (London: Institute of African Alternatives) pp. 96-113.

Foster, H.J. (1983) "African Patterns in Afro-American Family" *Journal of Black Studies* Vol. 16 No. 2 pp. 201-232.

Haas, H. (2007) *Remittances, Migration and Social Development: A Conceptual Review of the Literature* Social Policy and Development Paper Number 34 (Geneva: United Nations Research Institute for Social Development).

Hermandez-Coss, R. and Bun, C.E. (2006) *The U.K.-Nigeria Remittance Corridor: Challenges of Embracing Formal transfer systems in a Dual Financial Environment* Second International Conference on migrant Remittances, London, November 13-14, 2006.

Ihonvbere, J. (1991) "Structural Adjustment in Nigeria" in B. Turok (ed) *Alternative Strategies for Africa: Debt and Democracy* (London: Institute of African Alternatives) pp. 73-95.

Joseph, A. (2007) "Nigerians Abroad Sent N 702bn home in 2006" *Punch* October 30.

Kapur, D. and McHale, J. (2003) "Migratio's New Payoff" *Foreign Policy* No. 139 pp.48-57.

McCornick, B. and Wahba, J. (2000) "Overseas Employment and Remittances to a Dual Economy" *The Economic Journal* Vol. 110, No. 463 pp. 509-534.

Mohan, G. and Zark-Williams A.B. (2002) "Globalisation from \below: Conceptualising the Role of the African Diasporas in Africa's Development" *Review of African Political Economy* Vol. 29 No. 92 pp. 211-236.

National Bureau of Statistics (2006) *Abstract of Statistics* Chapter 13 Retrieved from www.nigerianstat.gov.ng/annual_report.htm on 12 January 2009.

Ogundele, S.O. (2001) *Human Origins: A Critical Perspective* (Ibadan: John Archers (Publishers Limited).

Olutayo, A.O. and Omobowale, A.O. (2006) "The Youth and the Family in Transition in Nigeria" *Review of Sociology* Vol. 12 No. 2 pp. 85-95.

Omobowale, M.O. and Omobowale, A.O. (2009) "Culture and the Identity of Yoruba Women in a Globalized World" in Adebayo, A.G. and Adesina, O.C. (eds.) *Globalization and Transnational Migrations: Africa and Africans in the Contemporary Global System* (Newcastle upon Tyne) pp. 202-213.

Orozco, M. (2002) Globalization and Migration: the Impact of Family Remittances in Latin America" *Latin American Politics and Society* Vol. 44, No. 2 pp. 41-66.

Osili, U.O. (2007) "Understanding Migrants' Remittances: Evidence from the U.S.-Nigeria Migration Survey" from *Researching Migration: Stories from the Field* Accessed from www.ssrcm.org/org/pubs/researching_migration.pdf on January 5 2009.

Pearce, T.O. (2001) "Human Rights and Sociology: Some Observations from Africa" *Social Problems* Vol. 48 No. 1 pp. 48-56.

Pedersen, P. (2004) "Zimbabwe's Changing Freight Transport and Logistical System: Structural Adjustment and Political Change" *Journal of Southern African Studies* Vol. 30 no. 3 pp. 577-601.

Raghuram, S. Slevers, H. and Vyasulu, V. (1994) "Structural Adjustment: Industrial and Environmenttal Concerns" *Economic and Political Weekly* Vol. 29 No. 4 pp. 164-165.

Shariff, A., Ghosh, P., and Mondal, S. (2002) "State-Adjusted Public Expenditure on the Social Sector and Poverty Alleviation Programmes" *Economic and Political Weekly* Vol. 37 No. 8 pp. 767-787.

Shettima, K. (1993) "Structural Adjustment and Students Movement in Nigeria" *Review of African Political Economy* No. 56 pp. 83-91.

Sofola, J.A. (1973) *African Culture and the African Personality* IIbadan: African Resources Publishers)

# Endnotes

[1] Department of Sociology, University of Ibadan, Ibadan, Nigeria

[2] Department of Archaeology and Anthropology, University of Ibadan, Ibadan, Nigeria

[3] Department of Sociology, University of Ibadan, Ibadan, Nigeria

*Corresponding Author (e-mails: ao.omobowale@mail.ui.edu, muyiwaking@yahoo.com)

[4] The researchers tried to conduct interviews with Nigerians residents in the United Kingdom and Canada all to no avail. The contact persons in these countries also could not help.

# Chapter 8
## Religious Institutions

## Mode of Adaptation for African Immigrants in the U.S.A.

*Emmanuel K. Twesigye*

### Introduction

Drawing on the author's research[1] and personal story as an immigrant, this chapter looks at some characteristic religious traditions and practices of some recent African immigrants within the United States of America. Along with their diverse traditions, the African immigrants have brought with them their professional skills, African cultures, religions, and value systems. They pay most of the expenses for staying electronically connected with their relatives back in Africa. By doing so, the more recent African immigrants have been able to preserve their cultural, religious, and linguistic links with their countries of origin. At the same time, these African immigrants are also struggling to adopt new values and to modify their African cultures and religions at new destinations, where they also encounter more challenging liberal religious, moral, and secular cultural traditions.

It is interesting that most of the African immigrants, who came to Europe and North America in the last century, are not the products of the digital revolution. They represent more conservative traditional African values and heritage. In contrast to the more internationalized digital revolution generation, the older and more conservative African immigrants to North America, especially those, who consist of the pre-digital revolution African group, have faced more challenges, as they try to settle down in the USA. As a result, this paper focuses on some of the struggles to adapt to American cultural and religious environment. It will also show how African immigrants create new religious and cultural institutions or celebrate African cultural or religious events in order to provide new meaning and create a new identity within their host country as they seek to transform it into their new homeland. That is, they seek to create sacred African cultural spaces or institutions in order to replicate ways of life in their countries of origin.

### Creation of Conservative African Churches in the Diaspora

The Western conservative Christian missionaries created an African conservative Church[2] that currently condemns and rejects Western religious liberal traditions and secular values as manifestations of false Christianity. Today, many African Christians accuse the West of having become what Soren Kierkegaard had decried as "a pagan Christendom devoid of the essential and truly redemptive Christianity.[3] Subsequently, there are many African Evangelical Christians and fundamentalist leaders, who have affirmed that it was now the right time for the African Christian Church to send true Christian missionaries to re-evangelize and reconvert Europe back to true biblical Christianity. Some of these conservative Christians have come to the West as both African professionals and Christian missionaries. Some of them have settled in the West, including the United States of America. This group forms an important professional class of new African immigrants and spiritual leaders in both Europe and North America. They provide a professional, religious and cultural bridge between Africa and the West. They are effective conduits of both the African theocratic cultures or values and the Western values, including religions, languages, skills and the work ethic.

The African Christian leaders point to the fact that some American Catholic priests have betrayed the Church and Christ by engaging in alternative lifestyle such as homosexuality and by committing illegal acts including the molestation of the altar boys and girls. They also point fingers at the American Episcopal Church, which has accepted homosexuality and joined the Roman Catholic Church in accepting and teaching the theories of evolution as God's method for the creation of the universe, including human beings as the linguistic and intelligent creatures. The conservative African Evangelicals condemn Western Christians who accept such teachings as being false Christians who promote a false Christianity and sexual immorality in the Church.

The African Christian immigrants in Europe and the USA are dragged into these nasty theological feuds. As a result, many Africans have founded their own new African churches, temples and mosques to preserve the integrity of their religious, moral and cultural heritage. Homosexuality and secular Western values are still condemned as vices and sins to be rejected and avoided according to the African leaders and pastors of African Evangelical churches including the Anglican, Baptist, Methodist, Presbyterian and Pentecostal churches.

In the above respect, the African Muslims are akin to the Evangelical Christians on matters of homosexuality, family values, the subordination of women to men and scriptural literalism. They too have established either their own mosques or worship communities or joined the Sunni Muslim communities from North Africa and the Middle East. African Islam is ancient and more akin to the Sunni traditions of Saudi Arabia than the Shiite traditions of Iran and Southern Iraq. They have not joined the Nation of Islam. They are similar to the African Christian immigrants, who have preferred to either join the White Churches or establish their own new African congregations, instead of enthusiastically joining the existing African-American Churches, and both fully accepting them and adopting them as their own.

Many African Christians, especially the Anglicans, Baptists, Catholics, Methodists, Pentecostals and Presbyterians joined the well-established African-American churches, and found them more welcoming and liturgically exciting than the White churches. Nevertheless, some of them still wanted to establish their own culturally relevant African churches in which to feel at home. The African ministers, priests and pastors who were often invariably overlooked and marginalized in both white and African-American churches also wanted to establish their own churches in which they were the primary leaders and owners of the respective churches or temples' assets and control them as they wished.

Both the unemployed and the underemployed African immigrants with leadership experience in churches in their countries of origin found it more socially and economically pressing to establish their own African churches and other religious institutions. In these cases, it could be that economic motives are the main driving forces or it could also be that some religious leaders have "obeyed a higher spiritual calling." Moreover, the desire to worship according African socio-cultural norms are presented to the public and the African immigrants as the main reasons for establishing and running African-centered churches. This new African phenomenon is, in reality, parallel to what happened in the American history, when the African slaves were set free in the eighteenth century. In order to find their own identity, maintain freedom, dignity, and determine and assert their own values, they founded many African-American churches and co-related religious institutions, including schools and charitable organizations. Economic factors and the need to maintain their cultural identity appear to be the main motives behind the proliferation of Black churches and more recently, the founding of many African churches, temples, mosques, schools and other institutions connected with them.

In short, some Africans wanted to establish their own churches and mosques in order to serve as the leaders and determine the liturgy, language and preaching style as well as the topics and cultural or moral content of the sermons. For instance, some African Christians wanted sermons that promoted respect for the elders and the need for children to obey their parents.

**Immigration and Assimilation**

Most immigrants, including the Africans, tend to hang on tenaciously to their cultural, religious and social institutions and values in the host country until they have become secured enough to let them go. These societal institutions and their associated activities and membership rituals, serve as the new immigrants' and refugees' essential "life-line." The uprooted people hang on to them for their lives. In that context and understanding, African institutions, especially the religious institutions, such as churches and mosques, effectively perform psychological, religious, socioeconomic, and cultural functions that help to preserve moral values. To accomplish these goals, the majority of the African-led churches and other religious institutions have provided orientation programs and counseling services on matters dealing with immigration, education, employment, sexuality, marriage, and the American cultures and laws. They also provided charity and the needed fiscal resources, including funds for scholarships, housing and medical care. If an immigrant got into legal trouble, the religious community also collected money for bail and legal fees. In some cases, a member of the community volunteered to provide legal services *pro bono*, as a form of professional community service, religious piety and patriotism.

Furthermore, some American humanitarian and religious charitable organizations have assisted in immigration issues and secured the necessary visas and other travel documents for many Africans. This was particularly the case with the Sudanese refugees languishing in some squalid refugee camps in Northern Uganda, Kenya and Ethiopia, during the 1980s and 1990s. Some American churches and religious organizations provided bond and attorneys, when the new immigrants were in trouble, and legal advice or representation was required.

Moreover, some churches contributed money to pay the immigrants' airline tickets and to provide for housing while the immigrants were settling down. Others like those in Nashville, Tennessee, and some Muslims in Boston, Columbus, Ohio, Dallas, Dearborn, and St. Paul, often helped the newly arrived fellow Muslims. When an immigrant or close relative dies, the religious community also provides the necessary social, moral and fiscal support. The immigrant's religious community is expected to collect funds from its members or outside bodies and donate the money to defray the costs of the funeral and in some cases, for the transportation of the body for burial services in Africa. The immigrants' religious community also provides love, the ministry of presence, understanding, grief counseling, consolation, and thereby, effectively promoting spiritual and social healing to the bereaved family members. According to Lillian Asante, an African immigration attorney practicing law in Columbus, Ohio,[4] it is this African cultural and social overriding need for social belonging, community and mutual support which functions as the main driving force and identifiable main reason why most traditional Africans prefer to establish their own churches, mosques and temples.

## Challenges of Cultural Assimilation and Religious Adaptation: Creations of New Institutions by Immigrants

As some cases of the *Baganda* in Boston, the *Ethiopian Coptic* Christians in Washington, DC the *Somali* Muslims in Columbus and Minneapolis; the *Sudanese* Christians in Nashville and the *Ghanaian* Christians in Columbus and Baltimore; some *Nigerian* congregations in Boston and several other cities may indicate, many African immigrants have sought to preserve their own African cultural, linguistic and religious identity, while they settle down and live in the USA. Many of these groups have established their own religious congregations that use their own home languages for their African religious rituals, traditional ceremonies and religious services.[5]

An outsider can easily interpret this African religious and cultural phenomenon as a symbolic form of passive resistance to radical change and transformation of identity, or resistance to a threatening, or perceived life-transforming religious and major cultural changes, which would lead to surrendering their highly treasured African ethnic cultural and linguistic identity. That is, some more recent African immigrants will consciously adopt African cultural institutions in order to remain African and to resist cultural or religious changes that would lead them to become an "African-American" or a "Black-American," such as Louis Farrakhan, who simply identifies himself as a "Black Muslim" or as a member of the "Nation of Islam."

The above scenario is also in contrast to President Obama, who identifies himself as an "African-American," as opposed to being self-identified as a "Kenyan-American." Therefore, it is mainly due to cultural identity that the most recent African immigrants prefer to identify themselves with their ethnic group and members of their relatives, in their former home country. In contrast to their African immigrant parents, their children or the second generation is like President Obama, and they prefer to identify themselves merely as "African Americans." They are also both religiously and culturally distinctly American, and in many cases, they are also both culturally and religiously alienated from the Africa of their parents or grandparents. The East Africans sometimes derogatorily refer to this Westernized African generation as "*Bazungu*" (African Europeans),[6] whereas the *Twi* speakers of Ghana, in West Africa, call these Westernized Africans: "*Oburuni*" (cultural sell out or the cultural misfits).[7] However, these *Oburuni* also often despise the African religious and cultural traditionalists as the "*Okuraseni*" (native, rural, conservative or uncivilized).[8]

It is clear that religious and cultural adaptation or modification of the African immigrants is essential if they are to be fully culturally integrated. In the case of African students, the Western assimilation process takes place by careful design through programs of orientation and education. For instance, in the USA, citizens are socialized from birth to embrace American values such as free market economy (capitalist), patriotism, and the ability to use the English language as the main medium of communication. Accordingly, African immigrants to the United States are expected to adapt and adopt American values and other aspect of its cultural traditions if they are to succeed.

However, the majority of the Africans have continued to resist wholesale cultural and religious assimilation in order to fit into their societies of encounter. Some Somali Muslims have built mosques in their new USA residential communities in cities like Boston, Columbus in Ohio, Dallas, and both in Minneapolis and St. Paul in Minnesota. This is similar to the manner in which Jews have sought to preserve their own religious and ethnic identity by building synagogues in many cities in the USA. Similarly, the Muslims from the Middle East have built mosques in Toledo, Ohio, Dearborn and other cities in Michigan. Likewise, some wealthy American Hindus, as people of Indian descent, have built and opened a grand Hindu temple in Atlanta, Georgia. As such, the Africans who have both sought to establish, own and run their churches, temples and mosques in the USA are not unique in this cultural or religious aspect.

Historically, the African slaves also resisted complete assimilation by practicing their African Traditional Religions or Islam along with their slave masters' religions, including both Protestant and Catholic forms of Christianity. Subsequently, syncretic forms of new religions, such as *Santeria* and *Candamble,* emerged in the Caribbean where the former African slaves deliberately mixed their African religious traditions and Western Christianity in order to form something new that was uniquely African and yet, Western and Christian. This form of religious and cultural syncretism was designed to preserve the African religious world-view, religious beliefs and ritual practices in their new home-countries in the Christian West. This syncretism can also be regarded as cultural and religious resistance to western forms of cultural and religious assimilation and Western secularism. Hence, beliefs in the ancestral spirits, spirit possession, exorcisms, sacrifices and witchcraft are central to the African religious traditions and cultures. As such, when the African immigrants guard these cultural or religious traditions or practice them, it is a significant event for them. These practices represent deliberate attempts by these immigrants to preserve their own African heritage and cultures, as they remember or modify them and meaningfully seek to preserve them, especially within their new Western cultural and religious environment.[9] In any case, the new environment demands religious and cultural adaptation and reinterpretation of old African traditions, values and cultures in order to be able to confront and successfully meet the new challenges. As a result, Black churches that evolved from the experience of African churches during slavery and those that are created by recent African immigrants are different from white churches of the same denominations. This is because of their different cultures and world-views of their respective congregation members and ministers. For instance, most Black churches in America are characterized by their African style of worship, music, alter calls, use of drums, dancing, shouting, spirit filled, spirit led, healing sessions, and prophecy.

In spite of the differences, the African and the African-American institutions are culturally, politically and theologically unique as they are diverse. This is partly because these institutions are created and established as responses to a particular pressing need or set of challenges. Therefore, they are to be studied and understood in the specific cultural, religious, socioeconomic and political contexts in which they have emerged and operate. For instance, the Black Christian theology centers on issues of degradations of individual and institutional forms of racism, injustice, oppression, and Black consciousness.

The Nation of Islam, as "Black Islam" was founded by Elijah Muhammad and promoted by Minister Louis Farrakhan is also distinct from the traditional or mainline forms of Islam, such as Sunni or Shiite branches of Islam. The American form of Black Islam is characterized by Black consciousness, Black Liberation Theology, appeal to Black Power as an antidote to degradations of Western white-supremacist racism. Additionally, it seeks to reject the dehumanizing racist doctrines of innate Black racial inferiority and the promotion of positive family values and practical anti-poverty acts of socioeconomic self-empowerment and the establishment of Black businesses for self-development.

Likewise, American Black churches have also attempted to accomplish the same task of Black self-empowerment and economic advancement within the American society. That is partly why the mainline Black churches have finally embraced the scholarship of W. E. B. DuBois, Dr. Martin Luther's radical moral vision of Civil Rights and justice for all citizens as equals before God and the law; radical Liberation Theology and Black Power as cautiously articulated by some Black liberation movement leaders and theologians like Malcolm X, Louis Farrakhan, James Cone, G. Gilmore, Peter Paris, G. Washington and others. It was at the secular and more political level that the more radical Black youth wing of the Civil Rights Movement most eagerly adopted Stockley Carmichael's new militant ideology of Black Power.

## African Religion as Basis for African Human Consciousness, Meaningful Life and Identity

According to Professor John Mbiti, Africans are incurably religious people.[10] The traditional Africans view themselves, the community, life and the world through the theocentric cultural lenses of religion, community and nature as God's sacred gifts by God's eternal will, holiness and creation. Africans, based on their world-view and God-centered life, are essentially social and religious mystics. In other words, they are not necessarily intellectually aware of cultural nature and centrality of their spiritual and ritualistic activities of daily life. Africans are also not aware of the mystical and sacramental means to engage in supernatural communication with God, and attain redemptive fellowship with God, in communion with the ancestral spirits and other divine mysteries that reside within nature and the local environment, such as lakes, rivers, big trees, forests and holy mountains.

Some traditional African priests and mystics claim to possess the sacred powers to communicate with animals and to harness the supernatural powers of God as manifested in nature to effect cures of deadly diseases and perform miracles. These miracles include claims of rain making during dry seasons. Likewise, these rainmakers are expected to stop the rain when it becomes excessive or when there is a communal function such as a wedding or another festive occasion. However, those rainmakers who are ignored and not invited to attend such functions are believed to use their supernatural powers to cause it to rain and ruin the festive occasions. This is believed to be done so as to punish the people who had overlooked them and not paid them their due respect. To the skeptics, these claims are false because these priests have failed to produce badly needed rains in Ethiopia and Kenya during dry seasons and severe droughts that have killed many cattle and thousands of people whose livelihoods depended on the cattle and the agricultural produce. In any case, if the rain makers truly existed in Africa, there would not be any deserts like the Sahara and Kalahari.

Nevertheless, the above kinds of African uncritical traditional religious faith, teachings, beliefs, superstitions, and cultural beliefs, and their correlative magical practices exist even among many Western educated people. It is therefore, significant to note that these central African cultural and religious beliefs and practices are also transported with the Africans into their new countries including the USA. For instance, some African immigrants pray for good weather when they have their meetings, church parties and weddings despite their awareness of Western reliance on weather forecast. And if rain or snow ruins the planned functions, and if people were in the open, then the religious congregation may begin to believe that their priests, pastors, and Imam were not mystically powerful because they could not avert the destruction caused by nature. Therefore, they believed that God did not hear or honor their prayers for good weather because of their personal moral imperfections and sins.

For these Africans, religion is not just a holy path to God and the final attainment of salvation. It is the true power to energize the believers and other people and their communities to become truly human, and to become self-consciously aware that they are truly the unique divine creatures as sons and daughters of God in the world. This realization empowers the devout Africans to face the world courageously, defy the barriers of racism, homesickness, cultural or social isolation, loneliness, and depression.

Many devout African immigrants, regardless of whether they are Muslim or Christian work two jobs to feed, house and educate their children, and yet boldly affirm that since God is their heavenly Father and Provider, they cannot fear any adversity such as racism and underemployment. Most of them attend African-based churches. Some of the church members including pastors still use their African languages such as Twi, Yoruba, Amharic, Swahili as the medium of liturgy and worship in services so as to maintain their cultural and religious heritage and mystical links with the African ancestors and relatives who were left behind in their countries of origin.

Twi, for instance, is used as the preferred and most meaningful language of worship and preaching for the Ghanaian community because some recent immigrants cannot speak English or follow sermons in English. In essence, the Ghanaian Community Church re-created the African traditions of rural Ghana, thereby minimizing the sense of detachment from their culture. As a result, the church serves as a mechanism whereby a community of caring people provides love and mutual support for one another in the Diaspora. By establishing African religious churches or mosques, and by using African languages as the medium of the liturgy and worship, such as the African immigrant community minimizes the feelings of being uprooted. This process of African cultural, linguistic and religious self-reaffirmation provide the necessary African cultural, social and religious continuity. They also serve as practical and effective tools for the recent immigrants to enable them to become reasonably well-settled in their new country without losing their own essential and meaningful identity, language, religious traditions and values. This is because religion provides a nurturing environment that also enables recent immigrants to make new friends and to become integrated within the cultures and traditions of their newly adopted country.

## Conclusion: A Personal Story of Professional Trial, Faith and Experience as an African Immigrant

The story of African immigrants has some correlative names, professionals and faces that go with specific stories and experiences. It is not a faceless story. It is the story and existential experience of real people and their unique histories, experiences, cultures, values and religious traditions, which they brought with them to the USA as African immigrants, refugees, students and professionals. Some people's experiences may be unique but they may have relevance to the African collective experience, especially the first or second generation of immigrants in the USA. Given their varied background, the experiences of African immigrants can significantly contribute to the cultural and religious richness and international outlook of the United States; a country of great diversity with a capacity for both flexible pluralism and tolerance for inclusiveness. In this respect, I draw on my own story as one example of the many African stories of immigrants coming to America as either political refugees or professionals. The story is told to illustrate how some African professionals, priests, professors and politicians who were forced to emigrate to Europe and the USA, may significantly differ from each other. Nevertheless, they have all significantly contributed to the formation of this new important diverse group of African professionals, who are immigrants within the USA. Their work and experiences are part of the African immigrant experience. Some of them consciously contribute to the African programs to welcome, mentor and help new African students and immigrants to settle down and become meaningfully integrated within their new religious, cultural and political environment in the USA.

There are some other professionals who may relate to this story as political or religious refugees and immigrants in the USA. Some of these professionals include the Anglican bishops like Benon Ogwal who fled his Diocese in Northern Uganda due to civil war there in the 1980s and the Rt. Rev. Benjamin Omusebi of Kano Diocese, in Northern Nigeria, who fled from his diocese in the early 1990s as a result of violent clashes between Christians and the fundamentalist Muslims. These are some examples of alienated and persecuted African professionals who were forced to flee to Europe or North America either for their political views or religious activities that included liberation theology, truth telling and prophetic ministries critical of political leaderships in their countries of origin.

My own story of immigration is rooted in Uganda's political instability and President Idi Amin, a fundamentalist Muslim, who through his reign of terror made an attempt to force Islam on Ugandans, from 1971 to 1979. As a teacher of political history at Makerere University, an Anglican Chaplain and Head of the Department of Religious Education at the National Teachers College (University), I had been directed to conduct a special course to prepare selected Muslims as teachers and chaplains. After graduation, they were expected to serve as teachers of religion as well as Muslim chaplains in public Secondary Schools. I had previously conducted a similar two-year course that was open to students of all religious backgrounds; so I did not see the need to construct a course tailor-made for Muslim students. This did not sit well with President Amin. Tragically, he misinterpreted my professional activities as political defiance to his presidential decree, and personally held me and the Most Rev. Janani Luwum, the Anglican Archbishop of Uganda, as enemies of Islam and his policies.

President Amin and some of his advisors also believed that I was the real stumbling block to his programs for the Islamization of schools and colleges, since I was responsible for this professional aspect of education. He also suspected that I influenced the Anglican Archbishop and bishops to resist and denounce his Islamization programs in the government appointments and the military. He also viewed the play I had been commissioned to write in celebration of the Anglican Church's century in Uganda in 1977 as a form of sedition and treason. Subsequently, the Anglican Archbishop Janani Luwum was assassinated; an act that forced me to flee to Kenya and later to the USA as a political refugee.

As stated earlier, the role of religion has been extremely important to immigrants. For instance, in my own case, during my exile here in the USA, the Episcopal Church has served as my family's host, friend, protector and has provided the necessary fiscal and professional support. Without our friends in the Episcopal Church like the late Bishop David Birney and Professor Urban Holmes III, Dean of the University of the South, Sewanee, Tennessee, and the faculty members of the University of the South and Vanderbilt University, and the Sisters of St. Mary of Sewanee Saint Mary's Convent, in Tennessee, we would have been lost. Bishop Hebert Thompson, Jr. Diocesan bishop of Southern Ohio Diocese and the priests of St. Peter's Church and the chaplain and faculty of Ohio Wesleyan University have extended a warm welcome, friendship and support without which the quality of my life and that of my family in exile, and as African immigrants, would have been terribly diminished and impoverished. In my case as in others, religion has been a strong factor that has positively defined my life and enabled me to succeed. Religion has provided me with the necessary fundamental grounding in positive faith, and God's impenetrable destiny for my life. My parents' exemplary life of faith and prayer has been unconsciously inherited and has influenced me to hope for a better future and by faith to accept some reliance on God's providence, hope and power to exist meaningfully as a member of God's Global Family and community. My faith in divine providence and protection supported me, even when storms of life and uncertainty threatened my life.

Again in my case as well as in that of many African immigrants, while I gained some Western religious and cultural heritage long before I came to the West, at the same time, I lost the chance of ever becoming truly African in cultural, religious and social aspects of heritage. Further, my immigration to the West has alienated me from African roots and therefore it is a great opportunity to find African community and worship with them. It renews my soul.

On the positive side, my religious tradition being Catholic or universal in its theological and liturgical expression has provided me with the unique opportunities to belong to God's universal Church and community that transcends the barriers of nationality, race, color, gender and class. This is also the positive experience and testimony of many other religious Africans who belong to the mainline universal religious traditions, including the Sunni Muslims, Methodists, Presbyterians and Catholic Christians and others who belong to religious traditions which have global branches and operations.

## Endnotes

[1] For instance, see Emmanuel Twesigye, *Common Ground: Christianity, African Religion and Philosophy* (New York: Peter Lang, 1987); *The Global Human Problem: ignorance, Hate, Injustice and Violence* (New York: Peter Lang, 1988); *God, Race, Myth and Power: an Africanist Corrective Research Analysis* (New York: Peter Lang, 1991); *African Religion, Philosophy, and Christianity in Logos-Christ: Common Ground Revisited* (New York: Peter Lang, 1996); *Religion and Ethics for a New Age: Evolutionary Approach* (Cambridge: UPA, 2001).

[2] For example, see Roland Oliver & J.D. Fage, *A Short History of Africa* (Baltimore: Penguin Books, 3rd Edition, 1970), 135-262; Holger Bern Hansen and Michael Twaddle, editors, *Religion & Politics in East Africa* (Athens: OUP, 1995; Adrian Hastings, *African Christianity* (New York: Seabury Press, 1976); A. Hastings, *Church and Mission in Africa* (London: Burns and Bates, 1967); John Mbiti, *African Religions and Philosophy* (London: Heinemann), 1969; Kwensi Dickson and P. Ellingsworth, *Biblical Revelation and African Beliefs* (London: Lutterworth Press, 1969).

[3] Soren Kierkegaard, *Collected Works of Kierkegaard* (Princeton: Princeton UP, 1960).

[4]Lillian Asante is a Ghanaian Christian and a lawyer. She established her own law firm called: *Asante Law Firm, Inc.* She was interviewed on September 8, 2007, at her office. She works with African churches to meet legal needs of the African immigrants, especially those from West Africa. There were more that 20 people waiting to see her when I got there at 4: 00 pm. It was clear that immigration attorneys may have as much ministry to extend to the African immigrants as some African religious leaders. Their combined ministry to the African immigrants and refugees, especially those facing deportations or in trouble with the law for other reasons is essential to the well-being of the African immigrant communities in North America or other Western countries.

[5]I have attended some of these services. They are exuberant. The singing and dancing is very characteristic of these African services. They are Pentecostal-like or charismatic.

[6]Some of my own African traditionalist relatives have indicated that I am culturally alienated by derogatorily by referring to me, during my absence, as a rich "*Muzungu*" (European). The equivalent term is the African-American reference to as assimilated African-American as an "*Oreo.*" "*Oreo*" is a derogatory comparison of a Black person to a cookie, which is black on the outside and white in the inside. This cultural information was collaborated by Professor Trace Regan, Chair, Dept. of Journalism, Ohio Wesleyan University.

[7]See Professor Ali Mazrui's classic film documentary called, *The Africans*. It portrays some Africans worshipping and behaving as Europeans and White Americans, whereas the African-Americans were trying to dress, worship and behave as the native or traditional Africans. The film, *Roots* is another good illustration of this African religious and cultural dilemma.

[8]The information was confirmed by Professor Randy Quaye, the Director of Black World Studies, Ohio Wesleyan University. He comes from Ghana and he is also familiar with factors and problems of African generation tension and societal phenomena of cultural and religious Westernization, urbanization that lead to alienation of some Africans.

[9]This process is similar to what the African slaves did in the Caribbean and Latin America. *Rastafarianism, Voodoo* and traditions and practices represent these African attempts and results of syncretism or modification and adaptations of the African religious traditions to Christianity and Western culture.

[10]See John Mbiti, *African Religions and Philosophy*, 1-11.

# Chapter 9
## The African Diaspora's Impact on Homeland National Identity

*Okechukwu Iheduru*

## Introduction

This chapter examines the changing relations between African countries and their diasporic populations, using the interaction between recent Ghanaian and Nigerian immigrants and their homeland governments as a case study. It focuses on two major interrelated questions: First, how are homeland attitudes toward kin-diasporas and diaspora involvement in public life in homeland affairs being transformed over time and why? Second, how do these homeland/diaspora-related changes affect conceptions of national and cultural identities within the home country and among the diaspora themselves? These questions are particularly interesting in the context of new types of complex and elaborate opportunities and sites of interaction between emigrants the world over and their ancestral homelands which have developed as a result of the growth of transnationalism.[1] It argues that migrant transnationalism, i.e., a process initiated either by governments or the diaspora itself, to encourage the diaspora to reconnect with their homelands, has had significant impact on the national identities of many African emigrant states as evidenced by market reforms targeting the diaspora, redefinitions in the philosophy and practice of citizenship and nationality laws and exercise of the accompanying rights of citizenship, as well as the influence of new media and technologies of mass communication on national integration and identity formation.

In order to explore these transformations in diaspora-homeland relations, the chapter first maps out the transformations in African state's perception of emigration and situates these changes within the global scholarship focusing on the hitherto neglected repercussions of diasporas' influences on homelands. This is followed by an analysis of four dimensions of national identity-transforming African diaspora interventions, namely diaspora remittances, investments and other economic activities; renegotiation of citizenship and nationality laws; diaspora membership and participation in homeland political associations within the homeland and from abroad; and finally the impact of African diaspora cyber-citizenship and cyber-political activities on the conceptions of national and cultural identities within their home countries.

### Globalization, the Diaspora and Transformations in National Identity

Until recently, scholarship on the political impacts of immigrants or diasporas focused largely on the repercussions of diasporic influences on foreign policy and issues of national identity and loyalty within the host-states. Conceptualizations of transnational political activities were restricted to migrant political activities in the host-state dealing exclusively with issues of interest to the home-state;[2] activities to improve immigrants' social status in the host state;[3] or initiatives of migrants or their communities to provide concrete support to specific localities in their homeland.[4]

Over the last decades, scholars have begun to give due recognition to the critical roles played by several diasporas in helping to attain homeland political goals such as national self-determination and the removal of dictatorial regime; while others have explored the contributions of the diaspora to national economic rebirth. For instance, the Greek-American diaspora has had a great impact on the evolution of the Greek state.[5] More recently, newly democratized countries in Eastern Europe have looked to their U.S.-based diasporas as an important source of economic investment and as important players in mediating and improving relations between the United States and the homeland. In China, the financial flows from expatriate residents abroad, which in recent decades have generated much of the volume of foreign investment, have brought about significant changes in the perception of the national status of Chinese diasporic communities both inside China and in their countries of domicile—especially in southeast Asian countries such as Indonesia, Malaysia, and the Philippines. The diaspora also played a critical role in the development of the South Korean economy.[6] In Israel, where in the past diasporic money was a major influence on the general economy, today partisan flows to political and cultural factions have a substantial impact.[7]

Diaspora involvement in these emigrant states has led to fundamental changes in homeland perception of the diaspora, namely the concept of membership and national identity evidenced in "re-territorialization" strategies that define diaspora as imagined "national territory" where the emigration state can project national authority and identity extra-territorially.[8] Traditionally, citizenship encompassing legal status, rights, participation, and belonging was anchored in a particular geographic and political community; hence, the concept evokes notions of national identity, sovereignty, and state control.[9] As globalization has deepened, these relationships are increasingly challenged by the scope and diversity of international migration, scholarship on citizenship has consequently shifted from exclusive focus on nation-states where most discussion centered on ethnic versus civic citizenship, multiculturalism, and assimilation, to studies that look at transnational, post-national, and dual citizenships, especially the normative and empirical implications of citizenship shared between those residing within the country and those that reside far away beyond its borders.[10]

As many African states have joined the ranks of emigrant states, they have also responded to these transnational flows by re-calibrating the nexus between the state and citizens.[11] Their new postures towards their emigrants or diasporas contrast with the Marshallian concept of citizenship as an instrument of closure with legal-constitutional and political-institutional realms of membership which they adopted at independence.[12] From the 1960s to the 1980s, many Africans on the continent considered migrants, especially the skilled ones emigrating to developed countries or those of them that failed to return after their studies, as deserters from this imagined community who had forsaken their impoverished homeland for the comforts of Western societies after receiving their education at the expense of taxpayers. From the 1980s onward and as African economies fell into deep decline and many states faced serious fiscal crises, African citizens—at first the highly skilled but later the unskilled classes as well—embarked on "exodus" to escape the worsening crises.[13] Several others were forced out by wars, natural disasters, and repressive regimes unwilling to brook any opposition to stifling structural adjustment programs foisted on them by international financial institutions and donor nations that had intervened to rescue these African states from their fiscal crisis.[14] Inevitably, some used the relative freedom and safety of exile to mount campaigns against some of the homeland governments, while others sponsored anti-state and pro-democracy groups back home. Consequently, it is not uncommon to see the diaspora variously portrayed as "lost sons" or social deviants who would rather sell their souls to emigrate than tough it out in the country and "contribute their own quota" in nation-building;[15] or as "coward failures."[16] While not all African émigrés can be so broadly categorized, the economic and political development consequences of a disproportionate number of the region's highly skilled people streaming out of the continent in search of "greener pastures" the West and the rich petro-states of the Arabian Peninsula cannot be underestimated.[17]

Yet, many African emigrants are the unsung heroes who are substituting for collapsed social welfare systems in Africa, albeit at the level of the individual and the family, since the early 1980s as structural adjustment programs and fiscal crisis of the state led to retrenchments in government social welfare infrastructural functions in almost every country.[18] More than any immigrants from the developing world, Africans are routinely stigmatized by the impoverishment of their homeland and embarrassed by Africa's political and socioeconomic failures. Most of them have retained homeland affinities as evidenced by the proliferation of homeland associations and the passion with which they engage in homeland issues or respond to extreme loyalty initiatives, such as the 2 percent diaspora tax enthusiastically paid by the diaspora to the Eritrean state.[19]

As their economic and political profile began to change from temporary visitors to permanent residents and citizens of their adopted countries with attractive incomes and assets, African governments have moved to tap into their accumulating human capital and financial resources now seen as critical to homeland development.[20] At least tentatively, the view that national identity and citizenship could be exercised extra-territorially is being mulled over as the diaspora is exhorted to see their contribution to national development as a "moral obligation."[21]

The African experience thus fits the global trend by which diasporas who may at one point be considered enemies of a (dictatorial) home regime and as a result suffer from "blackmail, surveillance, threats and other intimidations abroad,"[22] may, over time, come to be considered by a new regime as the key population for domestic transformation.[23] Hence, Morton Grodzin observed years ago that home regimes tend to manipulate citizenship as a carrot-and-stick mechanism on the assumption that naturalization and denaturalization are not always final acts: "all patriots are potential traitors" and vice versa.[24]

### The Economic Dimension of Diaspora Impact

Although African states are relatively latecomers to diaspora engagements, the impact of the contributions of the African diaspora to homeland economic development surpasses those of traditional emigrant states. The economic dimension of this diaspora-homeland impact comes in various forms, namely remittance flows; support of poverty alleviation; diaspora investments; and new directions in the search for alternative investment funds by both the state homeland business communities.

*(a) Diaspora Remittance Gold Mine:* Over the last decade, diaspora remittances have turned into a gold mine for which African governments. Table 1 below shows that the aggregate amount of annual inward flows of remittances into sub-Saharan Africa grew from a mere US3.2 billion in 1995 to US$10.8 billion in 2007, while outward flows rose from US$2 billion to US$2.9 billion during the same period.

Table 1: Sub-Saharan Africa Migrants' Remittances (1995-2007)

| (US$ billion) | 1995 | 2000 | 2001 | 2002 | 2003 | 2004 | 2005 | 2006 | 2007e |
|---|---|---|---|---|---|---|---|---|---|
| **Inward flows** | 3.2 | 4.6 | 4.7 | 5.0 | 6.0 | 8.0 | 9.3 | 10.3* | 10.8 |
| All developing countries | 57.5 | 84.5 | 95.6 | 115.9 | 143.6 | 161.3 | 191.2 | 221.3 | 239.7 |
| **Outward flows** | 2.0 | 2.5 | 2.3 | 2.5 | 2.8 | 3.0 | 3.3 | 2.9** | |
| All developing countries | 12.4 | 11.5 | 13.6 | 20.4 | 23.8 | 30.9 | 36.0 | 44.2 | |

Notes

\* 1.6 percent of GDP in 2006.

\*\* 0.4 percent of GDP in 2006. This table reports officially recorded remittances. The true size of remittances, including unrecorded flows through formal and informal channels, is believed to be larger.

Source: *The World Bank, 2008*.

According to the World Bank, inward remittance flows to SSA per annum ballooned from US$3.2 billion in 1995 to roughly $10.8 in 2007, totaling about $93 billion to Africa from 1995-2005, and second only to foreign direct investment (FDI) as a source of external financing. According to the World Bank, in over nine years, $28 billion was sent through the Western Union to Nigeria alone, while the Bank of Ghana tracked $1.3 billion between 2002 and 2003.

The Top 10 recipients of these remittances (in raw dollar amounts) in 2007 were Nigeria ($3.3 billion), Kenya ($1.3 billion), Sudan ($1.2 billion), Senegal ($0.9 billion), Uganda ($0.9 billion), South Africa ($0.7 billion), Lesotho ($0.4 billion), Mauritius ($0.2 billion), Togo ($0.2 billion), and Mali ($0.2 billion). The attraction of diaspora remittances becomes much clearer when we consider remittances as a percentage of the GDP. The Top 10 remittance recipients in 2006 in this case were Lesotho (24.5 percent), The Gambia (12.5 percent), Cape Verde (12.0 percent), Guinea-Bissau (9.2 percent), Uganda (8.7 percent), Togo (8.7 percent), Senegal (7.1 percent), Kenya (5.3 percent), Swaziland (3.7 percent), and Benin (3.6 percent).

Specific country experiences amplify the significance of migrant remittances. According to the World Bank, the US$1.3 billion remitted by Kenya's émigrés in 2007 put the country in the second position (after Nigeria with $3.3 billion), and constituted about 5 percent of the share of the GDP.[25] Eritrea and Somalia critically depend on remittances, while Zimbabwe's economic collapse would have been far worse were more than half of its population to lose their lifeline from remittances from émigrés.[26] The Bank of Ghana (central bank) reports that the annual diaspora remittances of over US$1.5 billion now surpasses annual earnings from either cocoa or gold.[27] These amounts do not include undocumented funds brought in by returning emigrants who undertake a variety of albeit uncoordinated social and economic development projects across Africa. This makes the African diaspora Africa's biggest "aid donor;" changing the debate from "brain drain" to "brain circulation" or "brain gain" celebrating the development potential of the African diaspora via their remittances to the homeland.[28]

Consequently, many African states have designed a variety of migrant remittance capture strategies and policies. First, despite the persistence of old bureaucratic habits persist, many African states have recently liberalized the money transfer business, especially by breaking the monopoly of Western Union International Financial Services and allowing the entry of Moneygram and local money transfer operators and the post office (mainly in Ghana). They have also granted approval for banks and other financial institutions to create "Non-Resident Products" to enable them to tap into the diaspora wealth. In Nigeria, banks created a more liberal domiciliary accounts regime to entice the diaspora to open and operate a bank account in Nigeria while resident overseas. In some cases, the race to capture diaspora funds has led to deliberate refusal to enforce money laundering laws which Africa's commercial and central banks were compelled to adopt under the Basel II financial accords, and which would otherwise stifle the inflow of remittances.[29] In Kenya, the government established the Kenya Investment Authority in September 2007 to market Kenya to potential domestic and international investors and guarantee them of the safety of their investments. Some segments of the private sector were also recruited to join the hunt for diaspora wealth. For instance, since 2006, the East African Breweries—east and central Africa's primary brewing company—has been vigorously pushing the sale of its popular *Tusker Mart* beer brand to the regional diaspora. The brand can now be found in many mainstream grocery stores in the UK, Australia, Canada, and the United States.[30]

African state's remittance-capture strategies are also target the old African diaspora in the Caribbean and the Americas.[31] African-Americans reportedly control over US$600 billion of the U. S. GDP which is nearly twice the total GDP of all of sub-Saharan Africa. In addition to their wealth, African leaders value the entry points or access into the global civil society that a few of the more well-connected among them provide for their elite counterparts back on the continent.

*(b) Diaspora Investments and Extra-Territorial Capital Drive:* In alliance with the World Bank, International Organization for Migration, and other diaspora-targeted NGOs, several low income African countries have pursued a systematic policy of diaspora-financed development. A Ugandan exile and president of United African Federation USA thus claimed that:

> Ugandans living abroad are our unconditional donors and investors, and are the best economic partners that Uganda has at the moment. It is important to include Ugandans in the Diaspora in our ongoing debates, to be respectful, to listen to their input, and to avoid demonizing, dismissing, or deeming them irrelevant. Ugandans in the diaspora should become our economic ambassadors so that we can build on the achievements of the NRM [National Resistance Movement] Government [of Yoweri Museveni].[32]

Many countries also routinely hold investment "summits" or send official delegations (sometimes led by presidents and/or prime ministers, central bank governors or leaders of stock exchanges and banks) to Africans overseas to "sensitize" them about investment opportunities in their homeland. The state of Senegal which derives about 7.1 percent of its GDP from diaspora remittances perhaps has the most elaborate of these economic mission strategies. The Minister of Senegalese Diaspora regularly travels to major cities around the world with large concentrations of the Senegalese diaspora to hold "working sessions" with the diaspora about their living conditions and strategies to encourage large in-flows of savings back in the country.[33]

In Uganda, the $1 billion per year its diaspora remits to the country (about 8.7 percent of its GDP) compelled the government to quickly initiate a bill in 2007 to amend the law granting dual citizenship to the diaspora. If implemented, the amended law would allow Ugandan diaspora to enjoy the concessional rates of investment (US$50,000) given to Ugandans applying for investor licenses, instead of subjecting them to the same US$100,000 currently charged to foreigners.[34] In his keynote address at the 19th annual Ugandan North American Association conference in San Francisco on 1 September 2007, the Ugandan vice president implored the diaspora to scale up from "sending money to your mother to buy a blanket, or to eat for the next two weeks" to funding income-generating projects for their relatives, urging the diaspora to buy cows for producing milk, chickens for eggs, mango or apple trees, and even bees for honey. As he put it, "You can earn money everyday from this cow; why don't you buy her [a cow]?"[35]

Despite its anti-diaspora citizenship policies, the government of Zimbabwe sees its 3.4 million non-resident Zimbabweans as critical to the economic rejuvenation of its battered economy. In 2004, overseas Zimbabweans sent home US$55 million, representing 3.2 percent of total inflows, while a further US$13.6 million was received from abroad in the first quarter of 2005. In order to facilitate these remittances, the Reserve Bank of Zimbabwe in 2004 launched the "Homelink" money transfer scheme through a massive awareness campaign that took a team led by the central bank governor to the US, UK, and South Africa.[36] In the Great Lakes subregion, the Rwanda Diaspora Global Convention held in January every year focuses exclusively on how Rwandans living abroad—who remit an estimated US$40 million to the country annually—can contribute to the development of the country.[37]

The Malian government has since 2006 been sending economic missions to European and other capitals to promote the return to Mali of members of *Maliens de l'éntranger*—diaspora—who remit an estimated $150 million - $200 million per year to invest in irrigated commercial agriculture through the *Office du Niger irrigation* scheme. Similarly, the Government of Southern Sudan has invited the Sudanese diaspora to invest in development of information technology and particularly in FM radio stations, production and broadcasts in 10 provinces of southern Sudan, saying it is a lucrative business. The government offered to give priority to the issuance of operating license to the diaspora than other investors in this area.[38]

Since the re-introduction of democratic government in 1999, Nigeria has shown greater appreciation of the potentially positive contributions of migrant remittances to national development. The economic reforms embarked by the Obasanjo administration, namely the controversial privatization of large state-owned companies, rationalization of banking and insurance sectors, and legal and corporate governance reforms especially in the capital market, finally compelled the country's private sector with substantial prodding from government, to pursue a diaspora remittance development strategy.[39] Until the onset of the global economic melt-down in 2008, several Nigerian firms embarking on initial public offering (IPO) in the stock market undertook various "road shows" to market their offers to Nigerians and foreign investors in the United States and the United Kingdom who the Nigerian Stock Exchange (NSE) claimed collectively held assets in excess of US$100 billion outside Nigeria.[40] Diaspora IPO "road shows" were much more routine for banks scrambling to raise enough capital to meet the N25 billion base capital requirement imposed by the Central Bank of Nigeria as part of its "rationalization" program that pruned down the number of banks to 25 in 2006 from a previous high of 98 little extremely weak banks.[41] Other sectors of the economy such as investment securities, infrastructure, estate developers, insurers, etc. have similarly aggressively mobilized to develop attractive products for the Nigerian diaspora. The Nigerian diaspora are also credited with causing the steep growth and bull market run on the Nigerian capital market between 2000 and 2006, although this trend has been virtually halted as a result of the stock market crash resulting in a loss of over 60 percent of its value in late 2008 following the global financial meltdown.[42]

*(c) Poverty Alleviation Projects and Programs:* As noted earlier, African emigrants have engaged in a variety of long-distance social welfare obligations, albeit at the level of family and communities, years before their governments and their foreign development partners started making moves to publicly acknowledge and recognize them.[43] Recently, governments have begun to draw up strategies to recruit diaspora to shore up more than two decades of failed World Bank "poverty alleviation" programs generally instituted in response to criticisms arising from SAP-induced poverty in every country that swallowed this neoliberal pill since the early 1980s.[44] For instance, Nigeria's national *Poverty Reduction Strategy Program*—locally called National Economic Empowerment and Development Strategy (NEEDS)—seeks to "continue to actively strengthen links with Nigerians and other Africans in the diaspora to deepen technical and business ties with the rest of the world, and improve export market penetration, especially in textiles, food, and cultural artifacts" as part of government policy to half poverty by 2020.[45] In 2006, the National Poverty Eradication Program (NAPEP) initiated a program that enlisted the enthusiastic support of diaspora to implement its "Give Back Program" targeting wealthy Nigerians abroad in the fight against poverty.[46]

By pulling all the stumps in the quest for diaspora financial and human resources, African states are indirectly looking to on-load statutory functions they have clearly failed to accomplish on the diaspora, but at the same time, clinging to a firm grip on their juridical power. The role assigned to the diaspora (the *nkuba kyeyos*, as Ugandans call them) as legitimacy props for the state is amplified by none other than President Museveni himself in an address to the Ugandan Diaspora in Boston, USA in 2005:

> No country can develop unless its citizens invest their capital. The foreign investors are good, but they usually do not go beyond the search for profits. Therefore you are Uganda's most precious investors ...Last year [2004], Ugandans living abroad remitted [US]$358 million. This contrasts sharply with the [US]$480 million that your 24.7 million resident in Uganda earned for the country through export of goods. This means that you who live away from home make more significant per capita contribution than your brothers and sisters living inside Uganda.[47]

In the same vein, the chairman of the diaspora committee of the NRM USA—the country's ruling party—urged the Ugandan government to pursue a "guest worker visa" treaty with the United States to enable Ugandans to work in the US and return home with their earnings as another strategy to take full advantage of the economic potential for the Ugandan diaspora. Ironically, NRM USA and other pro-government diaspora organizations have been vociferous in their opposition to dual citizenship and granting of the vote to Ugandans abroad. Many of these emigrants were forced out by the authoritarianism and human rights abuses of the Museveni regime which has ruled Uganda since 1986. Other countries may even be testing the limits of their reliance on the diaspora miracle. Indeed, African leaders are literally placing their proverbial begging bowls at the feet of the diaspora now seen as alternative to aid-weary developed world.[48]

## African Diaspora and Changes in Citizenship Laws

Since colonial times, citizenship laws have played a central role in both exacerbating and managing conflict and development in Africa.[49] Over the past two decades, globalization pressures have heightened the saliency of migrant flows from and within these multi-ethnic societies, forcing African governments to re-juggle the contradictions of their erstwhile exclusionist citizenship and nationality laws, especially the idea of "autochthony" which has become increasingly subject to constant redefinition against new "others" and at ever-closer range."[50] The result is that many of these countries have now joined other emigration states in redefining citizenship through the adoption of dual citizenship laws,[51] although they still incorporate elements of individual and group identities as forms of social reproduction for the state.[52] For example, emigrants are often encouraged to contribute to national development via more particularistic affiliations based on hometown, religious, or ethnic origins which brings into light multiple and overlapping homelands and citizenships.[53]

In this vein, one of the most contentious policy changes arising from diaspora pressure is the issue of "dual citizenship" or "dual nationality" rights to emigrants. From a treasonable offence 10-15 years ago in many countries, the acquisition of the citizenship or nationality of other states is now seen as a practical survival issue of émigrés trying to improve their economic and professional prospects. In fact, many governments see their emigrants or diaspora as citizens waiting to return, anyway. There are, however, significant variations in the different citizenship postures so far adopted by these states because their choices are rooted in the ideological, political, and economic circumstances of each country.

The international good will enjoyed by Ghana following its transition from a failed state in the 1970s to a consolidated democracy and a poster child for the IMF and World Bank-imposed economic reform success story led to significant "reverse diaspora," permanent or long-term return of emigrants, in Ghana beginning from the late 1990s.[54] In 1995, the National Democratic Council (NDC) government of military-turned civilian President Jerry Rawlings announced government's decision to permit dual citizenship rights for Ghanaian emigrants. The law was eventually enacted in 2002 (Act 259, Republic of Ghana, 2002).[55] Nigeria followed suit in 1997 and since then, over a dozen African states such as Botswana, Burkina Faso, Cape Verde, Ethiopia, Eritrea, Lesotho, Mali, Mozambique, Niger, Senegal, and South Africa have adopted dual citizenship laws; or relaxed prohibitions against this practice, some of them doing so through judicial interpretations of the constitutions.[56] The government of John Kufuor (2000-2008) in Ghana went a step further in 2005 by promising to grant automatic citizenship to the Old African Diaspora.

Some legal or constitutional changes reflecting the specific historical circumstances of African states, however, impede the actualization of these rights of citizenship extended to the diaspora. For example, Article 16(1) of Ghana's Dual Citizenship Act of 2001 lists about 12 categories of senior level positions in the public service and judicial branches of government which are legally off limits to the diaspora with dual citizenships. Since their dual citizenship is interpreted as "dual nationality" and therefore "dual allegiance," these Ghanaians are also not eligible to run for parliamentary seats, even though they are now eligible to vote.[57] Hence, one Mr. Akwesi Agyeman Prempeh, a former resident of Washington, DC in the United States, was rejected as Deputy Regional Minister by the Ghana National Parliament in 2006 on account of his being a dual citizen.[58]

In 2004, the Nigerian senate introduced a bill to abolish current law that strips Nigerians of their political rights once they became citizens of other countries, even though the country began to permit acquisition of dual citizenship by its nationals back in 1997.[59] By July 2009, "the Non-Residence Act" which was expected to grant "permanent residence" status to dual-citizen Nigerians had still not been passed into law. The long delay is attributable to the end of the Obasanjo administration (1999-2007) which had warmed up to the diaspora unlike his successor, the ethnic, religious and regional imbalance in the potential beneficiaries of the proposed amendment, and the complexities arising from the notoriously indeterminate nature of Nigerian citizenship even for those physically residing in the country.[60]

Regime interests also explain why a handful of African states still cling to the Marshallian concept of citizenship and nationality laws, despite their public acknowledgement of the diaspora as development partners. For instance, while the government of Mrs. Ellen Sirleaf-Johnson in Liberia has persistently implored the country's émigrés to return and take part in the rebuilding process after almost two decades of war—and has indeed benefited from the cushioning effects of long-distance social obligations and belongings of its large diaspora—the government has resisted diaspora demands to repeal the country's Alien and Nationality Law which strips its citizenship from Liberians who have obtained another citizenship.[61] The potentially destabilizing effect of granting citizenship rights to about 34 percent of the population living outside its borders is not lost on the government all too familiar with problems created by previous regimes of Samuel Doe and Charles Taylor who allegedly politicized citizenship in favor of their Kran and Mandingo ethnic, respectively.[62]

Kenya's more than 250,000 nationals living abroad have complained about the country's constitution that automatically striped Kenyans of their citizenship—or required them to renounce it—once they successfully applied for another citizenship.[53] A draft constitution to allow for a restricted dual citizenship was defeated in a referendum in November 2005 largely due to the complicated citizenship and nationality politics in that country where the citizenship of several minority ethnic groups are still morally suspect.[54] In 2005, Uganda's Parliament similarly amended the law to allow dual citizenship, but the law is yet to take effect because the government of President Yoweri Museveni reportedly considers the majority of Ugandans who have acquired citizenship of other countries to be hostile to the regime.[65] Similarly, not only does Zambia not permit dual citizenship, it requires that any person entitled to Zambian citizenship and who has acquired the citizenship of another country automatically loses entitlement to claim Zambian citizenship—a provision used to revoke the citizenship of political rivals, as was done to Dr. Kenneth Kaunda, the country's founding president, in the 1990s.

Zimbabwe, with over 3.5 million of its nationals currently living outside its borders, is another notorious recent example of failure to resolve citizenship crisis due to the domestic political and economic calculations of the ruling regime.[56] Moreover, any attempts to liberalize nationality laws would have to contend with the cultural imagination of most Zimbabweans for whom minorities (migrants or their descendants), who are still predominantly located on the farms, the mines and urban ghettos, continue to be a cultural aberration—"foreigners without a 'proper, rural place of belonging"—because they lack a rural home in the native reserves (Communal Lands) which is still the crucial site that defines one's sense of belonging in Zimbabwe.[57] Similarly, the Democratic Republic of the Congo's failure to resolve its citizenship crisis has continued to frame contemporary debates about citizenship. Despite its long-standing constitutional insistence that Congolese nationality is "one and indivisible," ethnic minorities with past migrant history, such as the Congolese of Hutu and Tutsi descent, are often portrayed in both public and official discourse as "settlers" whose real home is in Rwanda.[58] Ironically, the nationality exclusion notions employed by Congolese governments against the Kinyarwanda have also been appropriated in Hutu-Tutsi conflicts, with Hutu extremists portrayed as "settlers" with an indigenous home elsewhere outside Rwanda.[59] In Namibia, the fear of the deluge of white "return migration" from South Africa which could exacerbate the already delicate racial wealth imbalance in favor of the country's three percent white minority accounts for the tightening of the country's citizenship laws.[70]

That some of the most restrictive measures bucking the global trend of liberalized citizenship have occurred in the Great Lakes region is a reflection of the complications of colonially imposed boundaries that split ethnic groups into two or more countries some of whom have been implicated in cross-border wars, insurgencies and other conflicts as different states redefine citizenship rights that called into question individual and group identities.[71] The resurgence of colonially manufactured notions and policies of "native" vs. "settler" has equally rattled recent citizenship debates because while the discourses on "self-evident" claims of autochthony "promise the certainty of belonging... [they] in practice raise basic uncertainties because autochthony is subject to constant redefinition against new 'others' and at ever-closer range."[72] While the institutionalization of ethnic entitlements, rights, and privileges which create differentiated and unequal status of citizenship is not unique to this sub-region,[73] its tendency to de-individualize citizenship and make it more of a group phenomenon; hence a major source of conflicts when empirical statehood fails, has had more tragic consequences in this part of Africa.[74] Not surprisingly, fewer states in the region have joined the global trend of adopting liberal dual citizenship and nationality laws. SADC countries also provide an interesting paradox because in the unassailable attempts to dismantle racialized imbalances entrenched under "settler colonialism," their policies have inadvertently ended up sometimes disenfranchising African supporters of the regimes.

## Diaspora Membership and Participation in Homeland Political Associations

Membership and participation in homeland political associations is the epitome of immigrant transnationalism, which Martiniello and Lafleur define as:

> any political activity undertaken by migrants who reside mainly outside their homeland and that is aimed at gaining political power or influence at the individual or collective level in the country of residence or in the state to which they consider they belong. Such power or influence may be achieved by interacting with all kinds of institutions (local, subnational, national or international) in the country of residence and/or the country of origin or by intervening in the country of origin's politics.[75]

The clearest manifestation of this change involves interactions between emigrants and homeland political parties and interest groups. From the Sierra Leone Peoples Party (SLPP) to the Cameroon Peoples Democratic Movement (CPDM), Nigeria's People's Democratic Party (PDP), to Ghana's NPP, and the NDC, etc., government and opposition political parties have established vibrant branches in major world cities with large concentrations of their activists.[76] Consequently, many African homeland politicians seeking office or current occupants of high office, routinely jet off to woo or undertake Western-styled election campaigns among their diaspora populations and activists.

By the same token, many candidates for political office and their sponsoring political parties in many countries increasingly finance their domestic activities from diaspora sources—for example, by channeling funds to so-called voluntary associations that endorse political parties or oppose their rivals. In Cameroon, for instance, the state-owned *Cameroon Tribune* and the ruling CPDM have often alleged that some opposition party "militants" in the diaspora surreptitiously solicit and receive funds from sources beyond the national frontiers "in blatant violation of existing laws," just as diaspora communities have been implicated in providing financial and logistical support for the movement for self-determination in Anglophone Southern Cameroon.[77] In Nigeria, the military has repeatedly claimed that ethnic militant movements in the Niger Delta are sustained by logistic and strategic support by their kith and kin outside Nigeria.

At other times, the diaspora have posed serious threats to the ruling elite within its borders, especially in the case of those diaspora activists that worked to overthrow authoritarian regimes or override national or sectional interests of the political elite through the franchise—from Charles Taylor's Liberia to Gnasingbe Eyadema's Togo, Ethiopia and Robert Mugabe's Zimbabwe, Cameroon and of course, in the anti-apartheid struggles. For example, massive numbers of Ghanaians fled to Europe and North America in the 1980s and 1990s from where they launched campaigns against the military dictatorship of Jerry Rawlings in Ghana until 1992. The Nigerian diaspora was even more militant in their mobilization against the Sani Abacha dictatorship from 1993-1998. Many members of the National Democratic Coalition and other human rights organizations fled the country following the annulment of the June 12, 1993 election and the emergence of the Abacha dictatorship. They became an important voice in, and raised financial and logistical support for, the pro-democracy movement demanding for the restoration of multi-party democratic government in Nigeria in 1999. Some of them later became federal ministers and legislators, while others sought office as governors and state and local government officials following the return to civilian rule in 1999.

In Togo, to further illustrate, the National Congress of the Civil Society (CNSC), a network of 150 NGOs, community development associations, trade unions, women coalitions, religious groups, and student organizations, was founded in 2002 to advance democracy, human rights, and development in the country. CNSC itself was allied to, and received substantial financial support from the Togolese Diaspora for Democracy and Development (DIASTODE), a Montreal (Canada)-based coalition of Togolese diaspora organizations in Europe, Ghana, Burkina Faso, and South Africa created in 1992 to fight the Eyadema dictatorship. Since 2003, CNSC and DIASTODE have engaged in common advocacy and effective citizen-participation programs, such as publications, conferences, and open discussion forums, etc. aimed at ushering in democratic change in the country. Following the death of President Eyadema on 5 February 2005, the Togolese Parliament hastily changed the constitution to enable the army to impose his son, Fauré on the country as president. The CNSC and DIASTODE immediately mobilized local and regional pro-democracy organizations to protest in front of Togolese diplomatic and consular offices throughout the sub-region and worked with regional and international organizations to reverse this coup d'état.[78]

Similarly, in Cape Verde (where only about 475,947 of the country's 975,947 nationals still reside on the islands), the diaspora not only supported the struggle against Portuguese brutal colonialism by backing the socialist African Party for the Independence of Guinea-Bissau and Cape Verde (PAIGC, later PAICV) during the struggle, they were also instrumental in ending the one-party state in 1991 through their support for the opposition Movement for Democracy (MPD) that won the multi-party elections that year. In 2001, only 7,558 (27 percent) of the 28,022 registered diaspora voted, overwhelmingly for the PAICV as punishment for the mismanagement and corruption that characterized the MPD government.[79] Cape Verde has been described as Africa's "most democratic nation;"[80] yet, a series of "undisciplined voting" by a small percentage of the diaspora has produced an unfriendly posture toward the electoral interests of local politicians, most of whom have few tools at their disposal to influence or contain such non-resident communities.[81]

Liberia, however, provides an interesting example of diaspora involvement in national political life, other than through elections from their foreign locations. In 2007, the country's Truth and Reconciliation Commission provided for the establishment of Statement-Taking Centers for the Liberian diaspora where *pro bono* immigration lawyers and mental health counselors, and Liberian community volunteers helped the TRC to gather testimonies from the diaspora. The Liberian TRC is the first of its kind to give members of a diaspora community a voice in promoting international justice and human rights as part of the TRC process for national healing, unity and peace.[82]

### Diaspora Voting Rights in Homeland Elections

Another highly contentious impact on African homeland-diaspora relations arises from its growing demand for the right to vote and/or be voted for in homeland elections. Ghana and Nigeria best illustrate the hopes and impediments associated with this dynamic relationship over the past two decades.

On 26 February 2006, the Ghana National Parliament passed "the Representation of the People Amendment Act" (ROPAA) that extended voting rights to Ghanaian emigrants, a decision that suddenly led to a widening of the transnational scope of Ghanaian electoral campaigns.[83] Supporters of ROPAA praised it as "a simple case of correcting what is wrong and what came into being by decree promulgated by a non-elected government."[84] Indeed, while Article 42 of the 1992 Constitution gives all Ghanaians "aged 18 and above and of sound mind" the right to register for the purpose of voting in elections and referenda, the actual operation of this constitutional "guarantee" is dependent on PNDC Law 284 "Representation of the People Law, 1992". Section 7(1) (c) of the PNDC law states that a Ghanaian qualifies to vote if "he (sic) is a resident of the polling division," while section 7(4) states that "a person shall not be deemed to be a resident in a polling division if he (sic) has been absent from his (sic) place of abode for a continuous period of six months." This, according to one ROPAA advocate "means that for someone who generally lives in say Denmark to register at *Ghanakrom*, that poor fellow has to abandon work and come to live in *Ghanakrom* for six months."[85]

ROPAA was fiercely opposed by the NDC—the party of former strongman Flt. Lt. Jerry Rawlings which was elected back into office in December 2008—whose members had walked out of the Parliament in 2006 in protest over the adoption of the bill they claimed was intended to perfect the then ruling NPP's alleged "Golden Age of Election Rigging."[86] Statements by some Ghanaians abroad during and after the ROPAA debate, perhaps lends credence to NDC's fears. According to one Florida, USA-based Ghanaian, "February 23, 2006 will go down in the history books as a day when the friends of democracy defeated the *dictator babies*. It will also go down as the day when Ghana became part of the Africa Elite 11, joining Botswana, Burkina Faso, Cape Verde, Lesotho, Mali, Mozambique, Namibia, Niger, Senegal, and South Africa to give the power to vote to its Diaspora citizens."[87] The NDC was concerned about the perception that the diasporan vote would be strongly weighted in favor of the NPP, partly because a large number of vocal Ghanaians overseas were forced out of the country during the Rawlings' years of economic and political discontent.[88] Ironically, it was Rawlings' NDC government that actually allowed Ghanaians overseas to register and vote in national elections for the first time in 1992, although section 8(1) of PNDC Law 284 grants the exemption to the residency requirement to a very limited group of Ghanaians resident abroad, namely employees of Ghana's missions overseas and of international organizations, as well as students on government scholarship.

Although Nigeria seems to have followed a different trajectory than Ghana, its experience of diaspora-homeland state relations equally reflects the limits, or even emptiness, of the reification of "migration" or "diasporic civil society." For a long time following the adoption of dual citizenship rights in 1997, Nigerian emigrant citizens were content to "agitate in silence" for the right to vote in Nigerian elections from their overseas locations.[89] The agitations were tepid at best, and did not make much impact due to lack of organization and fractious leadership and political crisis bedeviling many Nigerian diaspora organizations. The creation of state-sponsored "offshore" diaspora organizations, such as NIDO, and the capturing of several of other emigrant organizations by Nigerian governments and politicians equally undermined their credibility and ability to actualize this aspiration.

Following the adoption of ROPAA by Ghana in 2006, however, several Nigerian diaspora groups began to organize and openly demanded for a "Bill on Diaspora Voting Rights" to enable them to vote in elections in Nigeria from their bases abroad. Several umbrella Nigeria-in-Diaspora Association members, especially the ethnically-based ones, namely the World Igbo Congress (WIC), Zumunta Association USA, and Egbe Omo Yoruba—North America presented their demand for diaspora voting rights to President Obasanjo in December 2005 who promised to look into their request.[90] The ruling PDP in the USA also organized a public hearing in Houston, the first of its kind outside the shores of Nigeria, to which thousands of the Nigerian diaspora attended and expressed support for diaspora voting rights. Although the diaspora voting bill was eventually introduced and passed the first reading in the National Assembly in 2005, it did not advance further until the retirement of the Obasanjo regime in May 2007.[91] In 2009, a bill seeking the establishment of a Nigerian Diaspora Commission to "meticulous and accurate collation of data of the Diaspora and the fostering of economic cooperation with resourceful nationals working and living abroad" was introduced into the House of Representatives. The chairman of the Diaspora Affairs Committee in charge of piloting the affairs of the bill, however, noted that Nigerian diaspora could only vote if sections of the 1999 constitution prohibiting such extra-territorial exercise of the franchise were amended.[92] The lack of voting rights by overseas Nigerians, however, has not dampened the zeal with which homeland politicians campaign and/or faithfully attend ethnic and/or national homeland association annual conventions (often bankroll such events).

The African diaspora have also taken the legal option wherever homeland governments claimed that logistical requirements obviated diaspora exercise of the franchise in homeland elections; and a few national courts have sided with the emigrants against the governments. For instance, a Nigerian federal high court in Abuja in January 2009 granted the plea of a United States-based diaspora group and ordered the Independent National Election Commission (INEC) to put in place relevant machinery to assist Nigerians to register and vote from abroad in any election in Nigeria "without having to travel for that purpose." The court, however, directed INEC to sponsor a bill at the National Assembly to implement its order.[93] INEC at first agreed to implement the court decision, but later reneged by arguing that the court only ruled that "the right to participate in the government of Nigeria and to register as voters (are) exercisable within the territorial boundaries of Nigeria."[94] The dream of diaspora vote advocates was finally shattered on 6 May 2009 when Nigeria's House of Representatives voted down a bill seeking to implement the court decision on the grounds that its provisions contravened the 1999 Constitution.[95] A Pretoria High Court in February 2009 similarly directed that South Africans living abroad should be allowed to vote in the April 2009 elections, but the order was not implemented, even though this did not happen in the end.[96]

## Diaspora Cyber-citizenship Activities and Transformations in National Identity

When the internet appeared in the early 1990s, many social scientists and commentators predicted that it would threaten the cultural integrity of nations; that the non-territorial character of the internet would lead to fragmentation and unprecedented cultural differentiation, making it difficult, eventually impossible, to uphold a collective sense of national identity based on shared images, representations, myths and so on. Today, nations are thriving in cyberspace, thanks to their diasporas as well to the realization by states that the internet can be a key technology for keeping nations and other abstract communities together, and projecting their identities to wider audience. Today, nations with large permanent or temporary diasporas appear in many sites on the internet—from online newspapers and magazines to semi-official information sites and "virtual community" homepages.[97]

Even though Africa came late to the internet, there is today a dizzying array of websites and often riotous online discussion and virtual community sites where homeland political activities are played out;[98] or where constituencies for country-specific or continent-wide issues and platforms now mobilize for action.[99] More importantly, the internet and new information communication technologies (ICT) offer unprecedented plurality that challenges the hitherto excessive powers and influence of the continent's ruling elites over information dissemination and freedom of expression. Before the advent of ICTs, many African leaders tightly controlled information dissemination, allowing only the dominant political views to be aired on state-controlled radio, television, and print media.[100] Currently, the most worrisome cyber challenge (from the perspective of some African governments) are internet-based ambush and muck-racking investigative blog sites, otherwise known as "guerrilla news agencies,"[101] that provide outlets for émigré journalists to expose corruption and misgovernance, or that provide space for civil society organizations and other critics of the regime to air their views from the safety of exile, and also from within the homeland.

In some countries, intrepid homeland or diaspora bloggers and virtual communities—"cybernauts"—are emerging as "the voice of the opposition," often publishing contemporaneous news and video recordings which expose alleged human rights violations, while others use these platforms to advocate exclusive identity agendas or to attack socio-political groups opposed to the state or other identity groups.[102] The blogosphere has also made it possible for some of Africa's most passionate state critics to write on issues that would never be published even in the privately owned mainline press. Quite often "scoops" from fairly popular diaspora-run online blog sites on Nigeria, especially http://www.empowerednews.com and http://www.saharareporters.com noted for their fairly accurate reporting about on-going corruption and lack of transparency in the Nigerian and other African governments, are re-published in mainline homeland press. Today, "Saharareporters.com is the only remaining space where Nigerians can dare to hope and aspire to a modicum of humanity. Saharareporters is the worst nightmare of Nigeria's internal colonizers, the traducers of our destiny."[103] Similarly, blogs sites—run mostly by Ugandans living outside the country—have become the watchdog of the society following the ban on live broadcasts by the government.[104] In Zimbabwe, the regime has been harassed ceaselessly by several online publications, virtual communities, and blogs run by Zimbabwean exiles, while several governments have been hopelessly unable or ineffective in countering the cacophony of anti-state, religious fundamentalist, and downright racist and/or rabid ethnic jingoism and divisive rhetoric on the internet.[105]

Yet, most African émigrés today obtain news about the homeland from online versions of media publications—often published by government-owned, ruling party-affiliated, or other privately owned media outlets—that have yet to operate without occasional state interference or dependence on state largesse by their proprietors. Moreover, many governments are catching up by creating interactive websites often targeting the diaspora and potential investors. Some have also sponsored or fostered the emergence of surrogate virtual communities, or planted their "moles" to represent, monitor anti-government activities, and/or defend government's positions on popular diaspora virtual community sites. Finally, many emigrant groups and organizations have deployed internet technology to mobilize their members and other sympathizers to promote conflict resolution in their homelands, often "transforming hawks into doves."[106]

## Conclusion

Many African countries have finally joined the ranks of emigrant states, with their citizens or nationals—most of whom never forgot the homeland—spread across the world and within the continent. As they have moved to either partner or structure the African diaspora's well-known long-distance social obligations to the homeland with a view to extending the frontiers of their citizens loyalty, their conceptions of the diaspora have been transformed, just as the diaspora itself has taken advantage of this rapprochement to impact the homeland in many ways unimaginable three decades ago.[107]

This chapter attempted to explore the outline of these transformations by focusing on two interrelated themes: transformations of homeland attitudes toward kin-diasporas and diaspora involvement in public life in homeland affairs and their impact on national and cultural identities within the home countries and among the diaspora themselves. It first maps out the in African state's perception of emigration, situating them within the global scholarship focusing on the hitherto neglected repercussions of diasporas' influences on homelands. Next it analyzes four dimensions of diaspora-homeland interactions, namely diaspora remittances, investments and other economic activities; renegotiation of citizenship and nationality laws; diaspora membership and participation in homeland political associations within the homeland and from abroad; and finally the impact of African diaspora cyber-citizenship and cyber-political activities on the conceptions of national and cultural identities within their home countries.

While the outcome of most diaspora-homeland interactions is a negotiated process, a review of the experiences of African emigrant states across the region shows that African migrant transnationalism has begun to alter the way African countries now redefine the philosophy and practice of citizenship and nationality laws and exercise of the accompanying rights of citizenship. The focus on diaspora cybercitizenship and cyberpolitical activities in particular highlights the way new media and technologies of mass communication are being deployed to shape national integration and identity formation. This and the other homeland-targeted activities of the African diaspora clearly demonstrate the discursive and institutional dimensions of migrant transnationalism to the extent that they are generating new national narratives, as well as new institutions to mediate the relations between society and state in Africa. These themes are often glossed over in recent scholarship on the African diaspora; they should be fruitful areas of future research on global Africa.

## Endnotes

[1] Among early publications that showed interest in the subject were Luis Eduardo Guarnizo and Michael Peter Smith, eds., *Transnationalism from Below* (New Brunswick, NJ: Transaction Publishers, 1998); and Nancy Foner, "What's New About Transnationalism? New York Immigrants Today and at the Turn of the Century," *Diaspora* 6 (Winter 1997): 355–75. Two recent publications clearly demonstrate that transnationalism has become a substantive theme in the cottage industry that diaspora studies appears to be turning into. See Eliezer Ben-Rafael and Yitzhak Sternberg (eds.), *Transnationalism: Diasporas and the Advent of a (Dis)Order* (Leiden and Boston: Brill, 2009; and Steven Vertovec, *Transnationalism* (London: Routledge, 2009).

[2] See Tony Smith, *Foreign Attachments: The Power of Ethnic Groups in the Making of American Foreign Policy* (Cambridge, MA: Harvard University Press, 2000); Yoshi Shain, *Marketing the American Creed Abroad: Diasporas in the U.S. and Their Homelands* (Cambridge: Cambridge University Press, 1999).

[3] Eva Østergaard-Nielsen, *Transnational Politics: Turks and Kurds in Germany* (London: Routledge, 2003).

[4] Luis Guarnizo, Alejandro Portes, and William Haller, "Assimilation and Transnationalism: Determinants of Transnational Political Action Among Contemporary Migrants," *The American Journal of Sociology*, vol. 108, no. 6 (2003), pp. 1211-1248.

[5] Alexander Kitroeff, "Continuity and Change in Contemporary Greek Historiography" in Martin Bilinkhorn and Thanos Veremis (eds.), *Modern Greece: Nationalism and Nationality* (Athens: Sage-Eliamep, 1990), pp. 170–171; and Richard Clogg

(ed.), *The Greek Diaspora in the Twentieth Century* (Basingstoke, UK: Macmillan Publishers, 1999).

[6] Alan Smart and Jinn-Yuh Hsu, "The Chinese Diaspora, Foreign Investment and Economic Development in China," *The Review of International Affairs*, vol. 3, no. 4 (Summer 2004), pp. 544-566; and Laurence J. C. Ma and Carolyn Cartier, *The Chinese Diaspora: Space, Place, Mobility, and Identity* (Lanham, MD.: Rowman & Littlefield, 2002).

[7] Gabriel Sheffer, *Diaspora Politics: At Home and Abroad* (Cambridge University Press, 2003).

[8] See, for examples, Mark I. Choate, *Emigrant Nation: Italians and the Global Fatherland* (Cambridge, MA: Harvard University Press, 2008); Mark I. Choate, "Sending States' Transnational Interventions in Politics, Culture, and Economics: The Historical Example of Italy," *International Migration Review*, vol. 41, no. 3 (Fall 2007), pp. 728-768; Østergaard-Nelson (ed.), *International Migration and Sending Countries*; Robert C. Smith, "Migrant Membership as an Instituted Process: Transnationalization, the State and the Extra-Territorial Conduct of Mexican Politics," *International Migration Review*, vol. 37 (2003), pp. 297-343.

[9] William Rogers Brubaker, *Citizenship and Nationhood in France and Germany* (Cambridge, MA: Harvard University Press, 1992), p. 12.

[10] Thomas Faist, "Transnationalization in International Migration: Implications for the Study of Citizenship and Culture," *Ethnic and Racial Studies*, vol. 23, no. 2 (March 2000), pp. 189-222; and Irene Bloemraad, Anna Korteweg and Gökçe Yurdakul, "Citizenship and Immigration: Multiculturalism, Assimilation, and Challenges to the Nation-State," *Annual Review of Sociology*, vol. 34, no. 1 (2008), pp. 153-179; and Richard Bellamy, Dario Castiglione and Emilio Santoro, *Lineages of European Citizenship: Rights and Belonging in Eleven Nation-States* (London: Palgrave Macmillan, 2004).

[11] See Chachage S. L. Chachage and Karuti Kanyinga, "Introduction: Special Issue on Globalization and Citizenship in Africa," *Africa Development*, vol. 28, nos. 1 & 2 (2003), pp. 1-16.

[12] Thomas H. Marshall, *Class, Citizenship and Social Development: Essays by T. H. Marshall* (New York: Anchor Books, 1964).

[13] See John A. Arthur, The African Diaspora in the United States and Europe: The Ghanaian Experience (Ashgate, 2008), pp. 25-44.

[14] See Edward Opoku-Dapaah, "Ghana 1981-1991: A Decade of Forced Repression and Migration," *Refugee*, vol. 11, no. 3 (1993), pp. 8-113; Margaret Peil, "Ghanaians Abroad," *African Affairs*, vol. 94 (1995), pp. 345-365; and Alice Bloch, "Emigration From Zimbabwe: Migrant Perspective," *Social Policy & Administration*, vol. 40, no. 1 (February 2006), pp. 67-87. On the impact of the structural adjustment programs, see Thandika Mkandawire, "Maladjusted African Economies and Globalization," *Africa Development*, vol. 33, nos. 1 & 2 (2005), pp. 1-33.

[15] See Oluwaekemi A. Adesina, " 'Checking Out': Migration, Popular Culture, and the Articulation and Formation of Class Identity," presented at the African Migration Workshop on "Understanding Migration Dynamics in the Continent", 18-21 September 2007, Accra, Ghana.

[16] Zarina Geloo, "Zambian Expatriates Scoff at President Mwanawasa's Remarks," *Inter Press Service*, 2 December 2004.

[17] See F. Nii-Amoo Dodoo, Baffour K. Takyi and Jesse R. Mann, "On the Brain Drain of Africans to America: Some Methodological Observations," *Perspectives on Global Development & Technology*, vol. 5, no. 3 (2006), pp. 155-162; Solomon A. Getahun, "Brain Drain and Its Impact on Ethiopia's Higher Learning Institutions:

Medical Establishments and the Military Academies Between 1970s and 2000," *Perspectives on Global Development & Technology*, vol. 5, no. 3 (2006), pp. 257-275.

[18] Giles Mohan, "Embedded Cosmopolitanism and the Politics of Obligation: The Ghanaian Diaspora and Development," *Environment & Planning*, vol. 38, no. 5 (May 2006), pp. 867-883; Tekie Feshatzion, "Eritrea's Remittance-Based Economy: Conjectures and Musings," *Eritrean Studies Review*, vol. 4, no. 2 (2005), pp. 165-184.

[19] See Tricia M. Redeker Hepner, "Transnational Governance and the Centralization of State Power in Eritrea and Exile," *Ethnic and Racial Studies*, vol. 31, no. 3 (March 2008), pp. 476-502.

[20] Sandra Lavenex and Rahel Kunz, "The Migration-Development Nexus in EU External Relations," *Journal of European Integration*, vol. 30, no. 3 (July 2008), pp. 439-457; and Thomas Faist, "Migrants as Transnational Development Agents: An Inquiry into the Newest Round of the Migration-Development Nexus," *Population, Space and Place*, vol. 14 (2008), pp. 21-42.

[21] See Hein de Haas, *International Migration and National Development: Viewpoints and Policy Initiatives in Countries of Origin—The Case of Nigeria*. Working Papers Migration and Development Series Report 6 (International Migration Institute, University of Oxford, 2006); Mohan, "Embedded Cosmopolitanism and the Politics of Obligation," pp. 867-883; and "Why One Would 'Want to Return to One of the World's Poorest Countries'," *The Reporter* (Addis Ababa), 19 November 2006.

[22] See Jack I. Garvey, "Repression of Political Empire – The Underground to International Law: A Proposal for Remedy," *Yale Law Journal*, vol. 90 (1980), p. 79.

[23] Shain, *The Frontier of Loyalty*, pp. 145–62.

[24] Morton Grodzin, *The Loyal and the Disloyal: Social Boundaries of Patriotism and Treason* (Chicago: University of Chicago Press, 1956), p. 213.

[25] The World Bank, *Migrations and Remittances Fact Book 2008* (Washington, DC: The World Bank).

[26] Kevin Savage and Paul Harvey (eds.), *Remittances During Crises: Implications for Humanitarian Response* (London: Overseas Development Institute, May 2007), http://www.odi.org.uk/HPG/remittances.html; accessed ... 2008.

[27] Cameroon Duodu, "Tapping Investments from Ghanaians in the Diaspora," *Ghanaian Times* (Accra), 7 March 2006.

[28] Saxenian, "Brain Circulation," pp. 28-31.

[29] Stijn Classens, Geoffrey R. D. Underhill and Xiaoke Zhang, "The Political Economy of Basle II: The Cost for Poor Countries," *The World Economy*, vol. 31 (2008), pp. 313-344.

[30] Charles Wachira, "Kenya Flush With Money From Expatriates," *Inter Press Service News Agency*, 31 October 2008 (http://ipsnews.net/print.asp?idnews=44533); accessed 8 November 2008.

[31] "African Diaspora Seen as 6th Region of Continent," *The Financial Times*, 8 February 2006; "Jamaica Hosts AU, Caribbean Diaspora Conference," *The Financial Times*, 15 March 2005; and Lydia Polgreen, "Ghana's Uneasy Embrace of Slavery's Diaspora," *The New York Times*, 27 December 2005.

[32] Abbey Walusimbi, "Involve Ugandans Abroad in Local Politics," *The Monitor* (Uganda), 30 May 2005.

[33] "A Senegalese Envoy at MINREX," *Cameroon Tribune*, 26 July 2005; and Marie Angelique Diatta and Ndiaga Mbow, "Releasing the Development Potential of Return Migration: The Case of Senegal," *International Migration*, vol. 37, no 1 (1999), pp. 243-266.

[34]Sylvia Juuko, "Ugandans Working Abroad Send $1 Billion Home Each Year," *New Vision*, 29 January 2007; and Julius Barigaba, "Ugandans Abroad Want Dual Citizenship to Invest at Home," *The East African*, 23 January 2007.

[35]Quoted in *Mobilizing the African Diaspora for Development* (Addis Ababa: Capacity Development Management Action Plan Unit, AFTCD, 2007), p. 42.

[36]"Zimbabwe: Summit Endorses Homelink," *The Herald*, 7 June 2005.

[37]Oscar Kimanuka, "The Clout of Africa's Diaspora," *The East African* (Kenya), 4 January 2006; "Central Africa: Diaspora Committed to Poverty Alleviation," *IRIN News*, 17 July 2006.

[38]*Mobilizing the African Diaspora for Development*, p. 43.

[39]Haas, *International Migration and National Development*, p. 16.

[40]Gbenga Agbana, "Transcorp Markets N60 Billion to Nigerians in Diaspora," *Guardian* (Lagos), 16 January 2007. Transcorp, touted as Nigeria's answer to the rise of "mega corporations" behind the business-government synergy that led to rapid industrialization of Southeast Asia, has since failed. The Nigerian government stripped it of its equity in the original state-owned telephone conglomerate it had purchased at its founding in 2006 and awarded them to other core investors. See Ebere Onwudiwe and Okey Iheduru, "Transcorp: a Dream Unfulfilled," *Business Day* (Lagos), 15 January 2009.

[41]"Lucky Fiakpa, "Success Story of Banks' Diaspora Account Products," *Vanguard* (Lagos), 22 September 2008.

[42]See "Bank PHB Extends Service to Nigerians Abroad," *THIS DAY*, 19 October 2006; and "Bank PHB Subsidiary to Manage $200m Diaspora Investment Fund," *Vanguard* (Lagos), 12 March 2008; and Abdul Imoyo, "Whither the Market in 2009," *Business Day* (Lagos), 8 January 2009.

[43]Valentina Mazzucato and Mirjam Kabki, "Small is Beautiful: The Micro-Politics of Transnational Relationships Between Ghanaian Hometown Associations and Communities Back Home," *Global Networks*, vol. 9, no. 2 (2009), pp. 1470-2266. Arthur, *The African Diaspora in the United States and Europe* pp. 121-138 describes it as "sharing the migration dividend."

[44]See Emmanuel C. Onwuka, "World Bank Development Policies and Poverty Alleviation in Africa," *Africa Development*, vol. 31, no. 4 (2006), pp. 104-120.

[45]*Meeting Everyone's Needs: National Economic Empowerment and Development Strategy* (Abuja: Nigerian National Planning Commission, 2004), p. 83.

[46]Emma Ujah, "NAPEP Enlists Nigerians in Diaspora on Funds Repatriation," *Vanguard* (Lagos), 24 March 2006.

[47]Quoted in Godfrey M. Sseruwagi, "Ugandans in the Diaspora Have Big Dreams," *The Monitor* (Uganda), 18 May 2005.

[48]"Ex-African Leaders Call on Diaspora to Help Development," *Agence France Presse*, 21 April 2006.

[49]Jeffrey Herbst, "The Role of Citizenship Laws in Multiethnic Societies: Evidence From Africa," pp. 267-284, in Richard Joseph (ed.), *State, Conflict, and Democracy in Africa* (Boulder, CO.: Lynne Rienner Publishers, 1999).

[50]Bambi Ceuppens and Peter Gershiere, "Autochthony: Local or Global? New Modes in the Struggle Over Citizenship and Belonging in Africa and Europe," *Annual Review of Anthropology*, vol. 34 (2005), pp. 385-407 (http://www.anthro.annualreviews.org).

[51]Linda Bosniak, "Multiple Nationality and the Postnational Transformation of Citizenship," pp. 27-49 in David A. Martin and Kay Heilbronner (eds.), *Rights and Duties of Dual Nationals: Evolution and Prospects* (The Hague: Kluwer Law International, 2003); Tanja Brondsted Sejersen, " 'I Vow to Thee My Countries'—The Expansion of Dual Citizenship in the 21st Century," *International Migration Review*, vol. 42, no. 3 (Autumn 2008), pp. 523-549; and Christian Joppke, "How Immigration Is Changing Citizenship: A Comparative View," *Ethnic and Racial Studies*, vol. 22, no. 4 (July 1999), pp. 629-652. and Michael T. Luongo, "Carrying Several Passports? It's Not Just for Spies," *The New York Times*, 20 January 2009 (http:www.nytimes.com/2009/01/20/business/ 20dual.html?em=&pagewanted-print (22 January 2009);

[52]Michael Neocomos, "The Contradictory Position of 'Tradition' in African National Discourse: Some Analytical and Political Reflections," *Africa Development*, vol. 28, nos. 1 & 2 (2003), pp. 17-52.

[53]Giles Mohan, "Making Neoliberal States of Development: The Ghanaian Diaspora and the Politics of Homeland," *Environment and Planning D: Society and Space*, vol. 26 (2008), p. 465, 476.

[54]Richard Black and Adriana Castaldo, "Return Migration and Entrepreneurship in Ghana and Côte d'Ivoire: The Role of Capital Transfers," *Tijdschrift voor Economische en Sociale Geografie*, vol. 100, no. 1 (2009), pp. 44-58; and Arthur, *The African Diaspora in the United States and Europe*, pp. 139-156.

[55]William Shaw, *Migration in Africa: A Review of the Economic Literature on International Migration in 10 Countries* (Washington, DC: The Development Prospects Group, the World Bank, 2007), p. 28.

[56]For a partial early treatment, see B. Von Lieres, "New Perspectives on Citizenship in Africa," *Journal of Modern Africa*, vol. 25, no. (1999), pp. 139-148.

[57]"Is Dual Citizenship the Same as Dual Allegiance," *Accra Mail*, 25 June 2008.

[58]Agyenim Boateng, "A Diaspora Ghanaian on Ghana@50," *Accra Mail*, 4 April 2007.

[59]Shaw, *Migration in Africa*, p. 28; Hein de Haas, *International Migration and National Development: Viewpoints and Policy Initiatives in Countries of Origin—The Case of Nigeria*. Working Papers Migration and Development Series Report 6 (International Migration Institute, University of Oxford, 2006), p. 9.

[60]"Yar'Adua Urged to Enact Non-Residence Act," *This Day* (Lagos), 13 May 2007; and O. O. W. Idowu, "Citizenship, Alienation and Conflict in Nigeria," *Africa Development*, vol. 24, nos. 1 & 2 (1999), pp. 31-55.

[61]"US-Based Liberian Group Calls for Review of Dual Citizenship," *Star Radio*, Monrovia, in English 0700GMT, 4 April 2007.

[62]Augustine Konneh, "Citizenship at the Margins: Status, Ambiguity and the Mandingo of Liberia," *African Studies Review*, vol. 39, no. 2 (September 1996), pp. 141-154.

[63]Muhula, "Kenyans Abroad Must Be Heard," *The Nation* (Nairobi), 22 November 2006.

[64]Kevin J. Kelley, "Let Kenyans in Diaspora to Vote—Kalonzo," *The Nation*, 6 February 2007; and Matthew Carotenuto and Katherine Luongo, "*Dala* or Diaspora? Obama and the Luo Community of Kenya," *African Affairs*, vol. 108, no. 431 (April 2009), pp. 197-219.

[65]Sylvia Juuko, "Ugandans Working Abroad Send $1 Billion Home Each Year," *New Vision*, 29 January 2007; and Julius Barigaba, "Ugandans Abroad Want Dual Citizenship to Invest at Home," *The East African*, 23 January 2007.

[66] Brian Raftopoulos, "The State in Crisis: Authoritarianism, Selective Citizenship and Distortions of Democracy in Zimbabwe," in A. Hammer, Brian Raftopoulos and S. Jensen (eds.), *Zimbabwe's Unfinished Business: Rethinking Land, State and Nation in the Context of Crisis* (Harare: Weaver Press, 2003); James Muzondidya, "Jambanja: Ideological Ambiguities in the Politics of Land and Resource Ownership in Zimbabwe," *Journal of Southern African Studies*, vol. 33, no. 2 (June 2007); and Alice Bloch, "Emigration From Zimbabwe: Migrant Perspective," *Social Policy & Administration*, vol. 40, no. 1 (February 2006), pp. 67-87..

[67] Muzondidya, "Jambanja," p. 335; and B. Rutherford, "Belonging to the Farm(er): Farm Workers, Farmers and the Shifting Points of Citizenship," in A. Hammer, Brian Raftopoulos and S. Jensen (eds.), *Zimbabwe's Unfinished Business: Rethinking Land, State and Nation in the Context of Crisis* (Harare: Weaver Press, 2003), p. 200.

[68] Georges Nzongola-Ntalaja, "Citizenship, Political Violence and Democratization in Africa," *Global Governance*, vol. 10 (2004), p. 405.

[69] Mahmood Mandani, *When Victims Become Killers: Colonialism, Nativism and Genocide in Rwanda* (Princeton: Princeton University Press, 2001), pp. 13-14.

[70] See "Govt Caves in on Dual Citizenship," *The Namibian*, 16 October 2008; and "Constitutional Changes Coming," *The Namibian*, 17 February 2009

[71] Mahmood Mamdani, "African States, Citizenship and War: A Case-Study," *International Affairs*, vol. 78, no. 3 (2002), pp. 493-506. See also his *Citizen and Subject: Contemporary Africa and the Legacy of Late Colonialism* (Princeton: Princeton University Press, 1996).

[72] Bambi Ceuppens and Peter Gershiere, "Autochthony: Local or Global? New Modes in the Struggle Over Citizenship and Belonging in Africa and Europe," *Annual Review of Anthropology*, vol. 34 (2005), pp. 385-407 (http://www.anthro.annualreviews.org).

[73] See Brennan Kraxberger, "Strangers, Indigenes and Settlers: Contested Geographies of Citizenship in Nigeria," *Space and Polity*, vol. 9, no. 1 (April 2005), pp. 9-27; Peter Gerchiere and Stephen Jackson, "Autochthony and the Crisis of Citizenship: Democratization, Decentralization, and the Politics of Belonging," *African Studies Review*, vol. 49, no. 2 (September 2006), pp. 1-14; Open Society Justice Initiative, The African Citizenship & Discrimination Audit Preparatory Meeting: Report of a Conference Held in Dakar, Senegal on July 19-20, 2004 (http://www.justiceinitiative.org/db/resource2/fs/?file_id=14358); and R. Marshall-Fratani, "The War of 'Who is Who': Autochthony, Nationalism, and Citizenship in the Ivorian Crisis," *African Studies Review*, vol. 49, no. 2 (2006), pp. 9-43.

[74] See Stephen Jackson, "Of 'Doubtful Nationality': Political Manipulation of Citizenship in the D. R. Congo," *Citizenship Studies*, vol. 11, no 5 (November 2007), pp. 481-500; Stephen Jackson, "Sons of Which Soil? The Language of Autochthony in Eastern D. R. Congo," *African Studies Review*, vol. 49, no. 2 (2006), pp. 95-123; O'Laughlin, "Class and the Customary"; and Adejumobi, "Citizenship, Rights, and the Problem of Conflicts and Civil Wars in Africa."

[75] Marco Martiniello and Jean-Michel Lafleur, "Towards a Transatlantic Dialogue in the Study of Immigrant Political Transnationalism," *Ethnic and Racial Studies*, vol. 31, no. 4 (May 2008), p.653.

[76] See "SLPP Launches Continental Europe Branch," *The Concord Times* (Freetown), 11 July 2006; "CPDM USA: Combating Misconceptions," and "Joseph Mbu, Coordinator CPDM USA: 'We Are Running On All Pistons'," *Cameroon Tribune*, 2 August 2005.

[77] "Raising Funds for Political Goals: Need to Control Origin of Financing for Political Parties," *Cameroon Tribune*, 14 June 2005.

[78]See "Togo: Peer Pressure Plus," *Africa Focus*, 28 February 2005; and "West African Civil Society to Sue Togolese Leader for Rights Violations," *Agence France Presse*, 20 February 2005.

[79]See Marc-Antoine Pérouse de Montcios, "The Political Value of Remittances: Cape Verde, Comoros and Lesotho," in *Diaspora, Remittances and Africa South of the Sahara: A Strategic Assessment*. ISS Monograph 112 (Pretoria: Institute of Strategic Studies, 2007). http://www.iss.co.za/static/templates/tmpl_html.php?node_id=754&link_id=21; accessed 13 November 2007.

[80]See Bruce Baker, Bruce (2006), "Cape Verde: The Most Democratic Nation in Africa?," *Journal of Modern African Studies*, vol. 44, no. 4 (2006), pp. 493-511.

[81]See J. Peter Spiro, "Political Rights and Dual Nationality," p. 139 in David A. Martin and Kay Hailbronner (eds.), *Rights and Duties of Dual Nationals: Evolution and Prospects* (The Hague: Kluwer Law International, 2003).

[82]"TRC Statement Taking Starts in the U.S.," *The Analyst* (Monrovia), 24 January 2007.

[83]*Representation of the People (Amendment) Act, No. 690 of 2006* (Accra: Republic of Ghana, 24 February 2006). For commentary on the law, see Okyere Bonna, Kwasi Kissi and Kwaku Danso, "Voting Rights for the Ghanaian Diaspora: A Challenge for Ghana's Parliament," *Accra Mail*, 29 June 2005; Kofi A. Boateng, "Diaspora Vote—Ghanaians in North America Organize Themselves," *Ghanaian Chronicle*, 25 July 2005; and "Citizenship and ROPAB," *Ghanaian Chronicle*, 28 February 2006.

[84]Kofi A. Boateng, "Diaspora Vote: We Came, We Listened, We Answered," (http://www.ghanaweb.com/GhanaHomePage/NewsArchive/printnews.php?ID=94127).

[85]Boateng, "Diaspora Vote."

[86]"Dozens March Against Diaspora Vote," *Agence France Presse*, 16 March 2006—a parody on that government's "Golden Age of Business" program. See also "Canada-Based Ghanaian Warns of Chaos If Bill is Passed," *Ghanaian Chronicle* (Accra), 17 November 2005.

[87]"GCG Congratulates Parliament for Passing ROPAB!," *Modern Ghana News* (www.modernghananews.com), 23 February 2006.

[88]See Emil Rado, "Notes Towards a Political Economy of Ghana Today," *African Affairs*, vol. 85, no. 341 (1986), pp. 563-572; Jonathan A. Frimpong, *The Vampire State in Africa: The Political Economy of Decline in Ghana* (Trenton, NJ.: Africa World Press, 1992); Edward Opoku-Dapaah, "Ghana 1981-1991: A Decade of Forced Repression and Migration," *Refugee*, vol. 11, no. 3 (1993), pp. 8-113; and Margaret Peil, "Ghanaians Abroad," *African Affairs*, vol. 94 (1995), pp. 345-365.

[89]"Diaspora Voting Rights Bill," *Daily Champion* (Lagos), 14 September 2006.

[90]Vincent Ujumadu, "Nigerians in Diaspora to Initiate Voting Bill," *Vanguard* (Lagos), 31 October 2006.

[91]"Nass [National Assembly] Tasked on Voting Rights for Nigerians in Diaspora," *Daily Trust* (Abuja), 27 January 2007.

[92]Tordue Salem, "Voting Rights: Huddles Before Nigerians in Diaspora," *Vanguard*, 4 March 2009.

[93]Davidson Iriepken, "Polls: Court Okays Nigerians Abroad to Vote," *This Day*, 20 January 2009.

[94]"INEC Denies Alleged Court Order Over Citizens in Diaspora," *Daily Independent* (Abuja), 25 February 2009.

[95] Bola Badmus, "Reps Reject Voting for Nigerians Abroad," *Nigerian Tribune*, 7 May 2009.

[96] "Court Backs S. Africa Exile Vote," *BBC News*, 9 February 2009 (http://newsvote.bbc.co.uk/mpapps/pagetools/print/news.bbc.co.uk/2/hi/africa/7878858.stm?ad=1); accessed 10 February 2009; and Steven Firer, "Tax But No Vote," *Business Day* (Johannesburg), 12 February 2009.

[97] Thomas H. Eriksen, "Nationalisn and the Internet," *Nations & Nationalism*, vol. 13, no. 1 (January 2007), pp. 1-17. See also Anastasia N. Panagakos and Heather A. Horst, "Return to Cyberia: Technology and the Social Worlds of Transnational Migrants," *Global Networks*, vol. 6, no. 2 (April 2006), pp. 109-124.

[98] See Jennifer Brinkerhoff, "Digital Diasporas and Conflict Prevention: The Case of Somalinet.com," *Review of International Studies*, vol. 32, no. 1 (2006), pp. 25-47; Abdisalam M. Issa-Salwe and Anthony Olden, "Somali Web Sites, History and Politics," *Aslib Proceedings: New Information Perspectives*, vol. 60, no. 6 (2008), pp. 570-582; Victoria Bernal, "Diasporas, Cyberspace and Political Imagination: The Eritrean Diaspora Online," *Global Networks*, vol. 6, no. 2 (2006), pp. 161-179; and Gado Alzouma, "Identities in a 'Fragmegrated' World: Black Cyber-Communities and the French Integration System," *African and Black Diaspora: An International Journal*, vol. 1, no. 2 (July 2008), pp. 201-214.

[99] Jill M. Humphries, "Cyberorganizing United States Constituencies for Africa," *Perspectives on Global Development & Technology*, vol. 5, no. 3 (2006), pp. 163-211.

[100] For interesting discussions, see Okoth Fredrick Mudhai, "ICTs and the Civil Society as Challengers to the Ruling Elite in *Africa*," paper at the International Studies Association, 2004 Annual Meeting, Montreal, Canada; and Kehbuma Langmia, *The Internet and the Construction of the Immigrant Public Sphere* (Lanham, MD: University Press of America, 2007).

[101] See Sokari Ekine, "Nigeria: Media Repression as Security Clamp Down on 'Guerrilla News Agencies'," *New Internationalist* (London), (http://blog.newint.org/majority/2008/10/31nigerian-media-repression/); accessed 24 December 2008.

[102] See John Sorenson and Atsuko Matsuoka, "Phantom Wars and Cyberwars: Abyssinian Fundamentalism and Catastrophe in Eritrea," *Dialectical Anthropology*, vol. 26, no. 1 (2001), pp. 37-63; and Chika Anyanwu, "Virtual Citizenship and Diasporic Discourse," presented at the Annual Meeting of the Australian and New Zealand Communication Association, 4-7 July 2005, Christchurch, New Zealand.

[103] Pius Adesanmi, "Andrew and His Naija-Based Enemies," USAAfricaDialogue@googlegroups.com (posted and accessed on 24 January 2009).

[104] See "Uganda: Blogs Becoming 'Watchdogs of Society'," *Africa Research Bulletin: Political, Social & Cultural Series*, vol. 45, no. 1 (January 2008), p17407.

[105] Zimbabwean exiles are probably the most active in the evolving anti-state cyberpolitical activities as a quick visit to these websites shows: www.zimdaily.com, www.swradioafrica.com, www.zimbabwesituation.com, www.thezimbabwetimes.com, www.zimonline.com.

[106] Terence Lyons, "Engaging Diasporas to Promote Conflict Resolution: Transforming Hawks into Doves," available at: www.tamilnation.org/conflictresolution/lyons.htm (accessed 11 August 2007).

[107] Emmanuel Akyeampong, "Africans in the Diaspora: The Diaspora and Africa," *African Affairs*, vol. 99 (2000), p. 213.